R. Gupta's®

POPULAR MASTER GUIDE

ITBP Indo-Tibetan Border Police

Constable

KITCHEN SERVICES

Recruitment Exam

by

RPH Editorial Board

2025
EDITION

RAMESH PUBLISHING HOUSE, NEW DELHI

Published by
O.P. Gupta *for* Ramesh Publishing House

Admin. Office
12-H, New Daryaganj Road, Opp. Officers' Mess,
New Delhi-110002 ✆ 23275224, 23245124

E-mail: info@rameshpublishinghouse.com
For Online Shopping: www.rameshpublishinghouse.com

Showroom
• Balaji Market, Nai Sarak, Delhi-6 ✆ 23253720, 23282525
• 4457, Nai Sarak, Delhi-6, ✆ 23918938

Book Code: R-2763

ISBN: 978-93-5477-892-6

Price: ₹ 195

Printed at: Deepak Offset, Delhi

ELEMENTARY MATHEMATICS

16. The speed of P and Q are in the ratio 3 : 4, P takes 20 minutes more than Q to reach a destination. In what time does P reach the destination?

A. $1\frac{1}{3}$ hours B. 1 hour
C. $2\frac{2}{3}$ hours D. $1\frac{2}{3}$ hours

17. The length of a rectangle is increased by 10% and breadth is decreased by 10%. Then the area of the new rectangle is

A. Neither decreased nor increased
B. Increased by 1%
C. Decreased by 1%
D. Decreased by 10%

18. ₹ 395 are divided among P, Q and R in such a way that Q gets 25% more than P and 20% more than R. The share of P will be

A. ₹ 180 B. ₹ 195
C. ₹ 120 D. ₹ 98

19. Out of 7 given numbers, the average of the first four numbers is 21 and that of last four numbers is also 21. If the average of all the seven numbers is 20, the fourth number is

A. 30 B. 28
C. 32 D. 21

20. When an article was sold, there was a loss of 10%. If its selling price was increased by ₹ 30, there would have been a profit of 10%. Find its cost price.

A. ₹ 150 B. ₹ 130
C. ₹ 110 D. ₹ 200

21. Four bells are ringing at intervals of 12, 16, 24 and 36 minutes. They start ringing simultaneously at 12 O'clock. When will they again ring together?

A. 2:28 P.M.
B. 2:48 P.M.
C. 2:24 P.M.
D. 2:44 P.M.

22. 108 kg of ration is sufficient for 18 students for 15 days. For how many students will 70 kg of ration be sufficient for 25 days?

A. 7 B. 8
C. 9 D. 10

23. A man is 24 years older than his son, in 2 years, his age will be twice the age of his son. What is the present age of the son?

A. 20 yrs. B. 25 yrs.
C. 22 yrs. D. 24 yrs.

24. A shopkeeper wants to sell his goods at cost price, but uses a weight of 800 gm instead of a kilogram weight. Thus he makes a gain of

A. 2% B. 8%
C. 20% D. 25%

25. If $x = 5$, $y = -2$, what is the value of $(2x^2 - 3y^2)$?

A. 62 B. 38
C. 50 D. 60

ANALYTICAL APTITUDE & ABILITY TO OBSERVE AND DISTINGUISH PATTERNS

26. In a certain code language, 'MILK' is called as 'PURE', 'PURE' is called as 'BLOOD', 'BLOOD' is called as 'RED', 'RED' is called as 'BIRD', 'BIRD' is called as 'DRY'. Which colour is used to show danger?

A. BLOOD B. MILK
C. RED D. BIRD

27. In the following question, select the related word from the given alternatives.

Five : Pentagon :: Three : ?

A. Rectangle B. Square
C. Rhombus D. Triangle

28. Riya is younger than Ram. Kishan is younger than Ram but elder than Riya. Sandhya is elder than Sheetal and Ram both. Ram is younger than Sheetal. Among these five, who is the third youngest?

A. Riya B. Ram
C. Sheetal D. Kishan

29. In the following question, select the odd word pair from the given alternatives.

A. Cup : Crockery B. Stationery : Pen
C. Lizard : Reptile D. Ostrich : Bird

30. In the following question, select the related letter pair from the given alternatives.

GHLP : IKPU :: ?

A. CGKO : EJOT B. FGHI : HJMN
C. PSTW : WYZA D. ACDH : CFOR

31. Pointing to a woman in the photo, Keshav said that "It is a photo of the younger sister of my mother's only son's father" what is the relationship between the person in the photo with Keshav?

A. Wife B. Aunt
C. Sister D. Mother

32. In a certain code language, 'BULB' is written as '190', 'CALM' is written as '150'. What is the code for 'DOES' in that code language?

A. 180 B. 220
C. 210 D. 160

33. In the following question below are given some statements followed by some conclusions based on those statements. Taking the given statements to be true even if they seem to be at variance from commonly known facts. Read all the conclusions and then decide which of the given conclusion logically follows the given statements.

Statements:

I. All books are tables.
II. All chairs are books.

Conclusions:

I. Some tables are books.
II. All books are chairs.

A. Only conclusion II follow
B. Only conclusion I follow
C. Both conclusion I and II follow
D. Neither conclusion follow

34. In the following question, select the odd word from the given alternatives.

A. Fox B. Lion
C. Tiger D. Eagle

35. In the following question, select the missing number from the given series.

2, 8, 14, 20, 26, ?

A. 32 B. 30
C. 42 D. 36

36. Two figures given on the left side of (::) are related with some logic/rule/relation. Select the missing figure on the right of (::) from the given alternatives based on the same logic/rule/relation.

A.  B. 
C.  D. 

37. Identify the diagram that best represents the relationship among the given classes.

Sun, Moon, Earth

A.  B. 
C.  D. 

38. Rohan walks 10 km towards north from a point A. Then he turns right and walks 6 km. Then, he again turns right and walks 10 km. In which direction is he now from the starting point?

A. North B. North-east
C. East D. South-east

39. If 'W' means '÷', 'X' means '×', 'Y' means '+' and 'Z' means '–', then 2 Y 448 W 112 X 4 X 2 Y 8 Z 15 = ?

A. 27 B. 37
C. 36 D. 25

40. If TRAIN is written as WUDLQ then BUS would be written as ....

A. EXU B. DWU
C. EXV D. VXE

ENGLISH

41. Choose the word that best illustrates the meaning given below.

A person who pretends to be someone else in order to deceive or cheat others.

A. fake B. impostor
C. thief D. fraud

42. Choose the right antonym for the below word.

stimulate

A. disappoint B. dishearten
C. discourage D. stifle

43. Choose the right answer to complete the sentence.

Who spilled tea on my ____ carpet?

A. Turkish blue floral B. blue floral Turkish
C. Turkish floral blue D. floral blue Turkish

44. Choose the right synonym for the underlined word.

It is a <u>perilous</u> journey through the mountains.

A. safe B. tiring
C. dangerous D. enjoyable

45. Choose the word with the wrong spelling.

A. prankster B. trickster
C. youngster D. ganster

46. Choose the right answer to complete the sentence.

Consumers are anxious _____ the rise in prices of cereals.

A. about B. of
C. on D. for

47. Choose the right answer to complete the sentence.

Don't panic. The film _____ by the time we get there.

A. will not have been started
B. will not be starting
C. will not start
D. will not have started

48. Choose the correct conjunction to complete the sentence.

The team members managed the work _______ the manager not being there.

A. although B. despite
C. though D. inspite

49. Choose from the four options, the word that best substitutes the given phrase.

The study of the origin and history of words.

A. Linguistics B. Etymology
C. Verbose D. Anthology

50. Use the appropriate article for the sentence given below.

He has gone to .... hospital to visit a sick friend.

A. A B. An
C. The D. No article

OR

हिन्दी

41. 'आठ बार नौ त्यौहार' लोकोक्ति का अर्थ है:

A. कठिनाई का अनुभव करना B. मौजमस्ती का जीवन
C. निरन्तर कार्य करना D. मेल से न रहना

42. 'अनायारा' शब्द में प्रयुक्त उपसर्ग है :

A. अ B. अना
C. अन D. अनाया

43. निम्नलिखित में शुद्ध वाक्य है :

A. उसने पुरस्कार का तिरस्कार कर दिया।
B. उसने पुरस्कार का अवमान कर दिया।
C. उसने पुरस्कार का अनादर कर दिया।
D. उसने पुरस्कार का अपमान कर दिया।

44. 'पर्णकुटी' का विलोम होगा :

A. तुष्टि B. तटस्थ
C. प्रसाद D. प्रासाद

45. निम्नलिखित शब्दों में से तत्सम शब्द को पहचानिए।

A. दूध B. दाँत
C. दीवाली D. पुत्रवधू

46. निम्नलिखित शब्दों में कौन-सा शब्द रेखांकित शब्द का पर्यायवाची **नहीं** है?

सोहन मेरा <u>मित्र</u> है।

A. मीत B. सहचर
C. केसरी D. दोस्त

47. नीचे दिए गए शब्दों के लिए एक शब्द क्या है?
जो स्त्री मीठी बात करती हो।

A. वाचाल B. प्रियंवदा
C. बातूनी D. कर्कशा

48. जहाँ वर्णों की पुनरावृत्ति होती है वहाँ कौन-सा अलंकार होगा?

A. यमक B. अनुप्रास
C. उपमा D. उत्प्रेक्षा

49. 'जीवन + अनुकूल' का संधिरूप क्या होगा?

A. जीवनानुकूल B. जिवनानुकुल
C. जीवनअनुकुल D. जीवनाकुल

50. निम्नलिखित वाक्य में रेखांकित शब्द का समास क्या होगा?
मुंबई में <u>गगनचुंबी</u> इमारतें बहुत-सी हैं।

A. तत्पुरुष समास
B. द्विगु समास
C. कर्मधारय समास
D. बहुब्रीहि समास

ANSWERS

1. (B) **2.** (A) **3.** (D)
4. (B) **5.** (D) **6.** (C)
7. (B) **8.** (C) **9.** (C)
10. (B) **11.** (D) **12.** (D)
13. (B) **14.** (B) **15.** (B)

16. (A): Speed ratio = 3 : 4 (given)

Let Q takes time t minutes.

then P takes time $(t + 20)$ minutes to cover the same distance.

that means

$$4.t = 3.(t + 20)$$

or, $t = 60$ minutes.

Hence, time taken by P

$$= (60 + 20) \text{ minutes} = 80 \text{ minutes}$$

$$= 1\frac{1}{3} \text{ hours.}$$

17. (C): Area of rectangle A = length (ℓ) × breadth (b)

i.e., $A = \ell b$

when length increases by 20%

$$\ell' = \ell\left(1+\frac{10}{100}\right) = 1.1\ell$$

when breadth decreases by 10%

$$b' = b\left(1-\frac{10}{100}\right) = 0.9b$$

$$\text{New Area A}' = \ell'b' = 1.1\ell \times 0.9b$$
$$= 0.99\ \ell b = 0.99\ \text{A}$$
$$\text{A}' = \text{A}\left(1-\frac{1}{100}\right) = \text{A} - 1\%\text{A}$$

Hence, New Area is decreases by 1%.

18. (C)

19. (B): Sum of all 7 numbers = 20 × 7 = 140
Sum of first four numbers = 21 × 4 = 84
Sum of last four numbers = 21 × 4 = 84
Hence, fourth number = 84 + 84 – 140
= 168 – 140 = 28.

20. (A)

21. (C): L.C.M. of 12, 16, 24 and 36 = 144 minutes
So, in interval of 144 minutes all bell are ringing together
Hence, they will ring together at $\frac{144}{60}$ hours or, 2:24 P.M.

22. (A): 108 kg of ration is sufficient for 15 days for 18 students
108 kg of ration is sufficient for 1 day for 18 × 15 students
1 kg of ration is sufficient for 1 day for $\frac{18\times15}{108}$ students
∴ 70 kg of ration is sufficient for 25 days for $\frac{18\times15}{108}\times\frac{70}{25}$ students = 7 students.

23. (C): Let present age of his son is x years.
then father's age = $(x + 24)$ years.
According to the question,

$$(x + 24 + 2) = 2(x + 2)$$
$$x + 26 = 2x + 4$$

or, $x = 22$

Hence, Present age of the son = 22 years.

24. (D): If a trader professes to sell his goods at cost price, but uses false weights, then

$$\text{Gain \%} = \left(\frac{\text{Error}}{\text{True Value} - \text{Error}}\times 100\right)\%$$
$$= \left(\frac{1000-800}{1000-200}\right)\times 100 = \frac{200}{800}\times 100 = 25\%.$$

25. (B): ∵ $x = 5$ and $y = -2$
The value of $(2x^2 - 3y^2) = 2(5)^2 - 3(-2)^2$
$= 50 - 12 = 38.$

26. (D): Here, MILK → PURE
PURE → BLOOD
BLOOD → RED
RED → BIRD
BIRD → DRY
Red colour is used to danger,
RED is called as BIRD.

27. (D)

28. (B): Sandhya > Sheetal > Ram > Kishan > Riya
Here, Ram is the third youngest.

29. (B)

30. (A):

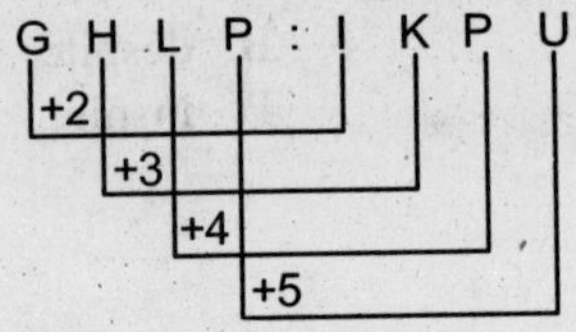

Similarly,

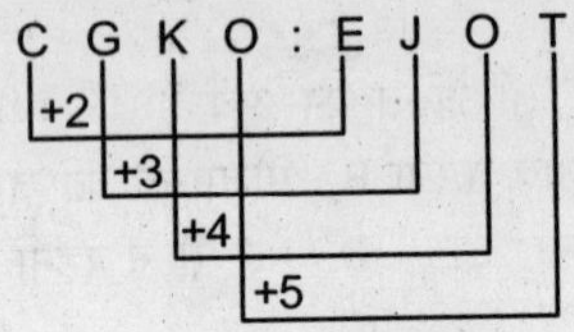

31. (B):

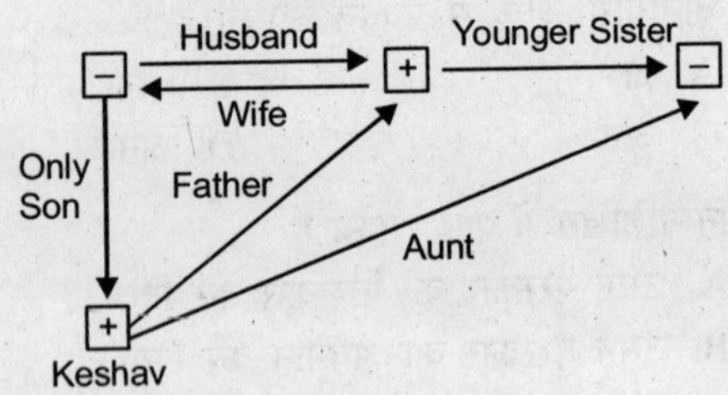

32. (B) **33. (B)**

34. (D)

35. (A):

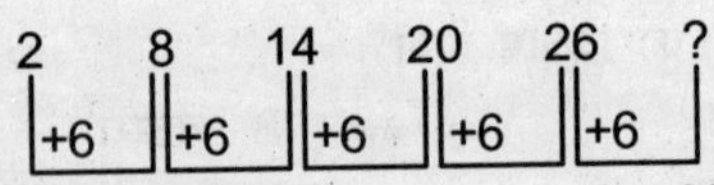

Here, Missing number = 26 + 6 = 32.

36. (D) **37. (A)**

38. (C):

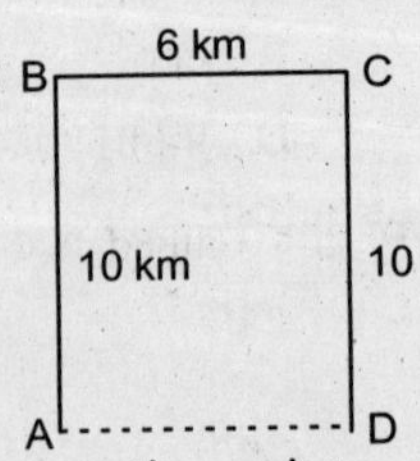

Here, starting point = A
Hence, Rohan is now east from the starting point.

39. (A)	**40. (C)**	**41. (B)**
42. (D)	**43. (B)**	**44. (C)**
45. (D)	**46. (A)**	**47. (D)**
48. (B)	**49. (B)**	**50. (C)**

OR

41. (B)	**42. (C)**	**43. (A)**
44. (D)	**45. (D)**	**46. (C)**
47. (B)	**48. (B)**	**49. (A)**
50. (A)		

ENGLISH LANGUAGE

CHAPTER

1

COMPREHENSION PASSAGES

ENGLISH LANGUAGE COMPREHENSION

The objective of language comprehension test is to ascertain the ability of the candidates to understand the passage properly. Therefore candidates are required to take notice of the following points:

1. Read the full passage very attentively and intelligently.
2. Try to comprehend the gist of it.
3. Make a mental note of all the important details and points given in the passage.
4. Read the passage for the second time in case you have not been able to understand it satisfactorily.
5. Divide the time proportionately for all the passages.
6. Answer the questions on the basis of facts, as given in the paragraph.
7. Don't waste much time in answering the questions of any one passage.
8. Check all the answers once again, very carefully, to see whether any question is left unanswered by mistake.

MODEL QUESTIONS (FOR PRACTICE)

Directions: *Each of the following passages is followed by five questions. Read the passage carefully and then answer the questions that follow each. For each question, four probable answers A, B, C and D are given. Only one out of these is correct. Choose the correct answer.*

PASSAGE-1

The use of words like 'welcome', 'thank you', 'please', etc., at the right moment reflects a polite nature. The civic sense also lies within the scope of good manners. We should not shout or talk loudly in public places like hospitals and libraries and create disturbance. We should not cheat people or make fun of them. Cleanliness is also necessary. We must not throw the waste on roads and make use of dustbins. We should not harm the public property as it belongs to all of us. While in a queue, discipline should be maintained. We must give fair chance to others.

1. Expressions like 'welcome' 'thank you' and 'please' reflect
A. happiness B. discipline
C. civic sense D. polite nature

2. While in a library, we should
A. respect others B. avoid arguments
C. talk in low tone D. be courteous

3. A public property belongs to
A. nobody B. all of us
C. government D. one who maintains it

4. Discipline is
A. the rule of proper conduct or action
B. the rule of road sense
C. making use of dustbins
D. forming a queue

5. The most appropriate title for this passage would be
A. Polite Nature B. Courtesy
C. Good Manners D. Civic Sense

PASSAGE-2

There is an old proverb 'Early to bed and early to rise makes a man healthy and wise.' I am in the habit of getting up early in the morning and have formed the habit of taking long morning walks in the past two years. It is a light exercise and best for physical fitness. The morning air which is fresh and pure is beneficial for the lungs. The early rays of the rising sun are good for healthy skin. 'Health is wealth' and doctors also recommend morning walk to their patients for gaining sound health and freshness of energy.

1. What is good for lungs?
   A. Sunrays B. Fresh air
   C. Sound sleep D. Light exercise
2. What is a light exercise?
   A. Early to bed B. Early to rise
   C. Morning walk D. Gaining sound health
3. What is good for skin?
   A. Fresh air B. Morning air
   C. Morning walk D. Rising sun's rays
4. What is best for physical fitness?
   A. Light exercise B. Long morning walk
   C. Early to rise D. Fresh and pure air
5. Long morning walk
   A. bring sound sleep
   B. ensures physical fitness
   C. ensures healthy skin
   D. keeps healthy, wealthy and wise

PASSAGE-3

Mahatma Gandhi lived a splendid long life and has set great moral standards before us. He showed to the world the true way to peace. He wished to see India prosper but he became a martyr for the noble cause of Hindu-Muslim unity at the time of partition when a religious fanatic, Nathuram Godse, shot him dead on January 30, 1948. His last words were 'Hey Ram'. He lived and died for his country and countryman.

1. Mahatma Gandhi showed the world the true way to
   A. prosperity B. love
   C. truth D. peace
2. Mahatma Gandhi became a martyr for the noble cause of
   A. truth B. non-violence
   C. freedom of India D. Hindu-Muslim unity
3. Mahatma Gandhi was shot dead
   A. before India achieved independence
   B. by a mad man
   C. by an intolerant religious person
   D. by a non-religious person
4. Mahatma Gandhi set great moral standards. It means
   A. he was a great religious teacher
   B. he was a great moralist
   C. he made India morally stronger
   D. moral was everything to him
5. Gandhiji lived and died for his country and countryman. It means
   A. he was born in India and died in India
   B. he was a patriot
   C. he was a great moralist
   D. he sacrified his life for India and her people

PASSAGE-4

On one hot day a crow felt very thirsty. He flew from one place to another in search of water. After long hours of labour he found a pitcher. Eagerly, he perched on the mouth of the pitcher. He found that the water was at the bottom of the vessel. He tried his best to dip his beak but did not succeed. He did not know what to do. Suddenly some pebbles lying nearby gave him an idea. One by one he dropped the pebbles with his beak into the pitcher. The level of water slowly came up to the mouth of the pitcher. The crow then drank the water and quenched his thirst.

1. The crow found a pitcher
   A. as it flew
   B. after many hours of labour
   C. full of water
   D. which was empty
2. What is the moral of the passage?
   A. No pains, no gains
   B. God helps those who help themselves
   C. Necessity is the mother of invention
   D. Try and try again, you will succeed at last
3. The crow flew from place to place
   A. in search of pitcher
   B. in search of pebbles
   C. in search of water
   D. in search of a vessel
4. The pitcher, the crow found
   A. was full of water
   B. was dry
   C. had little water in the bottom
   D. had water up to its mouth
5. As the crow dropped pebbles into the pitcher, what happend?
   A. The pitcher broke down
   B. The water leaked one of the pitcher
   C. The level of water into the pitcher rose up slowly
   D. Water level immediately rose to the mouth of the pitcher

PASSAGE-5

Once upon a time a crane and a fox lived in a forest. They were good friend. One day the fox invited the crane to a feast. He made a tasty food and served it before the crane on a plate. The crane could not eat anything because of the long beak. But the fox licked all his food. The crane felt insulted. He decided to teach the fox a lesson Next day he invited the fox. He prepared the same tasty food and placed it in front of the fox inside a narrow glass. The crane ate easily while the fox looked on. Now, it was the fox's turn to remain hungry.

1. What is the moral of the passage?
   A. Beware of the wicked
   B. One good turn deserves another

C. Be contented with what you have
D. Tit for tat

2. The crane could not eat tasty food because the
A. food was served in a shallow plate
B. food was very hot
C. food was served in a long jar
D. crane was not hungry

3. The fox had to remain hungry because
A. the food served was not enough in quantity
B. the food was served inside a narrow glass
C. the food served was not tasty
D. the food was all liquid

4. Why did the crane feel insulted?
A. Because he was invited to feast but he could not eat anything
B. Because the food was served in a shallow plate and he could not eat
C. Because the food was too hot
D. Because the fox gulped all the food quickly

5. The crane successfully taught a lesson to the fox when he invited the fox to a feast and served the food
A. in a narrow glass
B. in a large plate
C. in a broken plate
D. in a long jar

PASSAGE-6

The family set down at the table and began to talk about the summer holidays. They had to decide a place to visit during the vacation. Should they go to their village or to a hill station? The parents preferred the village while the children wished to go the hill station. After few moments of discussion the elders decided to visit both the places. First they shall go to the village for a week and then stay at the hill station for the remaining days. For the first time the family shall be together during the holidays. The children were happy with the holiday plan.

1. The purpose for which the family set down at the table was
A. to decide a place to visit during the vacation
B. to educate the children how to carry articles during a visit to a hill station
C. to decide the date when they should start their journey
D. to tell the children that they will visit a hill station during this vacation

2. The final plan was to visit
A. their village
B. a hill station
C. their village as well as a hill station
D. their home town

3. The final decision was made by
A. the boys　　B. the girls
C. the women　　D. the elders

4. They decided first to go to their village and stay there for
A. a day　　B. a week
C. ten days　　D. a fortnight

5. Why were children happy?
A. Because a hill station was included in their holiday plan
B. Because a visit to their village was excluded from their holiday plan
C. Because their choice prevailed
D. Because they were going all alone to the hill station

PASSAGE-7

Once Govind intended to go on pilgrimage with his family. He asked Mirind to accompany. But for his trade's reason, he did not go with him. So Govind thought it safe to leave the box of his jewellery with him, as it was dangerous to leave it in a lone house or take it on the journey. So he went to him with the box. He took him to a lonely place under a tree and handed it over to him. He told Mirind, "Keep it safe with you. I shall return from the journey after six month then I shall take it back from you." Mirind said, "Don't worry, I shall keep it as safe as own."

1. Govind intended to go
A. for a business trip
B. to a hill station
C. on a long journey to a sacred place
D. to his home town for a long period

2. Why did Govind leave his box of jewellery with Mirind?
A. Because it was not safe to take the box with him on a long journey
B. Because Mirind was his fast friend
C. Because the box was very heavy
D. Because his house was unsafe

3. Why did Govind take Mirind to a lonely place?
A. To tell him that the box contained valuable jewellery
B. So that no third person could see box
C. To show him what was within the box
D. To tell him that the box will remain with him

4. Where did Govind hand over the box of jewellery to Mirind?
A. At Mirind's house
B. At his own house
C. In a lonely place
D. In a lonely place under a tree

5. It was not safe to leave the box in a lone house. Here the word 'lone house' means
A. a house in a deserted place
B. a house where none lives
C. a house without door and lock
D. a house near the forest

PASSAGE-8

Zahir-ud-din Babar was the first Mughal emperor of India. A descendent of Timur on father's side and Changez Khan on his mother's side, Babar was a brave warrior. After defeating Ibrahim Lodhi in the First Battle of Panipat in 1526 he entered Delhi and soon gained control over Agra. After many more battles with Rajputs he extended his empire over Punjab, Uttar Pradesh and north Bihar. He died at a young age of 48 years in 1530 at his capital Agra without getting much time to consolidate his victories.

1. Zahir-ud-din Babar was the first
   A. Muslim ruler of India
   B. Mughal ruler of India
   C. Afghan ruler of India
   D. Turk ruler of India
2. Babar was born in the years
   A. 1480 B. 1482
   C. 1492 D. 1962
3. Babar first occupied
   A. Punjab B. Agra
   C. Delhi D. Panipat
4. Babar was a brave warrior. Here brave warrior means
   A. courageous soldier
   B. a kind hearted soldier
   C. a clever fighter
   D. a victorious general
5. Babar extended his empire over Punjab and Uttar Pradesh after many more battles with the
   A. Afghans B. Rajputs
   C. Mughals D. Lodhies

PASSAGE-9

Our National Flag is tricolour. It has three equal horizontal strips. The strip at the top is saffron, in the middle is white and at the bottom is green. The ratio of width to length of the flag is 2 : 3. In the centre of the white strip is a wheel in navy blue. The wheel represents the *chakra*. Its design is similar to the wheel which appears on the abacus of the Sarnath Lion Capital of Ashoka. Its diameter approximates to the width of the white strip. The wheel has 24 spokes. It was adopted by Constituent Assembly on July 22, 1947. We love our national flag. We respect it. We are ready to sacrifice our life to protect its honour. It represents the nation. So it is a symbol of national honour.

1. In our national flag the wheel is located in the centre of
   A. saffron strip B. white strip
   C. green strip D. blue strip
2. In our national flag which of the strips is at the bottom in our national flag
   A. blue C. saffron
   B. white D. green
3. Why do we love our national flag?
   A. Because it is tricolour
   B. Because it has three strips
   C. Because it has a wheel at the centre
   D. Because it is a symbol of national honour
4. Our national flag was approved by
   A. President B. Lok Sabha
   C. Parliament D. Constituent Assembly
5. The diameter approximates to the width of the white strip. Here the word 'approximates' means
   A. is more or less equal
   B. is exactly equal
   C. is not equal
   D. is related

PASSAGE-10

Distance in large cities are long. All the people do not have their own means of transport. They have to depend upon the state or private buses. The number of bus users is very large. Every bus stop is, therefore, crowded. The number of buses is not adequate. Thus people suffer the torture of long wait at the bus stop. Some bus stops are quite orderly. People form queues and get into the buses turn by turn. However, often this order is forgotten and confusion spreads when the bus comes and the law of jungle prevails.

1. Why are the bus stops crowded?
   A. Because they are small is size
   B. Because the number of passengers is very large
   C. Because they are situated at some busy centre
   D. Because people do not form queues
2. Long wait at the bus stop is the result of
   A. over-crowding in the buses
   B. late running of buses
   C. shortage of buses
   D. slow speed of buses
3. Some bus stops are quite orderly where
   A. there is no crowd
   B. the number of buses is adequate
   C. people do not have to wait for long
   D. people form queues and enter the buses one by one
4. Most of the people who travel by buses are
   A. non-working
   B. do not have their own vehicles
   C. have to go a long distance
   D. live in large cities
5. What happens when people do not have their own transport?
   A. They have to wait for a bus at a bus stop
   B. They have to depend upon the state or private buses
   C. They have to travel long distances
   D. They form queues and get into buses one by one

PASSAGE-11

A certain king once fell ill and doctors said that only a sudden fright would restore his health but the king was not a man for anyone to play tricks on, except his fool. One day, when the fool was with him in his boat he cleverly pushed the king into water but he was rescued and put to bed. The fright, the bath and bed cured the diseased king, but he was so angry with the fool that he turned him out of the country.

1. What did the doctor say about the king?
   A. Only a sudden fright would restore the king's health
   B. Only fool would cure the king
   C. Only a boat trick could cure the king
   D. The king had suffered a sudden fright
2. He cleverly pushed the king into water but *he* was rescued and put to bed. In this sentence *he* refers to
   A. the king B. the fool
   C. the doctor D. the river
3. When the fool pushed the king into water they were
   A. in the palace B. in the bed
   C. in the garden D. in a boat
4. Who played the trick on the king?
   A. The doctor
   B. The boatman
   C. The fool
   D. The fright
5. The fool who cured the king was
   A. rewarded
   B. thrown into water
   C. turned out of the country
   D. put into jail

ANSWERS

	1	2	3	4	5
Passage 1.	D	C	B	A	C
Passage 2.	B	C	D	B	B
Passage 3.	D	D	C	B	D
Passage 4.	B	C	C	C	C
Passage 5.	D	A	B	B	A
Passage 6.	A	C	D	B	A
Passage 7.	C	A	B	D	B
Passage 8.	B	B	C	A	B
Passage 9.	B	D	D	D	A
Passage 10.	B	C	D	B	B
Passage 11.	A	A	D	C	C

CHAPTER

2

ENGLISH GRAMMAR

PARTS OF SPEECH

Part of speech	Definition or Function	Examples
Noun	Name of a person, place, animal, quality or thing	Ram, boy, dog pen, sun, Delhi, truth, honesty
Pronoun	Used in place of a noun	I, you, he she, they
Articles & Determiners	Points out indefinite and definite nouns	a, an, the, few, some
Adjective	Describes a noun or pronoun	big, honest, wooden valuable, quiet, deep, soft, narrow
Adverb	Describes a verb, an adjective or another adverb	silently, widely, softly, quietly, very, carefully
Verb	Tells about action or state of something or someone	is, am, was, have, do, like, walk, work, make, throw, tell
Conjuction	Joins words, clauses or sentences	and, but, when, yet, while, else
Preposition	Links a noun or pronoun to another word	at, to, after, on for, under, over, with
Interjection	Expresses sudden feelings or emotions	Ah!, Alas!, oh!, ouch!, hi!, well!, Hurrah!

NOUNS

A word which denotes a person, a thing, an animal or a place is said to be a noun.

There are two noun numbers in English — the *Singular* and the *Plural*.

Singular Numbers : A noun that denotes one person or one thing, is said to be in the Singular number. For example — book, pencil, bird, dog, hen etc. are in singular number.

Plural Number : A noun that denotes more than one person or one thing is said to be in plural number. For example — boys, pens, lions, girls, men etc. are in plural number.

REMEMBER

Singular	*Plural*	*Singular*	*Plural*
Cat	Cats	Bamboo	Bamboos
Book	Books	Folio	Folios
Pen	Pens	Hero	Heroes
Room	Rooms	Volcano	Volcanoes
Tree	Trees	Mango	Mangoes
Bus	Buses	Potato	Potatoes
Bush	Bushes	Photo	Photos
Box	Boxes	Piano	Pianos
Glass	Glasses	Baby	Babies
Dish	Dishes	Fly	Flies
Judge	Judges	Country	Countries
Tax	Taxes	Lady	Ladies
Watch	Watches	Boy	Boys
Calf	Calves	Monkey	Monkeys
Thief	Thieves	Ox	Oxen
Knife	Knives	Child	Children
Scarf	Scarves	Man	Men
Wife	Wives	Woman	Women
Leaf	Leaves	Tooth	Teeth
Wolf	Wolves	Axis	Axes
Half	Halves	Basis	Bases
Monarch	Monarchs	Foot	Feet
Roof	Roofs	Goose	Geese
Hoof	Hoofs	Englishman	Englishmen
Gulf	Gulfs	Radius	Radii
Staff	Staffs	Vertex	Vertices
Radio	Radios	Stimulus	Stimuli

1. Note the plurals of the following nouns:

Singular	*Plural*	*Singular*	*Plural*
copy	copies	cry	cries
baby	babies	duty	duties
body	bodies	country	countries
family	families	diary	diaries
fly	flies	fairy	fairies
city	cities	spy	spies
army	armies	storey	storeys
bay	bays	monkey	monkeys

2. The following nouns do not undergo any change in plural form, in general.

Singular	*Plural*	*Singular*	*Plural*
deer	deer	sheep	sheep
thousand	thousand	pair	pair
hundred	hundred	score	score
dozen	dozen	gross	gross

Note: We can write—

(*a*) thousands of men; (*b*) two pairs of shoes; (*c*) dozens of mangoes; (*d*) scores of people etc. But—

(*a*) two thousand rupees; (*b*) three hundred men; (*c*) five dozen eggs, etc.

3. The following nouns are usually used in plural forms. They take a plural verb after them—

eatables	fetters	surroundings
riches	alms	spectacles
trousers	pants	scissors
premises	thanks	annals
congratulations	goods	shorts
tongs	pains	arms
breeches	(for troubles)	

4. The following are the nouns which are plural in appearance but are usually used in singular number. They are followed by a singular verb—

news	politics	physics
mathematics	economics	ethics
politics	classics	gallows
statistics	athletics	innings
mechanics	summons	mumps

5. Collective nouns often used as plurals—

public	police	cattle
audience	clergy	folk
people	poultry	nation
elite	gentry	glitterati

6. The nouns that are usually used in singular forms—

advice	hair	rice
fuel	alphabet	machinery
offspring	issue	furniture
mischief	stationery	luggage
bedding	information	abuse

7. Material nouns are always used in singular number—

gold	copper	milk
water	silk	wool

Note: They may be used in plural with a different meaning. copper coins (coppers), chains or fetters (irons), cans made of tin (tins).

GENDERS

The difference in sex is denoted by Gender in grammar. The various genders are as follows :

1. **Masculine Gender :** A noun that denotes a male is said to be of the masculine gender, as man, uncle, ox, boy etc.
2. **Feminine Gender :** A noun that denotes a female is said to be of feminine gender, as woman, aunt, princess, cow etc.
3. **Common Gender :** Nouns which denote both males and females are said to be of the common gender, as friend, cousin, person, parent, baby etc.
4. **Neuter Gender :** A noun that denotes the name of object without life is said to be of neuter gender, as file, table, pencil.

REMEMBER

Masculine	*Feminine*
Boy	Girl
Son	Daughter
Brother	Sister
Murderer	Murderess
Sorcerer	Sorceress
Son-in-law	Daughter-in-law
Father-in-law	Mother-in-law
Man-servant	Maid-servant
Land-lord	Land-lady
Bachelor	Maid
Gentleman	Lady
Monk	Nun
Earl	Countess
Lad	Lass
Sir	Madam
Duke	Dutchess
Emperor	Empress
Milk-man	Milk-maid
Pea-cock	Pea-hen
Step-father	Step-mother
Hero	Heroine
Viceroy	Vicerine
Mr.	Mrs.
Governor	Governess
Master	Mistress
Wizard	Witch
Heir	Heiress
Host	Hostess
Lion	Lioness
Mayor	Mayoress
Actor	Actress

Buck	Doe
Colt	Filly
Dog	Bitch
Horse	Mare
Count	Countess
Hunter	Huntress
Prince	Princess
Abbot	Abbess
God	Goddess
Author	Authoress
Ox	Cow
Widower	Widow
Grand-father	Grand-mother
He-goat	She-goat
Milk-man	Milk-woman
Bridegroom	Bride
Tiger	Tigress
Priest	Priestess
Poet	Poetess
Shepherd	Shepherdess
Nephew	Niece
Stag	Hind

PRONOUNS

The repetition of a noun in a sentence or a set of sentences is really boring. So, instead of repeating the noun, we can use a word (for that noun) called the pronoun.

"A pronoun is a word that we use instead of a noun".

Example:

This is *Sachin. He* plays cricket.

Note: *He* is the pronoun used in place of *Sachin.*

Kinds of Pronouns

1. **Personal pronouns :** A pronoun which is used instead of the name of a person is known as a 'Personal Pronoun'. A list of the 'Personal pronouns' is listed below :

I, my, mine, me, we	(First Person)
You, your, yours	(Second Person)
He, his, him, she, her, hers, it, its, they, their, theirs, them	(Third Person)

2. **Demonstrative, Indefinite and Distributive Pronouns:**

(a) Demonstrative Pronouns : Pronouns used to point out the objects to which they refer are called Demonstrative Pronouns.

Examples :

(i) *This* is a present from my uncle.

(ii) *These* are merely excuses.

(iii) Bombay mangoes are better than *those* of Bangaluru.

(b) Indefinite Pronouns : All pronouns which refer to persons or things in a general way and do not refer to any particular person or thing are called Indefinite Pronouns.

Examples :

(i) *Somebody* has stolen my watch.

(ii) *Few* escaped unhurt.

(iii) Did you ask *anybody* to come?

(c) Distributive Pronouns : Each, either, neither are called distributive pronouns because they refer to persons or things one at a time. For this reason they are always singular and followed by the verb in singular.

Examples :

(i) *Each* of the men received a reward.

(ii) *These* men received *each* a reward.

(iii) *Either* of you can go.

3. **Relative Pronouns :** A relative pronoun refers or relates to some noun going before, which is called its Antecedent.

Examples :

(i) I met Hari *who* used to live here.

(ii) I have found the pen *which* I had lost.

(iii) Here is the book *that* you lent me.

4. **Interrogative Pronouns :** These pronouns, are used for asking questions.

Examples :

(i) *Whose* book is this?

(ii) *What* will all the neighbours say?

(iii) *Which* do you prefer, tea or coffee?

Note : Interrogative pronouns can also be used in asking indirect questions. Consider the following examples :

(i) I asked *who* was speaking.

(ii) Tell me *what* you have done.

(iii) Say *which* you would like best.

Behaviour of the Pronouns

1. If three pronouns are used together in the same sentence they are arranged in the following order :

2	+	3	+	1
↓		↓		↓
Second Person		Third Person		First Person

Examples :

I, you and he must help *that* poor man. (Incorrect)

You, he and I must help *that* poor man. (Correct)

2. When two or more singular nouns are joined by and, the pronoun used for them should be plural.

Examples :

Mohan and Sohan are friends. *They* play football. *They* live at Lajpat Nagar.

3. But if these nouns joined by and refer to the same person or thing, the pronoun used should be singular.

Examples :

(*i*) Delhi, the beautiful city and the capital of India, is famous for *its* historical monuments.

(*ii*) The manager and owner of the firm expressed *his* views on the demands of the workers.

4. When two nouns are used with as well as, the pronoun agrees with the first subject.

Examples :

(*a*) Mohan as well as his friends is doing *his* work.

(*b*) The students as well as their teachers are doing *their* work.

5. When two singular nouns joined by 'and' are preceded by *each* or *every,* the pronoun used must be singular and should agree in gender with the second noun.

Examples :

(a) Every man and every woman will do *her* best for the nation.

(b) Each boy and each girl went to *her* house.

6. When two nouns are joined by using 'with', the pronoun agrees with the noun coming before 'with'.

Examples :

(a) The boy with *his* parents has gone to see a movie.

(b) The children with *their* parents have gone to picnic.

7. When two different nouns are joined by either......... or; neither .... nor, the pronoun is used according to the number and gender of the second noun.

Examples :

(a) Either your sister or you have done *your* work.

(b) Neither the students nor the teacher was in *his* class.

8. The pronoun coming after '*than*' must be in the same case as that coming before '*than*'.

Examples :

(a) She plays better than *me*. (Incorrect)
She plays better than *I*. (Correct)

(b) His elder brother is more intelligent than *him*. (Incorrect)
His elder brother is more intelligent than *he*. (Correct)

9. 'Many a' always takes a singular pronoun and singular verb.

Example :

Many a soldier has met *his* death in the battle field.

10. 'Who', 'Whose', 'Whom' are used only for persons.

Examples :

(a) *Who* is knocking at the door?

(b) *Whose* pen is this?

(c) *What* do you want?

11. 'Which' is used for things.

Example :

Which game do you like?

MULTIPLE CHOICE QUESTIONS

Directions: *In the following questions choose the correct options to fill the blanks.*

1. The place was so dirty that ..... wished to run away from there.
A. everybody B. anybody
C. few D. some

2. ..... was there to help me.
A. Somebody B. Anything
C. Anybody D. Nobody

3. Is there .... to eat?
A. some B. something
C. any D. few

4. ..... of the students were making a great noise.
A. Anyone B. Somebody
C. Many D. Nobody

5. ..... of the students can solve this sum.
A. Someone B. Anybody
C. Somebody D. None

6. ...... of us should try our best to make India a heaven.
A. Any B. Somebody
C. Anybody D. All

7. ...... of us do not know the real meaning of our lives.
A. Any B. Something
C. Several D. Many

8. My .... black.
A. hairs are B. hair is
C. hairs shall D. hair will

9. She saw two .... on the last Sunday.
A. thiefs B. theifs
C. thieves D. theives

10. My sister is a ....
A. bacheloress B. bachelor
C. unmaried D. spinster

11. One is supposed to do ....
A. our duty B. their duty
C. one's duty D. his duty

12. Take anything .... you want.
A. that B. which
C. than D. then

13. I cannot tolerate ....
A. separated you
B. your separation
C. separation from you
D. you separated

14. He is .... faithful partner.
A. Yours B. You
C. Your D. Your's

15. Ajay is more smart than ....
A. her B. hers
C. herself D. she

16. Vivek works harder than ....
A. me B. I
C. her D. his

17. They should help ....
A. the poor people B. the poor
C. the poor persons D. the poor peoples

18. .... are mad.
A. All his sons B. His all sons
C. Sons all his D. All sons his

19. The poor fellow .... to fate.
A. resigned
B. resigned himself
C. resigned itself
D. resigned themselves

20. Nobody will help you but ....
A. I B. me
C. ours D. his

21. It is a good chance, You must avail .... this opportunity.
A. of B. yourself of
C. for D. from

22. The person who is elected .... my relative.
A. is B. he is
C. his D. him

23. He made ....
A. yours mention
B. mention of you
C. mention for you
D. mention about you

24. .... I know, he is quite faithful.
A. As far as B. So far as
C. So far this D. So far so

25. It is a duty of a person to take .... for his family.
A. pain B. pains
C. pain-killers D. pained

26. She does not love .... husband.
A. his B. her
C. its D. their

27. Let .... work together.
A. him and me B. he and I
C. he and him D. I and me

28. Copper, Silver and Gold ....
A. each will do B. either will do
C. any one will do D. any will do

29. Jessica and Roma are very irregular .... habits.
A. in her B. in their
C. in its D. in every

30. One likes to enjoy .... who was a great poet.
A. The sonnets of Shakespeare
B. Shakespeare's sonnets
C. Sonnets
D. Shakespeare

31. That is the boy .... everybody loves.
A. whom B. who
C. that D. whose

32. That is the girl .... won the first prize.
A. whom B. who
C. whose D. which

33. That is the man .... purse was lost.
A. who B. whom
C. whose D. their

ANSWERS

1	2	3	4	5	6	7	8	9	10
A	D	B	C	D	D	D	B	C	D
11	**12**	**13**	**14**	**15**	**16**	**17**	**18**	**19**	**20**
C	A	C	C	D	B	B	A	B	B
21	**22**	**23**	**24**	**25**	**26**	**27**	**28**	**29**	**30**
B	A	B	A	B	B	A	C	B	A
31	**32**	**33**							
A	B	C							

ARTICLES

The family of the articles has only three members. They are: A, An and The. However, they fall under two groups :
(a) Definite Article *(b)* Indefinite Article

'The' is known as definite article whereas 'a' and 'an' are known as indefinite articles.

Use of the Definite Article 'The'

'The' is used before

1. The superlative degree :
He is the ablest man of the town.
(ablest is a superlative degree)

2. The name of states, countries etc. having a descriptive name :
   (i) The J & K is a small state. (J & K is a descriptive name)
   (ii) He lives in the U.S.A. (U.S.A. is a descriptive name) (But the Delhi and the America are wrong because neither Delhi nor America is a descriptive name)
3. The names of the scriptures :
   The Gita is a holy book. (Gita is a scripture)
4. Name of newspapers :
   The Tribune is published from Chandigarh.
5. Name of rivers, canals, seas, oceans, bays, gulfs, groups of islands etc. :
   (i) The Ganga is a holy river.
   (ii) The Indian Ocean is the deepest ocean.
   (iii) The Persian Gulf is a narrow gulf.
6. The name of famous buildings :
   The Taj is one of the best buildings in India.
7. The names of nationals, sects and communities:
   (i) The English defeated the Germans in the World War.
   (ii) The rich should help the poor.
   (iii) The Hindus believe in the caste system.
8. Proper nouns used as common nouns :
   (i) Kalidas is the Shakespeare of India.
   (ii) Delhi is the London of India.
9. Famous historical events :
   The Industrial Revolution changed the face of England.
10. The directions and the celestial bodies:
    The sun rises in the east.
11. Titles :
    Akbar, the Great was loved by his subjects.

Do not use 'the'

1. Before languages :
   The English is an international language. (Incorrect)
   English is an international language. (Correct)
2. Before the names of games :
   The hockey is a popular game. (Incorrect)
   Hockey is a popular game. (Correct)

Use of the Indefinite Articles 'A' and 'An'

'A' is used before :

1. All singular common nouns beginning with a consonant:
   (i) A boy sings a song.
   (ii) A black and a white cow were grazing in the field.
2. If a word begins with a vowel but gives the sound of a consonant, 'a' should be used before it :
   (i) He was helped in his work by a European.
   (ii) He is a one-eyed man.
   (iii) It is a useful work.

'An' is used as follows :

1. All singular common nouns beginning with a vowel (*i.e.*, a, e, i, o, u) :
   (i) He is an artist.
   (ii) He is an old man.
   (iii) I intend to buy an umbrella.
2. If a word starts with a consonant but gives the sound of a vowel, "an" should be used before it :
   (i) Brutus is an honourable man.
   (ii) He is an honour to his profession.
   (iii) He is an L.L.B.
   (iv) He is an M.A.
   (v) You will reach there in an hour.

Demonstratives, that, these and those

1. The demonstrative adjectives and pronouns are for objects nearby the speaker:
   this (singular) those (plural)
   and for objects far away from the speaker.
   That (singular) those (plural)
2. Demonstratives are the only adjectives that agree in number with their nouns.
   That hat is nice.
   Those hats are nice.
3. When there is the idea of selection, the pronoun "one" (or "ones") often follows the demonstrative.
   I want a book. I'll get this (one).
   If the demonstrative is followed by an adjective, "one"(or "ones") must be used.
   I want a book. I'll get this big one.

MULTIPLE CHOICE QUESTIONS

Directions: *In the following questions choose the correct options to fill the blanks.*

1. .... will have to be paid for this material.
A. Half rupee B. Half a rupee
C. A half rupee D. An half rupee

2. .... is taking keen interest in India.
A. The USA B. USA
C. An USA D. A USA

3. Only .... can save our country.
A. the Hitler B. a Hitler
C. Hitler D. an Hitler

4. I can run for ....
A. hundred miles
B. the hundred miles
C. a hundred miles
D. an hundred miles.

5. .... man-eater has been killed.
A. The B. A
C. An D. Either A or B

6. What .... fine idea!
A. the B. an
C. a D. No article

7. .... earth is moving around the sun.
A. An B. A
C. The D. No article

8. This is .... first example while I got.
A. the B. a
C. an D. No article

9. This is .... house which was built during earthquake.
A. a B. an
C. the D. No article

10. .... America is a rich country.
A. The B. An
C. A D. No article

11. .... U.S.A. is a developed country.
A. A B. An
C. The D. No article

12. .... Bible is a holy book.
A. A B. The
C. An D. No article

13. .... rich should help the poor.
A. The B. A
C. An D. No article

14. .... Gold is a costly metal.
A. The B. A
C. An D. No article

15. Kalidas is .... Shakespeare of India.
A. a B. an
C. the D. No article

16. I cannot do .... difficult work.
A. a such B. the such
C. such the D. such a

17. How foolish .... plan it is!
A. a B. an
C. the D. No article

18. An ink is .... useful article.
A. an B. a
C. the D. No article

19. They are .... husband and wife.
A. a B. an
C. the D. No article

20. He is learning .... French
A. the B. a
C. an D. No article

ANSWERS

1	2	3	4	5	6	7	8	9	10
B	A	B	C	D	C	C	A	C	D
11	**12**	**13**	**14**	**15**	**16**	**17**	**18**	**19**	**20**
C	B	A	D	C	D	A	B	D	D

ADJECTIVES & ADVERBS

An Adjective is a word which adds something to the meaning of a noun or a pronoun.

Mridula is an *intelligent* girl.
He has a *black* goat.
He is a *brilliant* student.
She is a *clever* girl.
It is a *beautiful* picture.

In the sentences given above, the words in italics are adjectives.

An Adverb is a word which qualifies the meaning of a Verb, an Adjective or another Adverb.

(*i*) He talks *slowly.*
(*ii*) He is a *very* good student.
(*iii*) He talks *very* slowly.

In sentence (*i*), *slowly* qualifies the verb *talks.*
In sentence (*ii*), *very* qualifies the adjective *good.*
In sentence (*iii*), *very* qualifies the adverb *slowly.*

Adjectives have three degrees of comparison :

1. **Positive Degree :** It expresses the common form of an adjective.
Example :
Ram is a *tall* boy.
In the above sentence *tall* is an adjective and expresses the common form.

2. **Comparative Degree :** It expresses the more of the same form.
Example :
Ram is *taller* than Mahesh.
In the above sentence *taller* is an adjective that expresses the more of the common form of the adjective *tall.*

"When and How to Use" Comparative Degree?

(a) Comparative Degree is used when two persons or two groups of persons or things are compared.
Examples :
(a) He is *wiser* than his younger brother.
(b) This glass is *cleaner* than the other.

(b) When two different qualities in the same person are compared, more is used instead of 'er' to form the comparative. The formula used in this case should be :

More + Positive Degree

She is *fairer* than polite. (Incorrect)

She is *more fair* than polite. (Correct)

(c) When selection of one out of two persons or things is meant, the degree of comparison is followed by of and *the* is used before it.

Example :

Zia is abler of *the* two sisters.

(d) If two comparatives are used in the same sentence to impress upon an idea, both should be preceded by the definite article.

Examples :

(i) The higher you go, the cooler it is.

(ii) The more we get, the more we desire.

(e) When one person or thing is compared with another of the same kind, other is used after the comparative degree. In such sentences other is normally preceded by any or all.

Examples :

(i) Kalidas is greater than any dramatist. (Incorrect)

Kalidas is greater than any other dramatist. (Correct)

(ii) Lead is heavier than all metals. (Incorrect)

Lead is heavier than all other metals. (Correct)

(f) Senior, junior, superior, inferior, prior, anterior (earlier than) and posterior (later than) are always followed by 'to'.

Examples :

(i) Ram is senior *to* Mohan by three years.

(ii) That pen is inferior *to* that.

(iii) He is junior *to* me in rank.

(iv) This event was posterior *to* that.

Note: Never use *than* after the above mentioned adjectives.

Important Information

(a) 'Preferable' is also used as an adjective of the comparative degree. As such, it is always followed by *to* and not *a*.

Death is preferable than dishonour. (Incorrect)

Death is preferable *to* dishonour. (Correct)

(b) To intensify the Degree of comparison, we use *far* or *much* before the comparative.

Examples :

(i) This book is *far* better than that.

(ii) His performance was *much* better than Mohan's.

Warning : Always avoid the use of double comparatives.

Don't say : Ram is more cleverer than his younger brother.

Say: Ram is cleverer than his younger brother.

3. **Superlative Degree :** It expresses the most of the common form of an adjective.

Example :

He is the ablest man of the town.

How and when to use the Superlative Degree?

(a) The Superlative Degree is used when more than two persons or things are compared.

(b) The Superlative Degree is generally preceded by 'the' and followed by 'of' in most of the cases or otherwise.

(c) When an adjective of the superlative degree is preceded by a Possessive Adjective or a Noun in the Possessive case, 'the' should not be used before it.

Example :

Which is Kalidas' best play?

It will be a blunder to use 'the' before the Superlative Degree in such cases.

Don't say : Which is Kalidas' the best play.

(d) To intensify the degree of comparison, *by far* is used before the superlative degree.

Example :

India is *by far* the most beautiful country of the world.

Note: Always avoid the use of double superlatives.

Don't say : He is the most strongest boy in the class.

Say : He is the strongest boy in the class.

Use of some Important Adjectives

1. (a) **'Some'** is used as follows :

(i) With countable nouns where it means— a little, a small quantity.

(ii) In a question which shows some request.

Examples :

(i) There is some water in the bottle.

(ii) Some of the students were absent yesterday.

(iii) Will you have some milk?

(iv) Will you buy some fruit for me?

(b) **'Any'** is used as follows :

(i) In negative sentences.

(ii) In interrogative sentences.

(iii) After 'Hardly', 'Scarcely' and 'Barely'.

(iv) After 'If'.

Examples :

(i) There isn't any sugar in the pot.

(ii) She didn't buy any tomatoes.

(iii) I have hardly any money.

(iv) There are scarcely any plants in this field.

(v) If there is any danger, blow the whistle.

2. (a) **Older :** Older (and oldest) are used for persons animals and things. But 'Older' and 'Oldest' refer to the persons who do not belong to the same family.

Examples :

(i) Radha is older than Shyama.

(ii) John is the oldest member of the staff.

'Older' and 'Oldest' refer to the persons who do not belong to the same family.

(b) **Elder** (and **eldest**) are used in respect of the members of the same family like sons, daughters, brothers, sisters.

Examples :

(i) My elder sister is a lecturer.

(ii) Meenakshi is the eldest of the three sisters.

Note :

(i) 'Elder' is not followed by 'than'.

(ii) 'Elder' and 'Eldest' cannot be used for things.

3. (a) **'Few'** is negative and is the opposite of 'Many'. It means 'not many'.

(b) **'A few'** is positive and means 'some at least'. It is the opposite of 'None'.

(c) **'The few'** means 'minority' and suggests 'whether there is'.

Examples :

(i) We have few holidays in school.

(ii) Only a few boys will fail in the examination.

(iii) The few poems that he wrote are very popular.

4. (a) **Further** means 'something additional'.

(b) **Farther** means 'a greater distance'.

Examples :

(i) Further discussion will be held in the office of the principal.

(ii) Amritsar is farther from Delhi than Ambala.

5. (a) **Little** is negative. It means, 'not much', or 'hardly any'.

(b) **A little** is positive. It means 'some quantity'.

(c) **The little** denotes quantity. It means, 'not much but all that is, or whatever quantity there is'.

Examples :

(i) There is little hope of his success.

(ii) He knows a little of everything.

(iii) I have spent the little money I had.

(iv) The little knowledge of shoe-making proved very useful to me.

6. (a) **'Much'** expresses 'quantity'.

(b) **'Many'** expresses 'number'.

(c) **'Many a'**—'Singular noun' and 'Singular verb' are used with 'many a'.

Examples :

(i) There is not *much* water in the jug.

(ii) *Many* boys are absent today.

(iii) *Many* a battle has been fought on the soil of India.

7. (a) **'Less'** denotes 'in a small degree'.

(b) **'Fewer'** denotes 'number'.

Examples :

(i) He devotes less time to his studies.

(ii) There are no fewer than ten chairs in this room.

8. (a) **'Each'** is used for a single number of 'two persons' or 'things'.

(b) **'Every'** is used for a single number of 'many persons' or 'things'.

Examples :

(i) Each boy must take part in games.

(ii) There are only two poets. Each poet recited his poem.

(iii) Every man dies in this world.

(iv) Every man is expected to do his duty.

9. (a) **'Either'** means one of the two or both.

(b) **'Neither'** is negative of the either.

Examples :

(i) You may buy either of these two chairs.

(ii) Neither of them could speak on the stage.

10. (a) **'Later'** expresses 'late in time'.

(b) **'Latter'** means 'second in position or order'.

Examples :

(i) My father reached later than I expected.

(ii) The latter position was better than the former.

Use of some Important Adverbs

1. (a) Also, too, enough:

(i) He taught English. Also, he edited the school magazine

(ii) He is a writer and also a painter.

(iii) He is too obstinate to listen to any reason.

(iv) This is too difficult a piece for the junior students.

(v) Sarla was kind enough to help the poor.

(vi) He is brave enough to help the truth.

Note: 'Too' is used in a negative sense, but enough is used in a positive sense.

(b) Fairly and rather: Both suggest the meaning 'moderately'. But, mainly 'fairly' is used with the words that denote a positive meaning and rather is used with the words that denote a negative meaning:

(i) Rita did fairly well in that competition, but her performance was rather poor in sports.

(ii) Mona is fairly rich, but she is rather stingy.

Note: 'Rather' can also be used in a positive sense.

(i) This is a rather interesting job.

(ii) That boy is rather smart.

(c) Hardly, barely, scarcely: These words mostly convey the negative suggestions and are almost similar.

(i) I have hardly any strength now.

(ii) There was barely any supply to the township,

(iii) There were scarcely a hundred guests present.

Note: With slight variance in the meaning, the words given above convey the idea of 'very little', 'not enough', 'lack of quantity and number'.

(d) Yet, Still: These adverbs can often be used to connect the sentence units:

(i) He has been defeated many times in the contest; still he wants to be a competitor.

(ii) Mona was sick; yet she went on doing her work.

(e) Alone:

(i) He alone (none else) is capable of handling that fire,

(ii) He hunted all alone in the forest. (not in any company)

Special Note:

(a) Apart from their conventional positions the adverbs might be used in different positions with different meanings and angles.

(i) He had only four books.

(ii) John only contacted his friend in need.

(iii) He greeted me only.

(iv) Only he greeted me there.

(b) Inversion: Some adverbs can be inverted *i.e.* placed in the beginning of the sentence and then be followed by an interrogative form. The most common of these adverb are: so, seldom, never, nowhere, under no circumstances, hardly, scarcely etc.

(i) So big was the bus that it could not enter the narrow lane.

(ii) Hardly had he reached the station when he received the message.

MULTIPLE CHOICE QUESTIONS

Directions: *In the following questions choose the correct options to fill the blanks.*

1. The girl whom you met is the .... sister of Ravi.
A. eldest B. elder
C. older D. oldest

2. The historical place is ....
A. seeing worth B. worthy of seeing
C. worth seeing D. worthy seeing

3. These flowers smell ....
A. sweet B. sweetly
C. more sweetly D. sweetest

4. .... aspirant cannot pass the entrance examination.
A. Each B. Every
C. All D. No

5. Harivansh Rai .... second Shakespeare.
A. is a B. is
C. is the D. is an

6. .... student in the class got prizes.
A. Each and every B. Every and each
C. Every D. Never

7. It is .... picture than the one we saw last Monday.
A. interesting B. much interesting
C. more interesting D. most interesting

8. She is clever ....
A. that her mother is B. as her mother is
C. to her mother is D. than her mother is

9. They will get ....
A. Red, green and black paper
B. Red, green black paper
C. Red and green and black paper
D. Red green black paper

10. Health is .... wealth.
A. preferable to
B. more preferable than
C. more preferable to
D. most preferable then

11. .... water that was in the jug evaporated.
A. Little B. The little
C. Small D. A small

12. He has not sung .... songs.
A. much B. most
C. more D. many

13. Srishti has searched .... office.
A. whole the B. the whole
C. a whole D. some whole

14. Premchand was .... best and .... famous writer.
A. a, the most B. the, a most
C. the, more D. the, the most

15. William Shakespeare is famous as ....
A. a poet and a dramatist
B. a poet and dramatist
C. the poet and the dramatist
D. a poet and the dramatist

16. What does .... leader suggest?
A. other B. another
C. others D. anothers

17. He .... money.
A. has few B. have few
C. has little D. have little

18. The .... boys are rewarded.
A. first two B. two first
C. firsts two D. two's first

19. He is .... brave.
A. stronger than B. stronger then
C. more strong then D. more strong than

20. No sooner said ....
A. so done B. and done
C. than done D. but done

21. She returned .... than I had thought.
A. quickly B. more quicker
C. more quickly D. quicker

22. He is .... foolish person.
A. rather the B. a rather
C. rather a D. rather

23. This pen .... rupees.
A. costs twenty B. twenty costs only
C. costs only twenty D. only costs twenty

24. It is .... pride.
A. nothing else but B. nothing else than
C. else nothing than D. but

25. This tea is .... to drink.
A. too hot B. very hot
C. enough hot D. much hot

ANSWERS

1	2	3	4	5	6	7	8	9	10
A	C	A	B	C	C	C	B	A	A
11	**12**	**13**	**14**	**15**	**16**	**17**	**18**	**19**	**20**
B	D	B	D	B	B	C	A	D	C
21	**22**	**23**	**24**	**25**					
C	C	C	A	A					

DETERMINERS

Determiners are actually Adjectives. They are always followed by nouns.

Determiners are of the following kinds:

1. Demonstrative Determiners
this, that, these, those

2. Possessive Determiners
my, our, your, his, her, its, their

3. Quantitative Determiners
some, any, much, enough, sufficient, whole, a little, the little, little, all, both

4. Numerical Determiners
a few, some, few, the few, any, several, many, no, etc.

One, two, three ... (Cardinals)

First, second, third ... (Ordinals)

5. Distributive Determiners
either, neither

6. Articles
Indefinite: a, an

Definite: the

MULTIPLE CHOICE QUESTIONS

Directions: *In the following questions choose the correct options to fill the blanks.*

1. Give me .... rice.
A. some B. few
C. a few D. any

2. .... sheep grazing on the slope of the hill had gone away.
A. Any B. The few
C. This D. Much

3. Have you got .... magazines to read?
A. all B. much
C. some D. little

4. I have .... money that I want to spend on shares.
A. any B. much
C. less D. some

5. There is .... owl on the branch of the tree.
A. a B. the
C. an D. some

6. My brother is .... MBA.
A. a B. an
C. the D. any

7. Have you got .... cheese?
A. some B. many
C. a few D. few

8. No, I have not got .... cheese.
A. many B. few
C. any D. some

9. There is only .... milk left in the bottle.
A. enough B. few
C. much D. a little

10. There is .... hope of his recovery.
A. any B. little
C. many D. few

11. .... dogs were barking at the strangers.
A. Some B. Any
C. Much D. Less

. The girl bought her father .... juice.

A. few | B. some
C. any | D. many

You should take .... honey everyday.

A. any | B. many
C. a little | D. a few

.... boy was punished by the teacher.

A. Either | B. All
C. Any | D. Many

.... girl was asked to join the army.

A. None | B. Neither
C. All | D. Any

.... water in the jug has been drunk by Mohan.

A. The little | B. The few
C. A few | D. Few

17. I shall play .... piano at the party.

A. some | B. any
C. the | D. few

18. .... labourers were found dead in the mine.

A. Any | B. Fewer
C. Many | D. Less

19. Could I borrow .... umbrella?

A. our | B. your
C. yours | D. my

20. My brother is standing in the .... row.

A. any | B. many
C. some | D. first

ANSWERS

1	2	3	4	5	6	7	8	9	10
A	B	C	D	C	B	A	C	D	B
11	**12**	**13**	**14**	**15**	**16**	**17**	**18**	**19**	**20**
A	B	C	A	B	A	C	C	B	D

THE VERB

Verb is a word that tells something about the action or te of or happenning to a person or thing.

A Verb tells the following:

1. What a person or thing does.
Sachin goes to school daily.
The bell *rang* loudly.
Many birds fly in the sky.
She *sang* a song.

2. What a person or thing is.
India *is* the biggest democracy in the world.
Ram Mehar *is* very rich.
They *are* happy.

3. What is done to a person or thing.
You *are liked* by all.
Two thieves *were arrested.*
Four students *were punished* by the teacher.

4. What happens to a person or thing.
His maternal uncle *died* last week.
Two ships *sank* yesterday.
Leaves *turn* yellow in autumn.

5. What a person or thing has, had, and so on.
I *have* a new car.
He *had* a scooter last year.
He *has* several cows and goats.

It goes without saying that a verb is the most important 't of a sentence. No sentence is complete without a Verb.

Important Information

1. If two or more singular nouns are joined by 'and' the verb used will be plural.

   Example:
   (i) He and I were going to the market.
   (ii) Ram and Mohan are friends.

2. If two singular nouns joined by 'and' points out to the same thing or person, the verb used must be singular.

   Example:
   (i) Rice and curry is the favourite food of the Punjabis.
   (ii) The Collector and District Magistrate is away.

3. In case two subjects are joined by 'as well as' the verb agrees with the first subject.

   Example :
   (i) Kanta as well as her children is playing.
   (ii) Children as well as their mother are playing.
   In the case of first sentence the verb (is) agrees with Kanta and in the case of second sentence the verb (are) agrees with the children.

4. 'Neither', 'Either', 'Every', 'Each', 'Everyone', and 'Many a' are followed by a singular verb. **Example :**
   (i) Either of the plans is to be adopted.
   (ii) Neither of the two brothers is sure to pass.
   (iii) Every student is expected to be obedient.
   (iv) Everyone of them desires this.
   (v) Many a person is drowned in the sea.

5. If two subjects are joined by 'Either .... or' / 'Neither .... nor', the verb agrees with the subject near to it.

Example :

(i) Either my brother or I am to do this work.

(ii) Neither he nor they are prepared to do this work.

6. 'A great many' is always followed by a 'plural noun' and a 'plural verb'. For example :

A great many students have been declared successful.

7. Similarly if two subjects are joined by 'with', 'together with', 'no less than', in addition to 'and not', etc. the verb agrees with the first subject.

Example :

(i) The boy with his parents has arrived.

(ii) He, no less than I, is to blame.

8. Nouns, plural in form, but singular in meaning, take singular verb.

Example :

This news was broadcast from television yesterday.

MULTIPLE CHOICE QUESTIONS

Directions: *In the following questions choose the correct options to fill the blanks.*

1. The bus with all its passengers .... lost.
A. were B. was
C. are D. would

2. You as well as I .... responsible for this work.
A. am B. are
C. was D. is

3. Raghava like all his companions .... a spoiled child.
A. are B. were
C. is D. will be

4. Pen and ink .... required for me.
A. are B. were
C. is D. has required

5. Every girl and every boy .... attended the seminar.
A. have B. has
C. is D. are

6. Not only she but all her sisters ...... been married.
A. has B. have
C. is D. are

7. There .... nothing but miseries in life.
A. is B. are
C. were D. will be

8. Neither prose nor poem .... given.
A. were B. was
C. has D. have

9. Either he or I .... wrong.
A. is B. are
C. am D. were

10. Either Sulekha or Rekha .... coming here.
A. are B. is
C. were D. have

11. .... the child or his parents to blame?
A. Is B. Are
C. Were D. Has

12. You and I .... neighbours.
A. am B. are
C. was D. has

13. The house with all its belongings ..... sold away.
A. were B. are
C. was D. must

14. Either water or juice .... required.
A. is B. are
C. were D. has

15. There were not as many tables as .... required.
A. was B. were
C. is D. are

16. They each .... a book.
A. have B. are
C. has D. is

17. He and I .... class friends.
A. is B. am
C. was D. are

18. She as well as I .... guilty.
A. is B. are
C. am D. must be

19. Purushottam .... not read more on this chapter.
A. needs B. has been need
C. need D. had been need

20. He came .... to his aunt.
A. run B. running
C. to run D. in run

21. She dislikes .... meat.
A. eat to B. to eat
C. eating D. to eating

22. He likes ....
A. sing to B. singing
C. to sing D. to singing

23. We are ready .... the match.
A. play to B. to playing
C. playing D. to play

24. .... is injurious to health.
A. Smoking B. To smoke
C. To smoking D. Smoke to

25. He loves .... raw vegetables.
A. eaten B. eating
C. to eating D. eat to

26. He seemed .... finished his homework.
A. have to B. to have
C. having D. to having

ANSWERS

1	2	3	4	5	6	7	8	9	10
B	B	C	A	B	B	A	B	C	B
11	**12**	**13**	**14**	**15**	**16**	**17**	**18**	**19**	**20**
A	B	C	A	B	A	D	C	C	B
21	**22**	**23**	**24**	**25**	**26**				
C	B	D	A	B	B				

CONJUNCTIONS

. conjunction is a word which connects words, clauses or entences.

Look at the following sentences.

(i) He bought apples *and* mangoes.

(ii) God made the country *and* man made the town.

(iii) The door was open *but* there was no one in the house.

(iv) He knows that I am here *and* that I want to see him.

In the sentence (i), *and* connects two words—*apples* and *angoes.*

In the sentence (ii), *and* connects two sentences—*God ade the country* and *man made the town.*

In the sentence (iii), *but* connects two sentences— *The door as open* and *there was no one in the house.*

In the sentence (iv), *and* connects two clauses—*that I am ere* and *that I want to see him.*

The main coordinating conjunctions are:

and, but, for, or, nor, also, either ..... or, neither ..... nor.

There are some conjunctions which are used in pairs. hey are:

either .... or, ... neither .... nor, both .... and, though .... yet, hether .... or, not only .... but also.

Example: *Either* take it *or* leave it.

It is *neither* useful *nor* ornamental.

They *both* like *and* respect me.

Though he is suffering from high fever, *yet* he does not ry.

He does not care *whether* you go *or* stay.

He is *not only* doltish, *but also* obstinate.

The conjunctions which are used in pairs in this way, are alled correlative conjunctions, or merely correlatives.

se of Important Conjunctions

1. **As soon as :** As soon as denotes simultaneous time.

   Example : As soon as he saw his enemy, he took to his heels.

2. **No sooner .... than :**

   (a) 'No sooner' is always followed by 'than'.

   (b) Please remember that 'No sooner' is always followed by do/does/did. As such only first form of the verb should be used after the subject.

   Example :

   No sooner did he see his enemy than he took to his heels.

3. **Hardly :** Hardly is followed by when.

   Examples :

   (i) Hardly had I left the house when it started raining.

   (ii) We had hardly come into the room when his father began chastising him.

   Note :

   A. Hardly is never followed by than.

   B. 'Scarcely' can also be used in the sense and manner of 'Hardly'.

4. **Lest :** Lest is used in the sense of so that .... not. It is always followed by should. Lest is negative in sense. Hence 'not' should never be used with it.

   Example :

   Work hard lest you should fail.

   Note : 'Lest' is always followed by 'should' and not 'may'.

5. **Unless :** Unless expresses condition. It is also used in the negative sense. Use of 'not' is not allowed with unless because unless is already in the negative sense.

   Example :

   Unless you labour hard you will not pass.

6. **Until :** 'Until' expresses time. It means 'till not'.

   Example :

   Wait here until I return.

   Note : Until is in the negative sense. So 'not' should not be used with it. Example :

   Wait here until I do not return. (Incorrect)

   Wait here until I return. (Correct)

7. **As well as :** When two subjects are joined by 'as well as', the verb always agrees with the first subject.

   Examples :

   (i) The teacher as well as students is playing.

   (ii) Students as well as the teacher are playing.

   Note : 'Both' and 'as well as' cannot be used together in the same sentence.

   Examples :

   Both Sita as well as Kanta are beautiful. (Incorrect)

   Sita as well as Kanta is beautiful. (Correct)

   Both Sita and Kanta are beautiful. (Correct)

8. **As if :** 'As if' is used in the sense of pretension. While using 'as if' in a sentence, we should see that even the third person singular subject gets 'were'.

   Example :

   He talks as if he were mad.

9. **Till :** Till expresses time. Till is always used in the affirmative.

Example :
We did not come back till sunset.

10. **Rather than :** 'Rather than' is used in the sense of 'preference'. 'Rather' is always followed by 'than'.

Example :
I would rather die than submit.

11. **As long as/so long as :** Both express time during which an action or event takes place.

Example :
As long as there is life, there is hope.

12. **However :** It is both a subordinate and co-ordin clause.

Examples :
(a) Mala worked hard, she however, failed.
(b) However hard he may work, he cannot pass.

13. **Such as :** 'Such as' gives us the sense of 'like'. Su is always followed by 'as'.

Example :
Life is such a puzzle as cannot be solved.

MULTIPLE CHOICE QUESTIONS

Directions: *In the following questions choose the correct options to fill the blanks.*

1. Neither he .... his friend is good.
   A. or B. and
   C. but D. nor
2. The officer asked the peon .... why he was late.
   A. that B. if
   C. but D. No word needed
3. Both Ajay .... Vijay are intelligent.
   A. or B. nor
   C. and D. No word needed
4. No Sooner did the thief see the public .... he ran away.
   A. then B. and
   C. but D. than
5. Abhinav .... his brothers was going to Mumbai.
   A. but B. yet
   C. No word needed D. together with
6. He behaves ....he were the captain of the team.
   A. as if B. as
   C. No word needed D. that
7. Either Rupali .... Sonali is going to attend the meeting.
   A. and B. but
   C. nor D. or
8. Neither Nirmal .... Ashwinee is going to listen the speech.
   A. and B. but
   C. nor D. or
9. Ravi .... Prakash are going to Kolkata.
   A. or B. nor
   C. but D. and
10. Rice .... curry is my usual breakfast.
   A. and B. but
   C. then D. than
11. Hardly had he left .... his brother came.
   A. then B. than
   C. when D. that
12. I would rather have a copy .... a book.
   A. then B. than
   C. when D. that
13. He is no other .... my friend.
   A. then B. than
   C. when D. but
14. He saw a snake ....he awoke.
   A. then B. when
   C. than D. No word needed
15. Ten years have passed .... my grandmother die
   A. since B. when
   C. then D. than
16. She is .... good .... bad.
   A. either, not B. neither, or
   C. neither, nor D. neither, than
17. The cellphone is both cheap .... best.
   A. than B. and
   C. then D. or
18. No sooner did the rogue see the police .... disappeared.
   A. then B. than
   C. so D. because
19. Srishti will go .... Sanju goes.
   A. if B. than
   C. then D. although
20. She is wise .... timid.
   A. and B. yet
   C. but D. however
21. Make hay .... the sun shines.
   A. though B. while
   C. after D. before
22. He is so weak .... he cannot walk.
   A. but B. that
   C. then D. so
23. Although he is rich, ... he is unhappy.
   A. but B. yet
   C. so D. still
24. Wait here .... I come back.
   A. till B. until
   C. before D. after

25. He is my friend .... I shall help him.
A. so B. hence
C. that is why D. therefore

26. He must go away .... he will be beaten.
A. otherwise B. and
C. or D. else

27. God loves good men .... good men love God.
A. and B. or
C. that D. those

28. He was late .... he was not punished.
A. but B. yet
C. still D. therefore

29. Walk slowly ...., you may fall.
A. and B. or
C. so D. otherwise

30. Work hard, ... you will fail.
A. and B. or
C. otherwise D. else

ANSWERS

1	2	3	4	5	6	7	8	9	10
D	D	C	D	D	A	D	C	D	A
11	**12**	**13**	**14**	**15**	**16**	**17**	**18**	**19**	**20**
C	B	B	B	A	C	B	B	A	C
21	**22**	**23**	**24**	**25**	**26**	**27**	**28**	**29**	**30**
B	B	B	A	B	C	A	C	D	D

PREPOSITIONS

A *Preposition* is a word which is placed before a noun or a pronoun to show its relation to some other word in the sentence.

1. I saw a goat *in* the field.
2. I am fond *of* hot coffee.

In sentence 1, the word *in* shows the relation between two things—*goat* and *field.*

In sentence 2, the word *of* shows the relation between the attribute expressed by the adjective *found* and *tea.*

The words *in* and *of* are here used as prepositions.

The noun or pronoun which is used with a preposition is called its object. The noun or pronoun is in the objective case. It is governed by the preposition. Now it is absolutely clear that in sentence 1, the noun *field* is in the objective case. The word *field* is governed by the preposition *in.*

A preposition may have two or more objects.

The road runs over *hill* and *plain.*

Here, the words *hill* and *plain* are used as objects.

Use of Important Prepositions

1. Among, Between

'**Among**' is used for more than two persons or things; '**Between**' is used only for two.

Examples :

(i) Distribute these sweets *among* the poor students of the class.

(ii) Distribute these books *between* Ram and Shyam.

2. Among, In

'**Among**' is used before collective plural nouns. '**In**' is used before collective singular nouns.

Examples :

(i) I found him standing *among* the crowd.

(ii) I saw him in the crowd.

3. Beside, Besides

'**Beside**' means 'by the side of'. '**Besides**' means 'in addition to'.

Examples :

(i) The daughter was sitting *beside* her mother.

(ii) *Besides* his relatives, he invited his friends also.

4. In, Within

'**In**' means at the expiry of a period of time in future, '**Within**' means before the expiry of a period of time in any tense.

Examples :

(i) She will return *in* a week.

(ii) I shall finish my work *within* a weak.

5. On, Upon

'**On**' is used for things at rest; '**Upon**' is used for things in motion.

Examples :

(i) He is sitting *on* the floor.

(ii) The dog sprang *upon* the table.

6. By, With

'**By**' denotes the agent or doer, '**With**' denotes the instrument with which anything is done.

Examples :

(i) The bird was killed *by* the hunter with an arrow.

(ii) He beat the dog *with* a stick.

(iii) I shall reach here *by* five o'clock.

7. After, In

'**After**' means at the end of a period of time in the past. '**In**' means at the end of a period of time in future.

Examples :

(i) I shall return your book *in* a week.

(ii) He returned the book *after* a week.

8. For, From, Since

'**For**' is used before a noun denoting a period of time with all the tenses. '**From**' is used before a noun or phrase denoting a point of time, it is used in all the tenses. '**Since**' is used before a noun or phrase denoting some point of time and is always produced by a verb in the perfect continuous tense or third form of a verb.

Examples :

(i) We have been playing cards *for* two hours.
(ii) She stayed with her uncle *from* the 15th of March to the 15th of May.
(iii) I have been reading this book *since* morning.

9. Above, Over

'**Above**' means 'higher from', **Over** is used in the following four senses :

(i) In the sense of 'above' :
At noon, the sun is *over* our heads.
(ii) In the sense of 'beyond' :
I cannot get *over* my disappointment.
(iii) In the sense of 'Superiority' :
God *over* all blesses for ever more.
(iv) In the sense of 'Conclusion' :
It is all *over* with me.

10. At, Towards

'**At**' denotes the idea of aim, '**Towards**' denotes the idea of destination.

Examples :

(i) He threw the stone *at* the cat.
(ii) He went *towards* the house.

11. At, In, On

'At' is used as follows :

(i) '**At**' is used with small towns and villages. **Examples:**
(a) He was born *at* Sonepat.
(b) He lives *at* village Bangra. (Bangra is a village)
(ii) '**At**' is used before a noun denoting a definite point of time.
Example :
He called on me *at* 9 p.m. yesterday.

'In' is used as follows :

(iii) '**In**' is used with the names of big cities, provinces and countries.
Examples :
(a) His father lives *in* England.
(b) His younger brother lives *in* Calcutta.
(iv) '**In**' is used before the names of months and years.
Example :
His elder sister was born *in* 1972 *in* the month of May.

'**On**' is used with dates and names of days. **Examples:**

(a) I joined college *on* the 26th April.
(b) He will leave for Kolkata *on* Wednesday next.

Important Information

1. '**In**' is also used in the following phrases :
In the morning; In the evening, In winter, In summer.
2. '**In**' also denotes a place inside anything.
He travelled *in* a crowded bus.
3. '**At**' is used in the following phrases :
At home, *At* the station, *At* work, *At* play.

12. Below, Beneath

Below means 'of lower level in position, dignity and expectation' etc. *Beneath* means 'under'.

Examples :

(i) It is *below* my dignity to talk to her.
(ii) They rested *beneath* the shade of a tree.

13. In, Into, To

'**In**' expresses Rest or Motion inside anything. '**Into**' expresses Motion towards the inside of anything or change from one medium to another. '**To**' denotes motion from one place to another.

Examples :

(i) The boys are *in* the room.
(ii) Translate this passage from English *into* Hindi.
(iii) Every morning he goes *to* the temple.

14. Till, By, Of, Off

- 'Till' means upto or not earlier than.
- 'By' means not later than.
- 'Of' shows cause, source, separation, quality, contents, possession, apposition, point of reference, space in time etc.
- 'Off' shows separation at a near distance, and detached condition.

Consider the following examples:

(i) I shall work *till* 5 a.m.
(ii) Madhu died *of* cancer.
(iii) The nib *of* the pen is made *of* gold.
(iv) He presented me a bottle *of* perfume.
(v) Our principal is a man *of* principle.
(vi) He lived in the house *of* his friend.
(vii) *By* this time tomorrow, I'll have finished my job.
(viii) My house is *off* the road.
(ix) The book fell *off* the table.

MULTIPLE CHOICE QUESTIONS

Directions: *Tick the correct preposition for the blank in each of the following sentences.*

1. He applied ...... the manager.
A. for B. to
C. with D. by

2. Trust ...... God and do the right.
A. in B. for
C. to D. with

3. She is worthy ...... a prize.
A. with B. for
C. to D. of

4. Mr. Gomes has no taste ...... music.
A. of B. for
C. with D. to

5. You are hard ...... hearing.
A. at B. of
C. with D. for

6. He is sure ...... his success
A. for B. with
C. on D. of

7. Preeti was warned ...... the danger ahead.
A. for B. at
C. of D. about

8. I am thankful ...... you for a good advice.
A. for B. with
C. to D. of

9. Deepak would not surrender ...... the police.
A. with B. to
C. for D. on

10. The small plant in your lawn is very sensitive ...... touch.
A. on B. with
C. to D. about

11. Divya was sure to succeed ..... the examination.
A. for B. in
C. to D. with

12. Geeta was jealous ...... Ravina's beauty.
A. to B. with
C. for D. of

13. He was ignorant ..... what was happening there.
A. for B. of
C. to D. with

14. Your pen is inferior ...... mine.
A. than B. with
C. from D. to

15. Reenu is no match ...... Meenu.
A. to B. for
C. with D. upon

16. It is necessary ...... you to apply for this job.
A. on B. with
C. for D. to

17. Be loyal ...... your country.
A. for B. to
C. on D. with

18. Mukesh is junior ...... me.
A. than B. to
C. from D. of

19. Deepika was innocent ...... the crime.
A. of B. with
C. from D. to

20. I am desirous.... joining the Indian cricket team.
A. for B. of
C. to D. on

ANSWERS

1	2	3	4	5	6	7	8	9	10
B	A	D	B	B	D	D	C	B	D
11	**12**	**13**	**14**	**15**	**16**	**17**	**18**	**19**	**20**
B	D	B	D	B	C	B	B	A	B

SYNONYMS

A synonym is a word which conveys a meaning similar to the given word.

REMEMBER

Words	*Synonyms*
Add	Increase
Adequate	Enough
Adjust	Adapt
All	Aggregate
Allow	Permit
Abode	Dwelling
Apt	Proper
Assess	Appraise
Accuse	Calumniate
Abashed	Timid
Annoy	Displease

Words	*Synonyms*
Ample	Enough, Sufficient
Amplify	Increase
Apathetic	Unenthusiastic
Accost	Address
Authentic	True
Adjust	Fit
Approve	Assent, Allow, Accept
Adapt	Conform
Adversary	Opponent, Rival, Competitor
Beat	Whack
Benign	Kind
Breeze	Zephyr
Baffle	Puzzle
Booty	Spoil
Beauty	Charm
Beast	Animal

Words	*Synonyms*
Bandit	Robber
Blaze	Shine
Bond	Tie
Bend	Twist
Bate	Diminish
Beg	Plead
Barbaric	Wild, Savage
Bashful	Shy, Reserved
Begin	Start
Blend	Mix, Mingle
Bizarre	Funny
Below	Under
Bedevil	Confuse
Bemoan	Lament
Babble	Nonsense
Blame	Fault
Behaviour	Demeanour
Call	Accost
Copy	Imitate
Close	Shut
Caress	Love
Camp	Stay
Connect	Attach
Cut	Injure, Curtail
Cling	Stick
Conical	Funny
Convey	Carry
Conspicuous	Prominent
Cheerful	Happy, Pleasant
Curtail	Decrease
Cheerless	Sad, Dejected
Curious	Strange
Circumstance	Factor, Situation, Condition
Competent	Capable
Congruent	Overlapping
Cope	Deal, Endure
Confident	Sure
Complex	Intricate
Cajole	Coax, Flatter
Cunning	Crafty
Delectable	Joyful, Delightful
Devilish	Diabolical
Delicate	Soft
Devil	Fiend
Delay	Postpone
Dislike	Repugnance
Destroy	Ruin
Dwell	Live, Dilate
Declare	Pronounce
Drunk	Flushed

Words	*Synonyms*
Deficient	Lacking
Damn	Condemn, Curse
Decrease	Diminish
Destruction	Devastation
Efficient	Competent
Ethnic	Racial
Enthral	Enslave
Earnest	Serious
Envious	Jealous
Ending	Final
Egg	Incite
Extempore	At once
Extensive	Far-ranging
Extra	Surplus
Existence	Life
Exceed	Overstep
Enormous	Vast
Excessive	Superfluous
Free	Unhindered
Frigid	Cold
Feed	Cater
Fame	Reputation
Frame	Make
First	Initial
Frighten	Terrorise, Intimidate
Fervent	Fervid
Fall	Decline
Feeble	Frail
Fickle	Changeable
Finish	Conclude
Fraud	Deception
Forgiving	Placable
Grow	Develop
Greed	Avidity
Greet	Welcome
Grave	Serious
Group	Constellation
Given	Bestowed
Gratitude	Thankfulness
Have	Possess
Hire	Rent
Hit	Strike
Handsome	Beautiful
Hinder	Prevent
Heap	Pile
Hope	Expect
Hard	Harsh
Help	Aid
Hymn	Song
Henpecked	Enslaved

Words	*Synonyms*
Hoodwink	Mystify, Cheat
Humble	Polite, Urbane, Modest
Harass	Vex, Trouble
Impart	Instil
Intact	Untouched
Instal	Establish
Indict	Impeach
Imitate	Ape
Instigate	Incite
Initiate	Start, Introduce
Inimical	Unfriendly
Insufferable	Intolerable
Impartiality	Justice
Jolly	Merry
Joyful	Delectable
Join	Conjoin
Kind	Benign
Kill	Murder
Kindred	Similar
Kinship	Relationship
Keen	Sharp
Knowledge	Scholarship
Lazy	Slothful
Large	Substantial, Gargantuan
Listless	Careless, Lackadaisical
Lax	Loose
Little	Small
Lifelike	Realistic
Lofty	High
Lenient	Soft, Gentle
Lacking	Deficient, Wanting
Lessen	Decrease
Middleclass	Bourgeois
Mitigate	Lessen, Abate
Modesty	Humility, Lowliness
Mix	Mingle, Blend
Mixture	Mingling
Mixed	Assorted
Modify	Decrease
Mean	Imply
Multifarious	Varied
Miscarry	Abort
Note	Notice
Noble	Stately
Native	Indigenous
Needful	Necessary
Notify	Declare
Nervous	Shaky, Tremulous, Timid
Natural	Spontaneous
Near	Close
Normal	Natural
Offend	Displease
Oppress	Persecute, Tyrannize
Opponent	Adversary
Obstruct	Hinder, Check
Offence	Fault
Offender	Villain
Overstep	Exceed
Overlapping	Congruent
Occult	Mystic
Profane	Unholy
Patience	Forbearance
Pornographic	Obscene
Plenitude	Abundance
Prominent	Important
Prodigal	Spender
Procrastinate	Postpone
Promote	Develop, Honour
Persecute	Tyrannise
Profess	Claim
Pliant	Flexible
Plebian	Common
Polished	Sophisticated
Quake	Shake
Quit	Leave
Queer	Eccentric
Quell	Suppress
Quantify	Allot
Reply	Answer
Relinquish	Retire
Read	Peruse
Relation	Reference
Render	Do
Remainder	Residuals
Repeat	Reiterate
Repentant	Contrite
Retaliative	Retaliatory
Rumour	Hearsay
Reveal	Divulge
Ritualistic	Ceremonious
Soft	Delicate
Sort	Kind, Choose, Select
Selfish	Egoistic
Sensual	Earthly
Suppress	Quell, Check
Stimulate	Provoke
Tasteless	Insipid
Travel	Journey
True	Authentic, Faithful, Truthful
Turbulence	Turmoil

Words	*Synonyms*
Tragedy	Calamity
Tasteful	Tasty, Delicious
Touching	Painful
Thankful	Grateful
Tremendous	Great, Huge
Tough	Strong
Terminate	Conclude, End
Theory	Doctrine
Tell	Relate
Tremble	Shake, Shiver
Urge	Spur
Unbeaten	Unsubdued
Use	Utilize, Practise
Underhand	Unfair, Undue
Unfair	Unjust
Unravel	Reveal, Divulge
Unimportant	Common
Unconcerned	Apathetic
Unimitated	Inimitable
Unfortunate	Unlucky
Understand	Perceive, Comprehend
Vain	Proud, Haughty, Conceited, Shameless
Vale	Valley, Dale, Dell
Vice	Fault
Virtue	Quality
Veracity	Reality
Value	Price, Prize
Vex	Tease
Vibrate	Quiver, Shake
Violent	Excessive
Vivid	Clear, Lucid
Victory	Triumph
Vulgar	Indecent
Virtuous	Honest
Variegated	Varied, Multifarious
Well	Good
Yell	Cry, Shout
Yonder	There
Yearn	Wish, Desire
Yoke	Slavery
Zest	Earnestness, Enthusiasm
Zealous	Earnest

ANTONYMS

A antonym is a word which conveys a meaning opposite to the given word.

REMEMBER

Words	*Antonyms*
Abhor	Love
Abnormal	Normal
Able	Unable
Acceptable	Unacceptable
Adequate	Inadequate
Amusing	Boring
Angry	Calm
Apex	Bottom
Attract	Repel
Bad	Good
Barren	Fertile
Beautiful	Ugly
Bitter	Sweet
Brave	Cowardly
Brief	Lengthy
Bright	Dull
Calm	Violent
Careful	Careless
Clear	Vague, Cloudy
Cold	Hot
Cruel	Kind
Dear	Cheap
Deep	Shallow
Difficult	Easy
Direct	Indirect
Dishonest	Honest
Disobey	Obey
Encourage	Discourage
Enormous	Tiny
Excellent	Bad
Expensive	Cheap
Eat	Fast
Fair	Unfair
Fake	Authentic
False	True
Famous	Obscure
Fool	Genius
Generous	Miserly
Genius	Fool
Genuine	Unauthentic
Gigantic	Tiny
Glad	Depressed
Good	Bad
Great	Little
Happy	Sad
Hard	Soft
Hate	Love
Honest	Dishonest
Idle	Busy
Immoral	Moral
Include	Exclude
Incorrect	Correct
Intelligent	Unintelligent
Kind	Cruel
Like	Dislike
Long	Short
Lucid	Vague

Words	*Antonyms*
Major	Minor
Naive	Experienced
Nadir	Apex
Neat	Clumsy
Obedient	Disobedient
Obscure	Clear
Oppose	Support
Optimistic	Pessimistic
Out	In
Patience	Impatience
Peaceful	Belligerent
Pious	Impious
Polite	Impolite
Potent	Impotent
Prominent	Unimportant
Proper	Improper
Pure	Impure
Quick	Slow
Quiet	Disturbance
Real	False, Unreal
Reject	Select, Choose
Reliable	Unreliable
Respect	Disrespect

Words	*Antonyms*
Right	Wrong
Robust	Feeble, Weak
Sad	Happy
Secret	Open
Sensible	Insensible
Severe	Mild
Sharp	Blunt
Simple	Complex
Sociable	Unsociable
Tall	Short
Tidy	Untidy
Uncanny	Canny
Violent	Calm
Vivid	Vague
Strong	Weak
Big	Small
Easy	Difficult
Fast	Slow
High	Low
Catchy	Unattractive
Ugly	Handsome, Beautiful, Tidy
Tasty	Insipid
Sonorous	Harsh

MULTIPLE CHOICE QUESTIONS

Directions (Qs. 1 to 20): *In the following questions choose the word which best expresses the meaning of the given word.*

1. ABSURD
A. Foolish B. Simple
C. Courageous D. Silly

2. ABANDON
A. Lose B. Profit
C. Vacate D. Foil

3. CAJOLE
A. Pause B. Lenient
C. Blast D. Lure

4. COMBAT
A. Fight B. Conflict
C. Shoot D. Quarrel

5. LAMENT
A. Condone B. Console
C. Complain D. Contribution

6. DEBACLE
A. Disgrace B. Defeat
C. Collapse D. Decline

7. SHIVER
A. Fear B. Tremble
C. Shake D. Ache

8. TORTURE
A. Terror B. Harassment
C. Torment D. Tranquility

9. LAUDABLE
A. Lovable B. Commendable
C. Profitable D. Oblivious

10. FIXED
A. Sterile B. Static
C. Stubborn D. Parennial

11. QUEER
A. Unfamiliar B. Cute
C. Curious D. Strange

12. SUFFICIENT
A. Fit B. Proper
C. Adequate D. Vast

13. GLOSS
A. Brightness B. Soothing
C. Rubbing D. Miracle

14. LONGING
A. Prune B. Apathy
C. Curtail D. Craving

15. JEER
A. Applaud B. Magnanimity
C. Avoid D. Scoff

16. ZENITH
A. Minimum
B. Nadir
C. Plant
D. Peak

17. GARB
A. Distort
B. Dress
C. Trivial
D. Rage

18. ABHOR
A. Rude
B. Reconcile
C. Crave
D. Detest

19. YIELD
A. Shum
B. Incisive
C. Retain
D. Surrender

20. YOKE
A. Twist
B. Release
C. Link
D. Extra

Directions (Qs. 21 to 38): *In the following questions choose the word which best expresses the opposite of the given word.*

21. TRAGIC
A. Dramatic
B. Strong
C. Gentle
D. Comic

22. ORAL
A. Verbal
B. Sane
C. Minor
D. Written

23. ADMIRE
A. Hate
B. Unlike
C. Dislike
D. Enough

24. VIOLENT
A. Gentle
B. Savage
C. Haughty
D. Decline

25. ADVERSITY
A. Windfall
B. Inprosperity
C. Prosperity
D. Slave

26. GENUINE
A. Spurious
B. Obscure
C. Countless
D. Apathetic

27. GRUDGE
A. Essence
B. Guile
C. Goodwill
D. Ill-will

28. STIFF
A. Soft
B. Courteous
C. Lively
D. Flexible

29. VANITY
A. Conceit
B. Pride
C. Ostentious
D. Humility

30. FRONT
A. Upper
B. Unusual
C. Back
D. Rear

31. ATTRACT
A. Lured
B. Longing
C. Repel
D. Disguise

32. COMFORT
A. Discomfort
B. Discontent
C. Uncomfort
D. Miscomfort

33. WELCOME
A. Repel
B. Accept
C. Resist
D. Fight

34. TACTFUL
A. Naive
B. Loose
C. Strict
D. Uncivilized

35. DUTIFUL
A. Harmful
B. Watchful
C. Forgetful
D. Remiss

36. RIGID
A. Flux
B. Adoptable
C. Yielding
D. Adaptable

37. RARE
A. Petty
B. Poor
C. Small
D. Common

38. ZEAL
A. Despair
B. Calmness
C. Passiveness
D. Indifference

ANSWERS

1	2	3	4	5	6	7	8	9	10
D	C	D	A	C	C	B	C	B	B
11	12	13	14	15	16	17	18	19	20
D	C	A	D	D	D	B	D	D	C
21	22	23	24	25	26	27	28	29	30
D	D	C	A	C	A	C	D	D	D
31	32	33	34	35	36	37	38		
C	A	C	A	D	D	D	D		

CHAPTER

3

SENTENCE COMPLETION

It is such an exercise which starts with the primary schools and continues in the highest level of competitive examinations. One must practise it regularly to score well.

MULTIPLE CHOICE QUESTIONS

Directions (Qs. 1 to 15): *Pick out the most effective word(s) from the given words to fill in the blanks to make the sentence meaningfully complete.*

1. The student .... that book from the library to study at home.

A. issued B. borrowed
C. hired D. lent

2. I wish I ...... a king.

A. was B. am
C. should be D. were

3. He ...... to listen to my arguments and walked away.

A. denied B. disliked
C. objected D. refused

4. The flow of blood was so ...... that the patient died.

A. intense B. adequate
C. profuse D. extensive

5. When I met her yesterday, it was the first time I ...... her since Christmas.

A. saw B. have seen
C. had seen D. have been seing

6. Can you pay ...... all these articles?

A. for B. of
C. off D. out

7. I ...... you to be at the party this evening.

A. expect B. hope
C. look forward to D. desire

8. ...... being a handicapped person, he is very cooperative and self-reliant.

A. Because B. Although
C. Since D. Despite

9. The child broke ...... from his mother and ran towards the painting.

A. away B. after
C. down D. with

10. With his ...... income, he finds it difficult to live a comfortable life.

A. brief B. sufficient
C. meagre D. huge

11. He could ...... a lot of money in such a short time by using his intelligence and working hard.

A. spend B. spoil
C. exchange D. accumulate

12. Though the brothers are twins, they look ......

A. alike B. handsome
C. indifferent D. different

13. Unfavourable weather conditions can ..... illness.

A. cure B. detect
C. treat D. enhance

14. No sooner did the bell ring, ... the actor started singing.

A. when B. than
C. after D. before

15. If I ...... realised it, I would not have acted on his advice.

A. was B. had
C. were D. have

Directions (Qs. 16 to 25): *In each question, an incomplete statement (Stem) followed by four fillers is given. Pick out the best one which can complete the incomplete stem correctly and meaningfully.*

16. Unless you work harder you will fail, means .....

A. if you fail you will work harder.

B. you must at least plan well than you will not fail.
C. hardly you will fail if you do not desire so.
D. if you do not put more efforts, then you will fail.

17. Even if it rains I shall come, means .....
A. if I come it will not rain.
B. if it rains I shall not come.
C. I will certainly come whether it rains or not.
D. whenever there is rain I shall come.

18. Dinesh is as stupid as he is lazy means .....
A. Dinesh is stupid because he is lazy.
B. Dinesh is lazy because he is stupid.
C. Dinesh is either stupid or lazy.
D. Dinesh is equally stupid and lazy.

19. He is so lazy that he .....
A. cannot depend on others for getting his work done.
B. cannot delay the schedule of completing the work.
C. can seldom complete his work on time.
D. dislike to postpone the work that he undertakes to do.

20. He always stammers in public meetings, but his today's speech .....
A. was fairly audible to everyone present in the hall.
B. was not received satisfactorily.
C. could not be understood properly.
D. was free from that defect.

21. In order to raise the company's profit, the employees ....
A. demanded two additional increments.
B. decided to go on paid holidays.
C. requested the management to implement new welfare schemes.
D. offered to work overtime without any compensation.

22. Although, he is reputed for making very candid statements, ...
A. his today's speech was not fairly audible.
B. his promises had always been realistic.
C. his speech was very interesting.
D. his today's statements were very ambiguous.

23. I felt somewhat more relaxed .....
A. but tense as compared to earlier.
B. and tense as compared to earlier.
C. as there was already no tension at all.
D. and tension-free as compared to earlier.

24. With great efforts his son succeeded in convincing him not to donate his entire wealth to an orphanage .....
A. and lead the life of a wealthy merchant.
B. but to a home for the forsaken children.
C. and make an orphan of himself.
D. as the orphanage needed a lot of donations.

25. Even though it is a very large house, ...
A. there is a lot of space available in it for children.
B. there is hardly any space available for children.
C. there is no dearth of space for children.
D. the servants take a long time to clean it.

ANSWERS

1	2	3	4	5	6	7	8	9	10
B	D	D	C	C	A	A	D	A	C
11	**12**	**13**	**14**	**15**	**16**	**17**	**18**	**19**	**20**
D	D	D	B	B	D	C	D	C	D
21	**22**	**23**	**24**	**25**					
D	D	D	C	B					

CHAPTER

4

SPOTTING ERRORS

The most common errors in English are of spellings, grammar and usage of words. By regular practice, the errors can be easily spotted and minimised.

MULTIPLE CHOICE QUESTIONS

Directions: *In the following questions some of the sentences have errors and some are correct. Find out which part of a sentence has an error, the number of that part is your answer. If a sentence is free from errors, then your answer is D i.e., No error.*

1. (A) Either Ram or/(B) you is responsible/(C) for this action./(D) No error.

2. (A) The student flatly denied/(B) that he had copied/(C) in the examination hall./(D) No error.

3. (A) By the time you arrive tomorrow/(B) I have finished/(C) my work./(D) No error.

4. (A) The captain with the members of his team/(B) are returning/(C) after a fortnight./(D) No error.

5. (A) After returning from/(B) an all-India tour/(C) I had to describe about it./(D) No error.

6. (A) The teacher asked his students/(B) if they had gone through/(C) either of the three chapters included in the prescribed text./(D) No error.

7. (A) Do you know/(B) how old were you/(C) when you came here?/(D) No error.

8. (A) Beware of/(B) a fair-weather friend/(C) who is neither a friend in need nor a friend indeed./(D) No error.

9. (A) Copernicus proved/(B) that Earth/(C) moves round the Sun./(D) No error.

10. (A) The property/(B) was divided/(C) among the two brothers./(D) No error.

11. (A) I am quite certain/(B) that the lady is not only greedy/(C) but miserly./(D) No error.

12. (A) The brilliant success in the examination/(B) as well as his record in sports/(C) deserves high praise./(D) No error.

13. (A) I cannot find/(B) where has he gone/(C) though I have tried may best./(D) No error.

14. (A) If I was/(B) the Prime Minister of India/(C) I would work wonders/(D) No error.

15. (A) If it weren't/(B) for you,/(C) I wouldn't be alive today./(D) No error.

16. (A) He looked like a lion/(B) baulked from/(C) its prey./(D) No error.

17. (A) Widespread flooding/(B) is affecting/(C) large areas of the villages./(D) No error.

18. (A) If we really set to/(B) we can get the whole house/(C) cleaned in an afternoon./(D) No error.

19. (A) It's arrogant for you/(B) to assume you'll/(C)win every time./(D) No error.

20. (A) The two books are the same/(B) except for the fact that this/(C) has an answer in the back./(D) No error.

21. (A) Your husband doesn't/(B) believe that you are older/(C) than I./(D) No error.

22. (A) I could not/(B) answer to/(C) the question./(D) No error.

23. (A) Two years passed/(B) since/(C) my cousin died./(D) No error.

24. (A) I am learning English/(B) for ten years/(C) without much effect./(D) No error.

25. (A) Ramesh has agreed/(B) to marry with the girl/(C) of his parent's choice./ (D) No error.

26. (A) When he was arriving./(B) the party was/(C) in full swing./(D) No error.

27. (A) The most studious boy/(B) in the class/(C) was made as the captain./(D) No error.

28. (A) I am participating/(B) in the two-miles race/(C) tomorrow morning./(D) No error.

29. (A) When the boy committed a mistake/(B) the teacher made him to do/(C) the sum again./(D) No error.

30. (A) Whenever a person lost anything/(B) the poor folk around/(C) are suspected./(D) No error.

ANSWERS

1	2	3	4	5	6	7	8	9	10
B	D	B	B	C	C	D	D	B	C
11	12	13	14	15	16	17	18	19	20
C	D	B	A	C	C	C	A	A	C
21	22	23	24	25	26	27	28	29	30
C	B	A	A	B	A	C	B	B	A

EXPLANATORY ANSWERS

1. Replace 'is' by 'are'.
2. No error.
3. Replace 'have' by 'would have'.
4. Replace 'are' by 'is'.
5. Replace 'had to describe' by 'described'.
6. Replace 'either' by 'any'.
7. No error.
8. No error.
9. Omit 'that'.
10. Replace 'among' by 'between'.
11. Add 'also'.
12. No error.
13. Replace 'has he' by 'he has'.
14. Replace 'was' by 'were'.
15. Replace 'wouldn't be' by 'would not have been'.
16. Replace 'its' by 'his'.
17. Replace 'areas' by 'area'.
18. Replace 'set to' by 'set on'.
19. Replace 'for' by 'of'.
20. Replace 'in' by 'on'.
21. Replace 'I' by 'me'.
22. Omit 'to'.
23. Replace 'passed' by 'have passed'.
24. Replace 'am' by 'have been'.
25. Omit 'with'.
26. Replace 'was arriving' by 'arrived'.
27. Omit 'as'.
28. Replace 'in' by 'at'.
29. Omit 'to'.
30. Replace 'lost' by 'loses'.

CHAPTER

5

ONE WORD SUBSTITUTION

There are many single words in English language which can be perfectly used for a number of words. These words help in expressing ideas in a short and correct manner for the right occasion. Such words not only increase the vocabulary but also enable you to economise in the use of words to a great extent.

Multiple Word Expression	*Substitution*
One who always looks towards the bright side of things	Optimist
One who always looks towards the dark side of things	Pessimist
The time when one develops from a child into an adult	Adolescence
The process of growing more plants in order to form a forest.	Afforestation
The science which deals with farming	Agriculture
From some other country or place etc.	Alien
A term, etc. giving more than one meaning	Ambiguous
A vehicle which is used to carry sick persons	Ambulance
An animal which can live both in water and on land	Amphibian
A lawless situation when there is no government	Anarchy
Belonging to the history of thousands of years old	Ancient
Once a year	Annual
A very old object but still valuable	Antique
Words of opposite meanings	Antonyms
Words of similar meanings	Synonyms
Signatures of a famous person	Autograph
A government led by one person with absolute authority	Autocracy
A written work of one's own life history	Autobiography
A person who has never been married	Bachelor
A person usually having no hair on his head	Bald
A place where one can deposit money and get interest	Bank
A person who cuts our hair	Barber
A building/group of buildings where soldiers live	Barracks
A person who makes buns and biscuits	Baker
A person who lives by asking people for food and money without doing any useful job	Beggar
The crime of having married to two persons at the same time	Bigamy
The branch of science which deals with the study of plants	Botany
Able to speak two languages	Bilingual
Able to speak more than two languages.	Polyglot
The branch of science which deals with the living organisms	Biology
A powerful snow storm	Blizzard
A great successful book or movie	Blockbuster
A short news on the radio or TV	Bulletin
A system in which the most important works are organised by the government officials	Bureaucracy
A person who has no vision in his eyes	Blind

Multiple Word Expression	*Substitution*
A page or a series of pages on which the information of days, weeks, months, etc. is given	Calendar
A person who eats human flesh	Cannibal
A complete list of items often arranged alphabetically	Catalogue
A sudden disaster	Catastrophe
A period of 100 years	Century
A branch of science which deals with chemicals	Chemistry
A printed leaf usually issued by banks that we sign to carry certain financial deal	Cheque
A person who makes or mends shoes	Cobbler
A group of people who has been chosen by others to make decisions on their own	Committee
A building in which nuns live	Convent
An animal which feeds on other animals	Carnivorous
A person who does criticism	Critic
A person who cannot hear	Deaf
A condition in which one loses a lot of water from one's body because of vomiting, etc.	Dehydration
A system of government in which the people cast their votes to elect their leaders	Democracy
The study of skin problems	Dermatology
A long piece of land covered with sand	Desert
The art of managing relationships between countries	Diplomacy
A piece of information about the words in a book form	Dictionary
A piece of information about the telephone numbers of the people in a book from	Directory
A person in charge of a newspapers, magazine etc.	Editor
A person who thinks he is better than the others	Egoist
To leave your country and settle in some other country	Emigrate
A book or series of books giving almost all knowledge about an area or some persons etc.	Encyclopaedia
Study of insects	Entomology
Time when day and night are of the same duration	Equinox
To sell things out of the country	Export
To purchase things from some other country	Import
A plant or animal no longer in existence	Extinct
A situation when there is a shortage of food for a long period of time	Famine
An amount of money that we pay for some action or services	Fee
Related to women	Feminine
An animal strong and aggressive	Ferocious
A piece of land where plants grow easily from the soil that is favourable to them	Fertile
A work of literature having some imaginary events	Fiction
A large amount of water covering certain area	Flood
A person who sells flowers	Florist
A religious ceremony for burying or cremating a dead person	Funeral
A substance which kills fungus	Fungicide
A person studying or having studied the diseases and the related things of female reproductory system	Gynaecologist
The murder of the person of the same group race or country	Genocide
A substance which kills germs	Germicide
A situation in which many people die because of fire during war	Holocaust
The act of killing a person deliberately	Homicide
A word having the pronunciation as the other one does but it differs in meaning	Homophone
A word having the same spelling as the other one does but it is pronounced in some other way	Homonym
A person who is attracted towards the person of the same sex	Homosexual
Go across and parallel to the ground	Horizontal
A substance which kills the insects	Insecticide
That cannot be corrected	Incorrigible
That cannot be defeated	Invincible

Multiple Word Expression	*Substitution*
That cannot be eaten	Inedible
That cannot be seen	Invisible
A place in a school or college where books are kept for the benefit of students, teachers etc.	Library
A place in a school or college where scientific experiments are performed	Laboratory
An official who is a judge in the lowest court	Magistrate
A piece of music or a book before it is printed	Manuscript
Related to men	Masculine
One who believes in the existence of God	A theist
One who does not believe in the existence of good	An atheist
That can be believed	Credible
That cannot be believed	Incredible
That which dissolves in a solvent	Soluble
That which does not dissolves in a solvent	Insoluble
Hard writing that can be read	Legible
Hard writing that cannot be read	Illegible
A person who does jobs beneficial to mankind	Philanthropist
A person who goes on foot	Pedestrian
A person who fights for his own country	Patriot
An act of killing oneself	Suicide
A woman whose husband is dead	Widow
A man whose wife is dead	Widower
A person who eats vegetarian and non-vegetarian diets	Omnivorous
Something which is everywhere at the same time	Omnipresent
One who knows everything	Omniscient
A child who does not have parents	Orphan
An award etc. given after the death of the person	Posthumous
The place where animals are kept for amusement and to increase the knowledge of the public	Zoo
The science which deals with the study of animals	Zoology

MULTIPLE CHOICE QUESTIONS

Directions: *In questions given below, out of the four alternatives, choose the one which can be substituted for the given words/sentences.*

1. Something that relates to everyone in the world
A. General B. Common
C. Usual D. Universal

2. An expression of mild disapproval
A. Warning B. Denigration
C. Impertinence D. Reproof

3. One who is not easily pleased by anything
A. Maiden B. Medieval
C. Precarious D. Fastidious

4. Murder of a king
A. Infanticide B. Matricide
C. Genocide D. Regicide

5. A remedy for all diseases
A. Stoic B. Marvel
C. Panacea D. Recompense

6. A dramatic performance
A. Mask B. Mosque
C. Masque D. Mascot

7. Study of birds
A. Orology B. Optology
C. Ophthalmology D. Ornithology

8. Ready to believe
A. Credulous B. Credible
C. Creditable D. Incredible

9. Incapable of being seen through
A. Ductile B. Opaque
C. Obsolete D. Potable

10. One who eats everything
A. Omnivorous B. Omniscient
C. Irresistible D. Insolvent

11. A place where bees are kept is called
A. An apiary B. A mole
C. A hive D. A sanctuary

12. One who cannot be corrected
A. Incurable B. Incorrigible
C. Hardened D. Invulnerable

13. One who is in charge of a museum
A. Curator B. Supervisor
C. Caretaker D. Warden

14. Continuing fight between parties, families, clans, etc.
A. Enmity B. Feud
C. Quarrel D. Skirmish

15. A voice loud enough to be heard
A. Audible B. Applaudable
C. Laudable D. Oral

16. A paper written by hand
A. Handicraft B. Manuscript
C. Handiwork D. Thesis

17. Habitually silent or talking little
A. Serville B. Unequivocal
C. Taciturn D. Synoptic

18. To slap with a flat object
A. Chop B. Hew
C. Gnaw D. Swat

19. A person who speaks many languages
A. Linguist B. Monolingual
C. Polyglot D. Bilingual

20. A light sailing-boat built specially for racing
A. Canoe B. Yacht
C. Frigate D. Dinghy

21. A fixed orbit in space in relation to earth
A. Geological B. Geo-synchronous
C. Geo-centric D. Geo-stationary

22. A style in which a writer makes a display of his knowledge
A. Pedantic B. Verbose
C. Pompous D. Ornate

23. A religious discourse
A. Preach B. Stanza
C. Sanctorum D. Sermon

24. A place that provides refuge
A. Asylum B. Sanatorium
C. Shelter D. Orphanage

25. Detailed plan of a journey
A. Travelogue B. Travelkit
C. Schedule D. Itinerary

26. A person who insists on something
A. Disciplinarian B. Stickler
C. Instantaneous D. Boaster

27. A drawing on transparent paper
A. Red print B. Blue print
C. Negative D. Transparency

28. One who believes that all things and events in life are predetermined is a
A. Fatalist B. Puritan
C. Egoist D. Tyrant

29. A school boy who cuts classes frequently is a
A. Defeatist B. Sycophant
C. Truant D. Martinet

30. The act of violating the sanctity of the church is
A. Blasphemy B. Heresy
C. Sacrilege D. Desecration

31. A place where monks live as a secluded community
A. Cathedral B. Diocese
C. Convent D. Monastery

32. One who is fond of fighting
A. Bellicose B. Aggressive
C. Belligerent D. Militant

33. Tending to move away from the centre or axis
A. Centrifugal B. Centripetal
C. Axiomatic D. Awry

34. Words inscribed on tomb
A. Epitome B. Epistle
C. Epilogue D. Epitaph

35. Leave or remove from a place considered dangerous
A. Evade B. Evacuate
C. Avoid D. Exterminate

36. Original inhabitants of a country
A. Abroge B. Aborger
C. Aborgory D. Aborigims

37. Government by the officials
A. Theocracy B. Plutocracy
C. Bureaucracy D. Democracy

38. Incapable of being exhausted
A. Inexhaustible B. Inaexhaustible
C. Exhaustable D. Non-tired

39. A person of good understanding, knowledge and reasoning power
A. Expert B. Intellectual
C. Snob D. Literate

40. One absorbed in his own thoughts and feelings rather than in things outside
A. Scholar B. Recluse
C. Introvert D. Intellectual

ANSWERS

1	2	3	4	5	6	7	8	9	10
D	D	D	D	C	C	D	A	B	A
11	**12**	**13**	**14**	**15**	**16**	**17**	**18**	**19**	**20**
A	B	A	B	A	B	C	D	A	B
21	**22**	**23**	**24**	**25**	**26**	**27**	**28**	**29**	**30**
D	A	D	A	D	B	D	A	C	C
31	**32**	**33**	**34**	**35**	**36**	**37**	**38**	**39**	**40**
D	A	A	D	B	D	C	A	B	C

CHAPTER

6

SPELLING ERRORS

There are thousands of words in English language. It is difficult to remember the spellings and meanings of all at once. Try to learn as many as you can. Use a dictionary regularly.

MULTIPLE CHOICE QUESTIONS

Directions: *Find the correctly spelt words.*

1. A. Damage B. Dammage C. Damaige D. Dammege

2. A. Efficiant B. Effecient C. Efficient D. Eficient

3. A. Schedule B. Schdule C. Schedale D. Schedeule

4. A. Occurad B. Occurred C. Ocurred D. Occured

5. A. Grieff B. Grief C. Grieef D. Grrief

6. A. Guarantee B. Garuntee C. Guaruntee D. Gaurantee

7. A. Meddicine B. Medicine C. Medicene D. Medicinne

8. A. Benefeted B. Benefitted C. Benifited D. Benefited

9. A. Acommodation B. Acomodation C. Accomodation D. Accommodation

10. A. Querrelsome B. Quarrelsame C. Quarrelsome D. Querralsome

11. A. Sympathetic B. Smypathetic C. Sympothetic D. Sympethetic

12. A. Prograssive B. Progressive C. Progresive D. Prograsive

13. A. Uncivilized B. Uncevilized C. Uncivillized D. Uncevelized

14. A. Extravagant B. Extreragent C. Extreregant D. Extravegent

15. A. Missunderstood B. Miesunderstood C. Misunderstood D. Misunderstod

16. A. Belligerent B. Beligirent C. Belligarant D. Belligerrent

17. A. Astonished B. Astronished C. Astoneshed D. Asstonished

18. A. Sincerely B. Sencerely C. Sincerelly D. Sincerrely

19. A. Rigourous B. Rigerous C. Rigorous D. Regerous

20. A. Satellite B. Sattellite C. Satelite D. Sattelite

21. A. Pesanger B. Passenger C. Pessenger D. Pasanger

22. A. Humurous B. Humorous C. Humoreus D. Humorrous

23. A. Exeggerate B. Exaggerate C. Exadgerate D. Exagerate

24. A. Fariegn B. Forein C. Foriegn D. Foreign

25. A. Excesive B. Excessive C. Exccessive D. Exccesive

26. A. Forcaust B. Forcast C. Forecast D. Forecaste

27. A. Paralleled B. Paralelled C. Parralleled D. Parallelled

28. A. Ocasion B. Occassion
C. Occasion D. Ocassion

29. A. Boquet B. Bouquet
C. Bouquete D. Bouquette

30. A. Chettering B. Chatering
C. Chattering D. Chatering

31. A. Discourage B. Disscourage
C. Discourege D. Discaurage

32. A. Curageous B. Courageous
C. Courrageous D. Couregeous

33. A. Abandon B. Abanddon
C. Abendon D. Abbandon

34. A. Embarassment B. Emberrassement
C. Embarrassment D. Embbaresment

35. A. Eccintric B. Eccentrie
C. Eccentric D. Eccintrie

36. A. Occasional B. Occassional
C. Occesional D. Occessional

37. A. Querrel B. Querral
C. Quarrel D. Quarel

38. A. Contrebution B. Contribution
C. Contributtion D. Conterbution

39. A. Desgrace B. Disgrece
C. Disgrice D. Disgrace

40. A. Harassment B. Herassment
C. Harasment D. Harassmient

41. A. Imaginative B. Imeginative
C. Imagenative D. Imaginetive

42. A. Suficient B. Suficiant
C. Sufficient D. Sufficiant

43. A. Adequate B. Edequate
C. Adaquete D. Edaquete

44. A. Expairienced B. Experianced
C. Experienced D. Experrienced

45. A. Flatering B. Fletering
C. Flattering D. Fletaring

46. A. Cuttiveted B. Culltrivated
C. Cultivated D. Caltivated

47. A. Praiceworthy B. Peiseworthy
C. Praiseworthy D. Praisaworthy

48. A. Profesional B. Professionel
C. Professional D. Profissional

49. A. Ameteur B. Amateur
C. Amataur D. Amateor

50. A. Unfevourable B. Unfevaurable
C. Unfavourable D. Unfivourable

ANSWERS

1	2	3	4	5	6	7	8	9	10
A	C	A	B	B	A	B	D	D	C
11	**12**	**13**	**14**	**15**	**16**	**17**	**18**	**19**	**20**
A	B	A	A	C	A	A	A	C	A
21	**22**	**23**	**24**	**25**	**26**	**27**	**28**	**29**	**30**
B	B	B	D	B	C	A	C	B	C
31	**32**	**33**	**34**	**35**	**36**	**37**	**38**	**39**	**40**
A	B	A	C	C	A	C	B	D	A
41	**42**	**43**	**44**	**45**	**46**	**47**	**48**	**49**	**50**
A	C	A	C	C	C	C	C	B	C

REASONING ABILITY

SERIES

Directions : *In each of the following series determine the order of the letters. Then from the given options select the one which will complete the given series.*

1. BMK, DLM, FKO, HJQ, ?

A. JIR B. JIT
C. JHS D. JIS

2. A, CD, FGH, ?

A. IJKL B. KLMN
C. JKLM D. LMNO

3. BXJ, ETL, HPN, KLP, ?

A. PHR B. NIR
C. NHR D. MHR

4. PUF, QVG, RWH, ?

A. SXI B. SYZ
C. SXJ D. SVI

5. DEF, HIJ, MNO, ?

A. RTV B. STU
C. PTU D. SRU

Directions : *Which of the following groups of letters will complete the given series?*

6. ab---b-bbaa-

A. babba B. abaab
C. abbab D. baaab

7. aa-ab--aaa-a

A. baaa B. abab
C. aaab D. aabb

8. -baa-aab-a-a

A. baab B. abab
C. aaba D. aabb

9. -a cca-ccca-acccc-aaa

A. ccaa B. acca
C. caac D. caaa

10. c-bbb--abbbb-abbb-

A. abccb B. bacbb
C. aabcb D. abacb

Directions : *In the following questions, select the number(s) from the given options for completing the given series.*

11. 3, 9, 27, 81, 243, ?

A. 486 B. 729
C. 972 D. 359

12. 1, 6, 12, 19, 27, ?

A. 38 B. 35
C. 36 D. 54

13. 2, 6, 14, 30, 62, ?

A. 126 B. 128
C. 120 D. 130

14. 8, 48, 16, 96, 32, ?

A. 192 B. 160
C. 64 D. 288

15. 2, 8, 14, 24, 34, 48, ?

A. 66 B. 62
C. 58 D. 64

Directions : *In the given series find the number which is wrong.*

16. 5, 25, 120, 625, 3125, 15625

A. 15625 B. 625
C. 120 D. 5

17. 4, 8, 11, 22, 18, 36, 24, 50

A. 8 B. 22
C. 36 D. 24

18. 2, 4, 12, 24, 72, 142, 432

A. 432 B. 12
C. 142 D. 72

19. 2, 3, 4, 4, 6, 8, 9, 12, 16

A. 3 B. 9
C. 6 D. 12

20. 97, 91, 86, 83, 79, 77, 76, 76

A. 86 B. 76
C. 91 D. 83

ANSWERS

1	2	3	4	5	6	7	8	9	10
D	C	C	A	B	D	C	B	D	A
11	**12**	**13**	**14**	**15**	**16**	**17**	**18**	**19**	**20**
B	C	A	A	B	C	D	C	B	D

EXPLANATORY ANSWERS

1. The letters in one group correspond to the letters in the next group in the manner +2, –1, +2 respectively.

BMK DLM FKO HJQ JIS

+2 +2 +2 +2

–1 –1 –1 –1

+2 +2 +2 +2

2. The letters are in natural sequence and from one group to the next one letter is dropped. Also the number of letters in groups is increased by one.

A CD FGH JKLM

↓ ↓ ↓

B E I

3. The letters in one group correspond to the letters in the next group in the manner +3, – 4, +2 respectively, *i.e.*,

BXJ ETL HPN KLP NHR

+3 +3 +3 +3

–4 –4 –4 –4

+2 +2 +2 +2

4. The three letters in each group are moved one step forward.

PUF QVG RWH SXI

+1 +1 +1

+1 +1 +1

+1 +1 +1

5. The letters are in natural order. The number of letters dropped in between the groups is increased by one at each step.

DEF HIJ MNO STU

↓ ↓ ↓

G KL PQR

6. The series is abbaab, abbaab

7. The series is aaaaba, aaaaba

8. The series is aba, aba, aba, aba

9. The series is c,a,cc,aa, ccc, aaa, cccc, aaaa

10. The series is cabbbb, cabbbb, cabbbb

11. The numbers in the series are multiplied by 3 to get the next numbers.

12. The difference between the numbers in the series increases by 1, after beginning from 5, *i.e.*,

1 6 12 19 27 36

+5 +6 +7 +8 +9

13. The difference between the numbers in the series doubles each time, after beginning from 4, *i.e.*,

2 6 14 30 62 126

+4 +8 +16 +32 +64

14. *Explanation I* : The sequence in the series is × 6, ÷ 3 which is repeated.

8 48 16 96 32 192

×6 ÷3 ×6 ÷3 ×6

Explanation II : There are two alternate series and the numbers are multiplied by 2.

×2 ×2

8 48 16 96 32 192

×2 ×2

Series I : 8, 16, 32

Series II : 48, 96, 192

15. The sequence in the series is :

2 8 14 24 34 48 62

+6 +6 +10 +10 +14 +14

The difference increases by 4 at alternate step.

16. The numbers in the series are multiplied by 5 to get the next number.

∴ 125 should be in place of 120.

17. Two numbers form a pair. The first number increases by 7 for the next pair and the second number is the double of first number.

4 8 11 22 18 36 25 50

×2 ×2 ×2 ×2

+7 +7 +7

∴ 25 should be in place of 24.

18. There are two alternate series and in each series, the numbers are multiplied by 6 to get the next number.

×6 ×6 ×6

2 4 12 24 72 144 432

×6 ×6

∴ 144 should be in place of 142.

19. There are three alternate series and in each series, the numbers are multiplied by 2 to get the next number.

×2 ×2

2 3 4 4 6 8 8 12 16

×2 ×2

×2 ×2

Series I : 2, 4, 8

Series II : 3, 6, 12

Series III : 4, 8, 16

∴ 8 should be in place of 9.

20. The difference between the consecutive numbers in the series decreases by 1 at each step.

97 91 86 82 79 77 76 76

–6 –5 –4 –3 –2 –1 –0

∴ 82 should be in place of 83.

ANALOGIES OR RELATIONSHIPS

Directions : *In the questions given below establish the relationship between the two words. Then from the given options select one which has the same relationship as of the given two words.*

1. ADULT : BABY : : FLOWER : ?
A. Seed B. Bud
C. Fruit D. Butterfly

2. WRITER : READER : : PRODUCER : ?
A. Creator B. Contractor
C. Creature D. Consumer

3. ENTRANCE : EXIT : : LOYALTY : ?
A. Treachery B. Patriotism
C. Fidelity D. Reward

4. MOTHER : MATERNAL : : FATHER : ?
A. Eternal B. Detrimental
C. Paternal D. Formidable

Directions : *In the questions given below one term is missing. Based on the relationship of the two given words find the missing term from the given options.*

5. GFC : CFG : : RPJ : ?
A. JRP B. JPR
C. PJR D. RJP

6. BCF : DEG : : MNQ : ?
A. OPR B. PQS
C. OPP D. QRT

7. NATION : ANITNO : : HUNGRY : ?
A. HNUGRY B. UNHGYR
C. YRNGUH D. UHGNYR

8. SSTU : MMNO : : AABC : ?
A. GGHH B. IJKK
C. XXYZ D. NOOP

ANSWERS

1	2	3	4	5	6	7	8
B	D	A	C	B	A	D	C

EXPLANATORY ANSWERS

1. The youngone of an adult is a baby and that of a flower is a bud.
2. A writer aims to please the readers by his writings, a producer aims to please the consumers by his products.
3. The related words are opposites.
4. Relations on the mother's side are maternal and on the father's side paternal.
5. The letters of the first group are reversed.

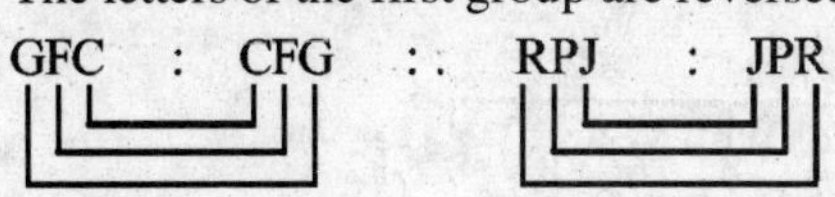

6. The three letters are moved 2, 2 and 1 steps forward respectively.

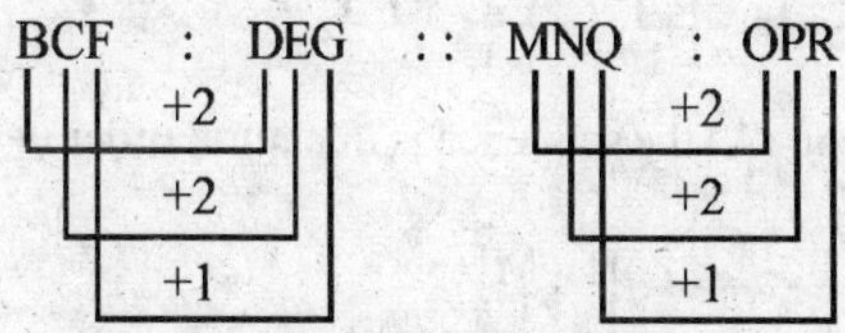

7. The word is divided in sections of two letters and the letters are reversed.

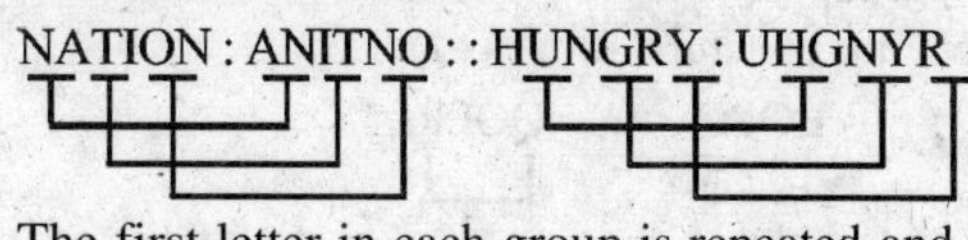

8. The first letter in each group is repeated and followed by two consecutive letters.

ODD ONE OUT

Directions : *Three of the following four in each question are alike in a certain way and so form a group. Select the group of letters that does not belong to that group.*

1. A. ACE B. LOR
C. GIK D. VXZ

2. A. TSR B. LKJ
C. PQO D. HGF

3. A. EF LM B. KJ SR
C. XW HG D. ED YX

4. A. JOPK B. BOPC
C. QOPR D. TOPS

5. A. DfH B. MoQ
C. UwY D. lnO

6. A. JKkL B. OPpQ
C. DEEf D. VWwX

7. A. BdfH B. FHJL
C. RTvX D. uVwX

8. A. DFHEG B. TWXUV
C. OQSPR D. JLNKM

9. A. FEUV B. DCXW
C. BAZY D. HGTS

10. A. UTSR B. XYZW
C. ONML D. IHGF

ANSWERS

1	2	3	4	5	6	7	8	9	10
B	C	A	D	D	C	D	B	A	B

EXPLANATORY ANSWERS

1. The sequence in each group is +2. Only option B has sequence in +3, *i.e.,*

ABCDE (+2 +2) LMNOPQR (+3 +3)

GHIJK (+2 +2) VWXYZ (+2 +2)

2. The sequence of alphabet in each group is in reverse order. Only option C has sequence in disturbed order.

3. Two consecutive alphabet in each group are in reverse sequence (–1), *i.e.,*

KJ SR; XW HG; ED YX

–1 –1 –1 –1 –1 –1

Only in option (A) the sequence is in natural order (+1), *i.e.,*

E F (+1) L M (+1)

4. In each group, letters 'OP' are common. The two corner alphabet are in natural order (+1); *i.e.,*

JOPK ; BOPC ; QOPR

+1 +1 +1

Only in option (D) they are in reverse order (–1); *i.e.,*

TOPS (–1)

5. In other groups, only the alphabet in the centre is of lower case. In this option letter 'L' on the left is also in lower case.

6. In other groups, the third letter which is a repeat of the second alphabet is in lower case.

7. In each group, the sequence of the alphabet, irrespective of the case, is +2; *i.e.,*

B D f H ; F H J L ; R T v X

+2 +2 +2 +2 +2+2 +2 +2 +2

Only in option (D) the sequence is in natural order (+1), *i.e.,*

u V w X

+1 +1 +1

8. In each group; the alphabet at positions-first, fourth, second, fifth and third, form a natural sequence.

In option (B), the alphabet at positions first, fourth, fifth, second and third, form the natural sequence.

9. In each group, two alphabets in the corner and two alphabets in the centre correspond to their reverse order positioned alphabet. *i.e.,*

natural order → A B C D E F G H I J K L M

reverse order → Z Y X W V U T S R Q P O N

natural order → N O P Q R S T U V W X Y Z

reverse order → M L K J I H G F E D C B A

As such—

D corresponds with W and

C corresponds with X.

B corresponds with Y and

A corresponds with Z.

H corresponds with S and

G corresponds with T.

Similarly,

F should correspond with U and

E should correspond with V;

i.e. letters 'UV' should be written as 'VU'

10. In each group, the alphabet are in reverse order.

In option (B), the order is disturbed.

7

CODING AND DECODING

Directions : *In the following questions select the right option which indicates the correct code for the word or letter given in the question.*

1. If CHAIR is coded as FKDLU then RAID is coded as:

A. ULGD B. ULKG
C. ULDG D. UDLG

2. If CONDEMN is coded as CNODMEN, then TEACHER is coded as :

A. TEACHER B. TAEECHR
C. TCAEEHR D. TAECEHR

3. In a code language COME is written as XLNV and ABLE as ZYOV. How will MOLLY be written in that code?

A. NLOBO B. NLBOO
C. LNOOB D. NLOOB

4. In a certain code PROFESSION is written as EFORPNOISS. In the same code DICTIONARY will be written as :

A. YRANOITCID B. ITCIDYRANO
C. ITCIDYRNAO D. ITCDIYARNO

5. JUNE is coded as NXPF, how will STAY be coded in the same manner?

A. WWCZ B. WVCZ
C. WWDB D. VWZC

Directions : *In the following questions study the coded patterns and then select the right option from the given alternatives.*

6. In a certain language, (a) 'go ju mi' stands for 'plenty of money'; (b) pao ju go nei vu' for 'money creates lots of problems'; (c) 'kol vu nei' for 'problems create tension'; and (d) 'sol tun ju haw' for 'still money is needed'. Which of the following words stand for 'money'?

A. nei B. ju
C. haw D. go

7. In a certain language, (a) 'FOR' stands for 'old is gold'; (b) 'ROT' stands for 'gold is pure'; (c) 'ROM' stands for 'gold is costly'. How will 'pure old gold is costly' be written?

A. TFROM B. FOTRM
C. FTORM D. TOMRF

8. In a certain code '415' means 'milk is hot'; '18' means 'hot soup'; and '895' means 'soup is tasty'. What number will indicate the word 'tasty'?

A. 9 B. 8
C. 5 D. 4

9. In a certain code '643' means 'she is beautiful', '593' means 'he is handsome', and '567' means 'handsome meets beautiful'. What number will indicate the word 'meets'?

A. 5 B. 3
C. 7 D. 6

10. In a certain code language, (a) 'dugo hui mul zo' stands for 'work is very hard'; (b) 'hui dugo ba ki' for 'Bingo is very smart'; (c) 'nano mul dugo' for 'cake is hard', and (d) 'mul ki qu' for 'smart and hard'. Which of the following words stand for 'Bingo'?

A. jalu B. dugo
C. ki D. ba

ANSWERS

1	2	3	4	5	6	7	8	9	10
D	D	D	B	A	B	A	A	C	D

EXPLANATORY ANSWERS

2. In this word, the second and third letters interchange their places and the fifth and sixth letters do the same. Other letters retain their position.

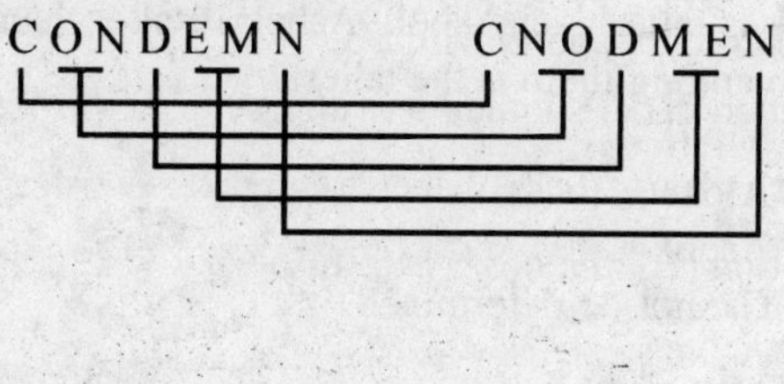

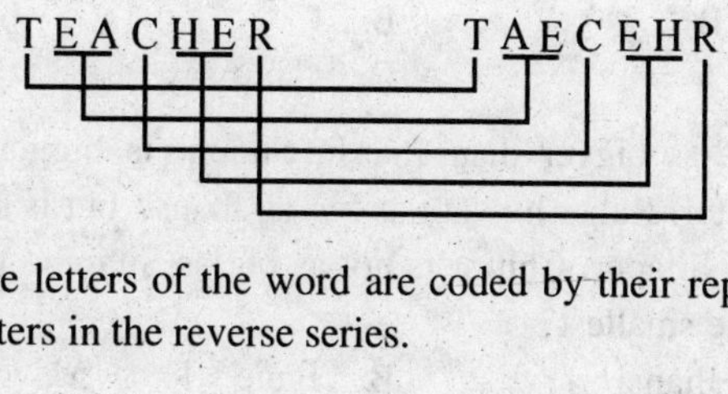

3. The letters of the word are coded by their represented letters in the reverse series.

C O M E → letters in natural series
X L N V → letters in reverse series
↓ ↓ ↓ ↓
3rd 15th 13th 5th → position of letters
A B L E → letters in natural series
Z Y O V → letters in reverse series
↓ ↓ ↓ ↓
1st 2nd 12th 5th → position of letters

Similarly,

M O L L Y → letters in natural series
N L O O B → letters in reverse series
↓ ↓ ↓ ↓ ↓
13th 15th 12th 12th 25th → position of letters

4. The word is divided into two equal parts and the letters of each part are written backwards.

PROFE SSION → EFORP NOISS

Similarly,

DICTI ONARY → ITCID YRANO

5. The word is coded by moving the letters +4, +3, +2, and +1 steps respectively.

J U N E → N X P F (+4, +3, +2, +1)

Similarly,

S T A Y → W W C Z (+4, +3, +2, +1)

6.

	Code	Sentence
1.	go *ju* mi	plenty of *money*
2.	pao *ju* go nei vu	*money* creates lots of problems
3.	kol vu nei	problems create tension
4.	sol tun *ju* haw	still *money* is needed

In 1st, 2nd and 4th codes and their sentences the word 'ju' is repeated and so is 'money'.

8.

	Code	Sentence
1.	415	milk is hot
2.	18	hot soup
3.	895	soup is *tasty*

From 3rd code and its sentence neither number '9' is repeated nor the word 'tasty'.

9.

	Code	Sentence
1.	643	she is beautiful
2.	593	he is handsome
3.	567	handsome *meets* beautiful

From 3rd code and its sentence, neither number '7' nor the word 'meets' is repeated.

10.

	Code	Sentence
1.	*dugo hui* mul zo	work *is very* hard
2.	*hui dugo* **ba** *ki*	**Bingo** *is very smart*
3.	nano mul *dugo*	cake is *hard*
4.	mul *ki* qu	*smart* and hard

From 2nd code and its sentence, neither 'ba' nor 'Bingo' is repeated.
(Words repeated are in italics)

STATEMENT ANALYSIS

1. Among five friends, A is heavier than B; C is lighter than D; B is lighter than D but heavier than E. Who among them is the heaviest?

A. B B. C
C. A D. Can't say

2. Pune is bigger than Jhansi, Sitapur is bigger than Chittor. Raigarh is not as big as Jhansi, but is bigger than Sitapur. Chittor is not as big as Sitapur. Which is the smallest?

A. Jhansi B. Pune
C. Chittor D. Sitapur

3. Ajay works more than Ram. Alok works as much as Raju. Pankaj works less than Alok. Ram works more than Alok. Who works the most of all?

A. Ajay B. Ram
C. Alok D. Raju

4. Vipul is taller than Hans. Hans is taller than Anand. Alok is taller than Ashok. Ashok is taller than Hans. Who among them is the tallest?

A. Vipul
B. Alok
C. Ashok
D. Cannot be determined

5. Pramod is taller than Gopal. Gopal is shorter than Madhu. To find out who among them is the tallest, which of the following further informations is necessary?
A. Madhu is taller than Gopal.
B. Madhu is shorter than Pramod's brother
C. Pramod is taller than Madhu.
D. Pramod is taller than Madhu's brother.

6. Among five friends P, Q, R, S and T, who is the youngest? To arrive at the answer which of the following information given in the statements (*a*) and (*b*) is sufficient?
(*a*) R is younger than P and T.
(*b*) S is younger than Q.
A. Only (*a*) alone is sufficient
B. Either (*a*) or (*b*) is sufficient
C. Both (*a*) and (*b*) together are needed
D. Both (*a*) and (*b*) together are not sufficient

7. Sushma is richer than Rashmi whereas Anand is richer than Priya. Arun is as rich as Rashmi. Shoba is richer than Sushma.
Which of the following statements is correct according to the above propositions?
A. Rashmi is poorer than Priya.
B. Priya is richer than Arun
C. Arun is poorer than Sushma.
D. Anand is richer than Rashmi

8. A is elder to B while C and D are elder to E who lies between A and B. If C be elder to B, which one of the following statements is necessarily true?
A. E is elder to B
B. A is elder to C
C. C is elder to D
D. D is elder to C

9. Vikram is taller than Rajan but shorter than Annie. Jamal is taller than Annie. Sita is taller than Vikram. Rajan is shorter than Sita. Who is the shortest of all in the group?
A. Sita
B. Rajan
C. Vikram
D. Cannot be determined

10. Suresh is as much older than Kamal as he is younger than Prabodh. Navin is as old as Kamal. Which of the following statements is wrong?
A. Suresh is older than Navin
B. Kamal is younger than Suresh
C. Prabodh is not the oldest
D. Navin is younger than Prabodh

ANSWERS

1	2	3	4	5	6	7	8	9	10
D	C	A	D	C	D	C	A	B	C

EXPLANATORY ANSWERS

1. The five friends in descending order of weight are : A/D, B/C, E or A/D, B, C/E. Either A or D is the heaviest.

2. The order of cities in descending order of size is : Pune, Jhansi, Raigarh, Sitapur, Chittor.

3. On the basis of doing work, the descending order will be : Ajay, Ram, Alok/Raju, Pankaj.

4. On the basis of height, the descending order will be Vipul/Alok, Ashok, Hans, Anand. Either Vipul or Alok is the tallest.

5. According to the information both Pramod and Madhu are taller than Gopal. Option (c) decides who is the tallest.

6. Statements are not inter-related.

7. On the basis of wealth, the descending order will be :
1. Shobha, Sushma, Rashmi/Arun
2. Anand, *and* Priya
(The two statements are not inter-related.)

8. The order in descending seniority will be : A/C/D, E, B.

9. On the basis of height the descending order will be :
Jamal/Sita, Annie, Vikram, Rajan.
or
Jamal, Sita/Annie, Vikram, Rajan.

10. On the basis of age the descending order will be : Prabodh, Suresh, Kamal/Navin.

PLACE ARRANGEMENT

Directions: *In the following questions, understand the arrangement pattern and then select the right answer from the given options :*

1. Five boys are sitting in a row. Raghu is not adjacent to Shyam or Amit. Ajay is not adjacent to Shyam. Raghu is adjacent to Mayank. If Mayank is at the middle in the row, then Ajay is adjacent to whom out of the following?

A. Amit B. Raghu
C. Mayank D. Shyam

2. Mini is to the right of Rajni but to the left of Ananta. Saya is to the right of Mini but to the left of Jaya. Who is on the extreme left if all the girls are facing North?

A. Jaya B. Mini
C. Rajni D. Saya

3. Kittu is in-between Mohan and Sohan. Raju is to the left of Sohan and Shyam is to the right of Mohan. If all of the friends are sitting facing South, then who is on their extreme right?

A. Mohan B. Sohan
C. Kittu D. Shyam

4. A, B, C, D and E are running one behind the other. C is not near E and A is not near D. B is next to A and E is not near D. Who is in the middle?

A. B B. E
C. A D. Cannot be said

5. O, P, Q, R, S and T are standing on a bench according to their height. P is taller than O but shorter than S. Only S is taller than T. R is shorter than P but taller than Q. Who is the shortest?

A. O B. Q
C. P D. Cannot be said

ANSWERS

1	2	3	4	5
B	C	D	A	D

EXPLANATORY ANSWERS

1. The order of sitting is :

Amit, Shyam, Mayank, Ajay, Raghu

or

Ajay, Raghu, Mayank, Amit, Shyam

2. The order in which the girls are positioned is :

Rajni, Mini, Ananta, Saya, Jaya

or

Saya, Jaya, Ananta

or

Saya, Ananta, Jaya

3. The order of sitting while facing South is:

Shyam, Mohan, Kittu, Sohan, Raju.

4. The positions while running behind the other is :

E		E
A		A
B	*or*	B
C		D
D		C

5. In descending order of height, the standing positions are :

S		S
T		T
P	*or*	P
R		R
O		Q
Q		O

Either O or Q is the shortest. The information given is not enough to clarify the answer.

DIRECTION SENSE

Directions : *In the following questions, select the right answer from the given options to depict the correct direction/distance.*

1. Kittu walks towards East and then towards South. After walking some distance he turns towards West and then turns to his left. In which direction is he walking now?

A. North
B. South
C. East
D. West

2. A person is driving towards West. What sequence of directions should he follow so that he is driving towards South?

A. left, right, right
B. right, right, left
C. left, left, left
D. right, right, right

3. Richa drives 8 km to the South, turns left and drives 5 km. Again, she turns left and drives 8 km. How far is she from her starting point?

A. 3 km
B. 5 km
C. 8 km
D. 13 km

4. Dingi runs 40 km towards North then turns right and runs 50 km. He turns right and runs 30 km, and once again turns right and runs 50 km. How far is he from his starting point?

A. 90 km
B. 50 km
C. 10 km
D. 5 km

5. Debu walks towards East then towards North and turning 45° right walks for a while and lastly turns towards left. In which direction is he walking now?

A. North
B. East
C. South-East
D. North-West

ANSWERS

1	2	3	4	5
B	D	B	C	D

EXPLANATORY ANSWERS

1.

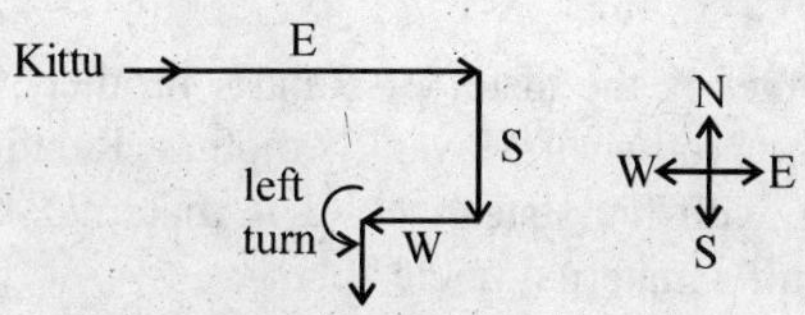

2.

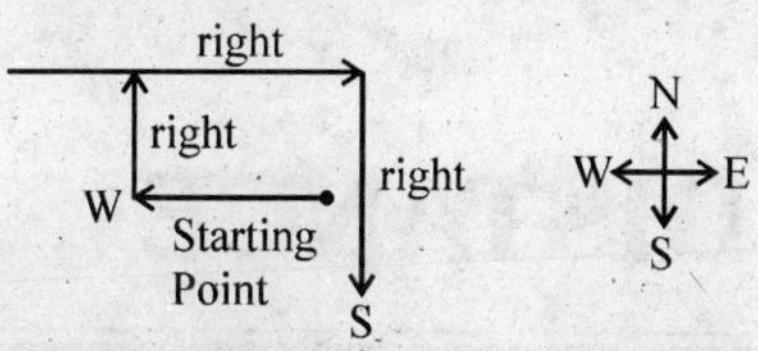

3.

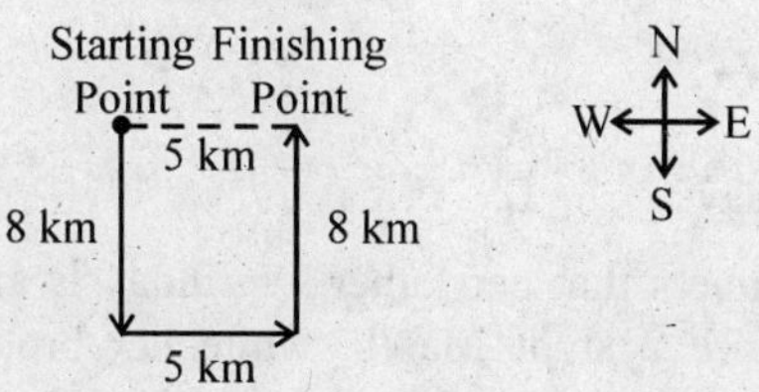

4.

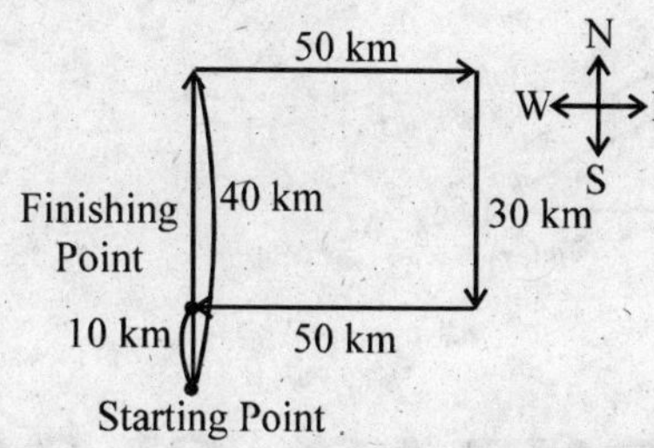

5.

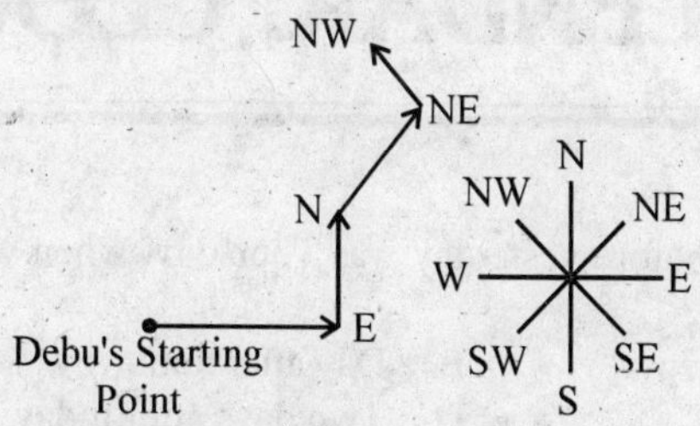

BLOOD RELATIONSHIPS

Directions : *In each of the following questions keenly study the relationship mentioned between the persons, and then from the given options select the right relationship as the answer.*

1. 'A' is the father of 'B' and 'C'. 'B' is the son of 'A' but 'C' is not the son of 'A'. What is 'C's' relation with 'A'?

A. Daughter
B. Son
C. Niece
D. Nephew

2. A lady said, "The person standing there is my grandfather's only son's daughter". How is the lady related to the standing person?

A. Sister
B. Mother
C. Aunt
D. Cousin

3. Ravi is the brother of Amit's son's son. What is Amit's relation to Ravi?

A. Cousin
B. Father
C. Grandfather
D. Son

4. Mayank said, "My mother is the sister of Rajat's brother." What is Rajat's relation with Mayank?

A. Cousin B. Maternal uncle
C. Uncle D. Brother-in-law

5. Introducing Lily, Raghav said, "Her father is my mother's only son". How is Lily related to Raghav?

A. Aunt B. Daughter
C. Mother D. Sister

ANSWERS

1	2	3	4	5
A	A	C	B	B

EXPLANATORY ANSWERS

1.

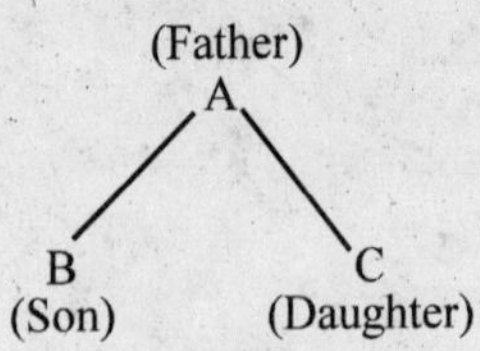

'C' is not the son of 'A', but 'A' is the father of 'C'. So, 'C' is the daughter of 'A'.

2.

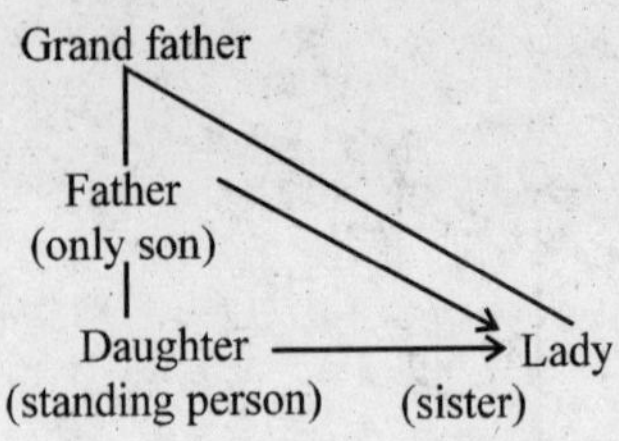

Lady's grandfather's son is lady's father and father's daughter will only be lady's sister.

4.

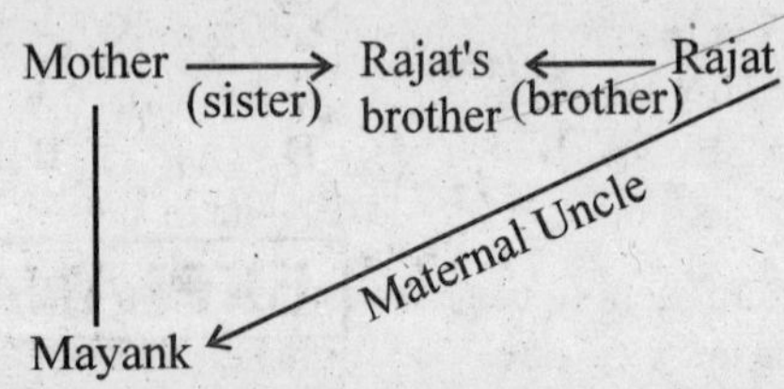

Mayank's mother is the sister of Rajat's brother. So Rajat is also the brother of Mayank's mother. Relation of the brother with his sister's child is maternal. So Rajat is Mayank's maternal uncle.

CALENDAR, CLOCK, TIME, DISTANCE

1. If the day before yesterday was Thursday, when will Sunday be?

A. Tomorrow B. Day after tomorrow
C. Today D. Two days after today

2. There are twenty people working in an office. The first group of five works between 8:00 A.M. and 2:00 PM. The second group of ten works between 10:00 AM to 4:00 PM. And the third group of five works between 12 noon to 6:00 PM. There are three computers in the office which all the employees frequently use. During which of the following hours the computers are likely to be used most?

A. 1:00 PM - 3:00 PM
B. 12 noon - 2:00 PM
C. 2:00 PM - 4:00 PM
D. 10:00 AM - 12 noon

3. If the seventh day of a month is three (3) days earlier than Friday, what day will it be on the nineteenth day of the month?

A. Sunday B. Monday
C. Wednesday D. Friday

4. Radha remembers that her father's birthday is after 16th but before 21st of March, while her brother Mangesh remembers that his father's birthday is before 22nd but after 19th of March. On which date is the birthday of their father?

A. 19th
B. 20th
C. 21st
D. Cannot be determined

5. A man is three (3) years older than his wife and four (4) times as old as his son. If the son attains an age of fifteen (15) years after three (3) years, what is the present age of the mother?

A. 45 years B. 51 years
C. 48 years D. 60 years

6. A clock is so placed that at 12 noon its minute hand points towards north-east. In which direction does its hour hand point at 1.30 P.M.?

A. East B. West
C. North D. South

7. If in the above question clock is turned through an angle of 135° in an anticlockwise direction, in which direction will its minute hand point at 8.45 P.M.?

A. East B. West
C. North D. South

8. A couple married in 1980 had two children, one in 1982 and the other in 1984. Their combined ages will equal the years of the marriage in?

A. 1986 B. 1985
C. 1987 D. 1988

9. Manoj left home for the bus stop 15 minutes earlier than the usual time. It takes 10 minutes to reach the stop. He reached the stop at 8.40 a.m. What time does he usually leave home for the bus stop?

A. 8.30 a.m. B. 8.55 a.m.
C. 8.45 p.m. D. None of these

10. Mamuni went to the movies nine days ago. She goes to the movies only on Thursday. What day of the week is today?

A. Sunday B. Tuesday
C. Thursday D. Saturday

11. If Thursday was the day after the day before yesterday five days ago, what is the least number of days ago when Sunday was three days before the day after tomorrow?

A. Two days ago B. Three days ago
C. Four days ago D. Five days ago

12. 1.12.91 is the first Sunday. Which is the fourth Tuesday of December 91?

A. 31.12.91 B. 24.12.91
C. 17.12.91 D. 26.12.91

13. If the third day of a month is Monday, which of the following will be the fifth day from 21st of that month?

A. Tuesday B. Monday
C. Wednesday D. Thursday

14. Keshav runs a factory in three shifts of eight hours each with 210 employees. In each shift minimum of 80 employees are required to run the factory effectively. No employee can be allowed to work for more than 16 hours a day. At least how many employees will be required to work for 16 hours every day?

A. 30 B. 60
C. Data inadequate D. None of these

15. If 15 horses eat 15 bags of gram in 15 days, in how many days will one horse eat one bag of grain?

A. 15 days B. 1/15 days
C. 1 day D. 30 days

16. A century leap year is divisible by :

A. 4 B. 16
C. 40 D. 400

17. If the fifth day of a month is Friday, which of the following will be the Seventh day from 10th of that month?

A. Tuesday B. Monday
C. Wednesday D. Thursday

18. Day after tomorrow is my birthday. On the same day next week falls 'Holi'. Today is Monday. What will be the day after 'Holi'?

A. Wednesday B. Thursday
C. Friday D. Saturday

19. A clock shows the time as 3 : 30 p.m. If the minute hand gains 2 minutes every hour, how many minutes will the clock gain by 4 a.m.?

A. 23 Minutes B. 24 Minutes
C. 25 Minutes D. 26 Minutes

20. Two brothers were expected to return home on the same day. Rajat returned 3 days earlier but Rohit returned 4 days later. If Rajat returned on Thursday, what was the expected day when both the brothers were to return home and when did Rohit Return?

A. Wednesday, Sunday
B. Thursday, Monday
C. Sunday, Thursday
D. Monday, Friday

ANSWERS

1	2	3	4	5	6	7	8	9	10
A	B	A	B	A	A	D	A	D	D
11	**12**	**13**	**14**	**15**	**16**	**17**	**18**	**19**	**20**
A	B	C	D	A	D	C	B	C	C

EXPLANATORY ANSWERS

1. Thursday —Day-before-yesterday
Friday —Yesterday
Saturday —Today
Sunday — Tomorrow

2. 1. 5 people work between 8 a.m. to 2 p.m.

2. 10 people work between 10 a.m. to 4 p.m.

3. 5 people work between 12 noon to 6 p.m.

So, computers are used most between 12 noon to 2 p.m.

3. 7th day is 3 days earlier than Friday so, 10th day is Friday, so also is 17th.

∴ 19th day will be 2nd day ahead of Friday, *i.e.,* Sunday.

4. Father's birthday

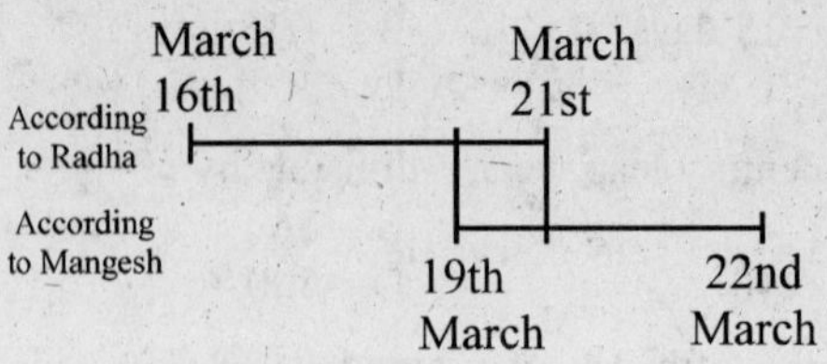

∴ Their father's birthday is on 20th March.

5. Present age of son is 15 – 3 = 12 years. Age of the man is 4 times the age of son, *i.e.*,

12 × 4 = 48 years

Man is 3 years elder to his wife/son's mother.

So Age of the mother is 48 – 3 = 45 years

6.

At 12 noon

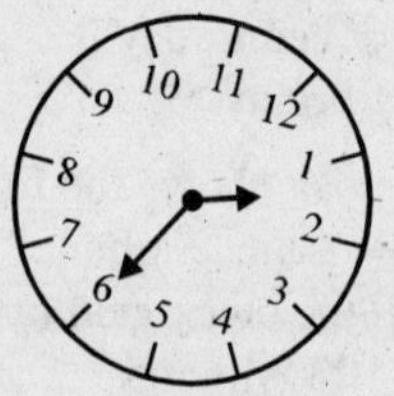

At 1.30 p.m. the hour hand will point towards East.

7.

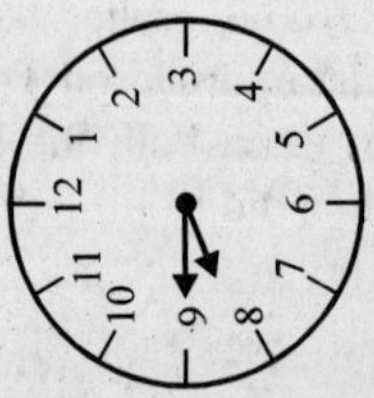

After rotating the clock in earlier question, its minute hand will point towards South at 8:45 p.m.

8. 1982 — 2 years later — 1st child

1984 — 4 years later — 2nd child

Total age of children — 2 years.

1985 — 5 years later — Total age of children: 4 years.

1986 — 6 years later — Total age of children : 6 years.

9. Manoj reached the bus stop at 8.40 a.m. He left his home at 8:40 – 10 minutes = 8:30 a.m. He left 15 minutes earlier than usual, so his actual time of leaving home is 8:30 am + 15 minutes = 8:45 a.m.

10. Mamuni goes to the movies on Thursday, so nine days ago was Thursday.

∴ Two days ago was also Thursday. So, today is Saturday.

11. Day after the day-before-yesterday five days ago is the 6th day which is Thursday. And so, the 3rd day will be Sunday. Three days before the day-after-tomorrow is Yesterday which is the 1st day of the five days. So, two days ago was Sunday.

12. First Sunday is on 1st December

First Tuesday is on 3rd December

3 weeks later, Fourth Tuesday will be on 3 + (7 × 3) = 24th December.

13. 3rd day of the month is Monday

5th day from 21st is 26th

26 – 3 = 23 days

23 days later, 23/7 leaves 2 days.

So, two days ahead of Monday will be Wednesday.

14. 80 employees are required for double shift.

15. 15 horses eat 15 bags of grain in 15 days

15 horses eat 1 bag of grain in 1 day

1 horse eats 1 bag of grain in 15 days

16. A leap year is divisible by 4 and a century leap year is divisible by 400.

17. Seventh day from 10th is 17th.

5th day is Friday. Next Friday is on 12th, 17 – 12 = 5, 5 days ahead of Friday will be Wednesday. So, 17th is Wednesday.

18. Today is Monday

Day-after-tomorrow is Wednesday

Next week 'Holi' is also on Wednesday

So, Day after Holi is Thursday.

19. Hours between 3:30 p.m. and 4 a.m. are — 12½ hours. Number of minutes gained will be 12½ × 2 = 25 minutes.

20. Rajat returned on Thursday. 3 days later was the day of expected return, *i.e.,* Sunday. Rohit returned 4 days after Sunday, *i.e.,* Thursday.

ROWS AND RANKS

1. In a row of trees, one tree is fifth from either end of the row. How many trees are in the row?
   A. 11 B. 8
   C. 10 D. 9

2. Jaya ranks 5th in a class of 53. What is her rank from the bottom in the class?
   A. 49th B. 48th
   C. 47th D. 50th

3. Mohan ranks twenty-first in a class of sixty-five students. What will be his (Mohan's) rank if the lowest candidate is assigned rank 1?
   A. 44th B. 45th
   C. 46th D. Data inadequate

4. If Rahul finds that he is 12th from the right in a line of boys and 4th from the left, how many boys should be added to the line such that there are 28 boys in the line?
   A. 12 B. 14
   C. 20 D. 13

5. In a row of boys, Rajan is tenth from the right and Suraj is tenth from the left. When Rajan and Suraj interchange their positions, Suraj will be twenty-seventh from the left. Which of the following will be Rajan's position from the right?
   A. Tenth B. Twenty-sixth
   C. Twenty-ninth D. None of these

6. Mahesh and Suresh are ranked 11th and 12th respectively from the top in a class of 41 students. What will be their respective ranks from the bottom?
   A. 32nd and 33rd B. 29th and 30th
   C. 30th and 31st D. 31st and 30th

7. Uma ranked 8th from the top and 37th from bottom in a class. How many students are there in the class?
   A. 47 B. 46
   C. 45 D. None of these

8. In a queue, Sadiq is 14th from the front and Joseph is 17th from the end, while Jane is in between Sadiq and Joseph. If Sadiq be ahead of Joseph and there be 48 persons in the queue, how many persons are there between Sadiq and Jane?
   A. 5 B. 6
   C. 7 D. 8

9. Rohan ranked eleventh from the top and twenty-seventh from the bottom among the students who passed the annual examination in a class. If the number of students who failed in the examination was 12, how many students appeared for the examination?
   A. 48
   B. 49
   C. 50
   D. Cannot be determined

10. Some boys are sitting in a row. P is sitting fourteenth from the left and Q is seventh from the right. If there are four boys between P and Q, how many boys are there in the row?
    A. 19 B. 21
    C. 25 D. 23

ANSWERS

1	2	3	4	5	6	7	8	9	10
D	A	B	D	D	D	D	C	B	C

EXPLANATORY ANSWERS

1. 

Total number of trees in the row are :
(5 + 5) –1 =9

2. 

Jaya's rank from the bottom is :
(53 – 5) +1 = 49th.

3. 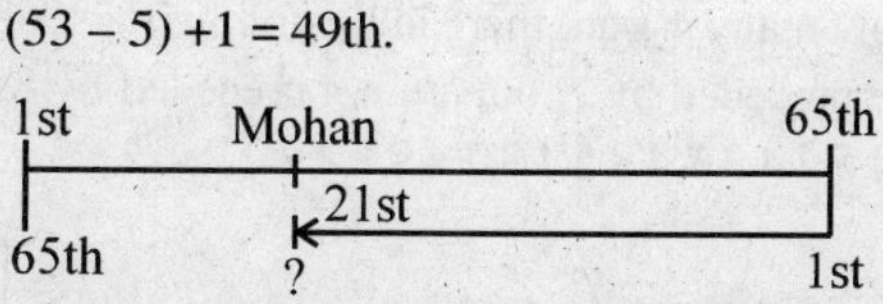

Note : Mohan's rank from the last or the question asked means the same.

Mohan's rank is (65 – 21) +1 = 45th

4. 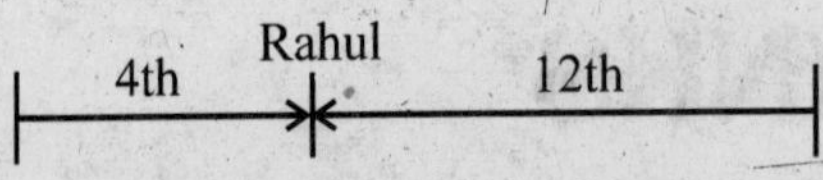

The number of boys in the line are :
(4 + 12) – 1 = 15
To make a line of 28 boys, (28 –15) *i.e.* 13 more boys are needed.

5. 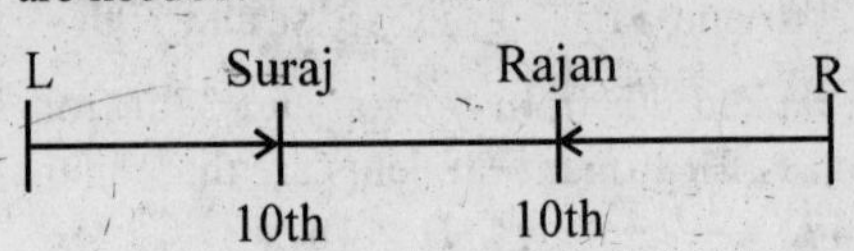

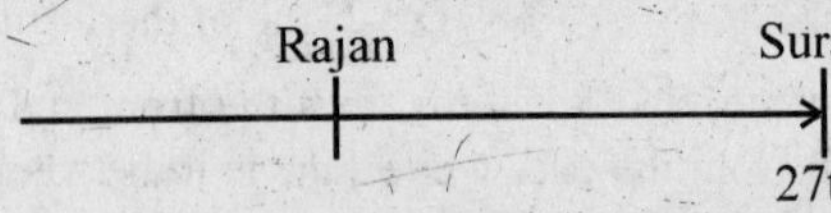

As the position of boys is equal from both ends, Rajan will also be 27th from the right after changing positions.

6. 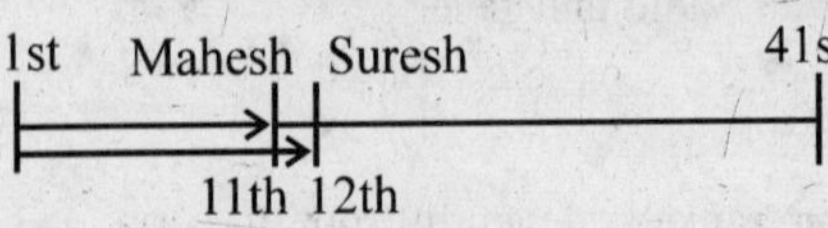

Mahesh's position from bottom is :
(41 – 11) + 1 = 31st
Suresh's position from bottom is :
(41 – 12) +1 = 30th

7. 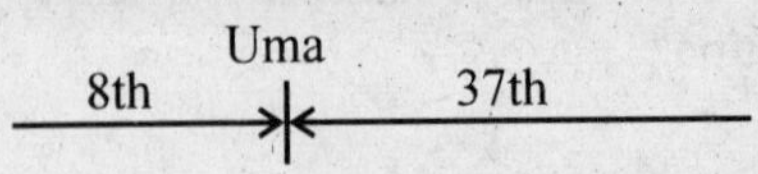

Total number of students in the class are :
(8 + 37) – 1 = 44

8. 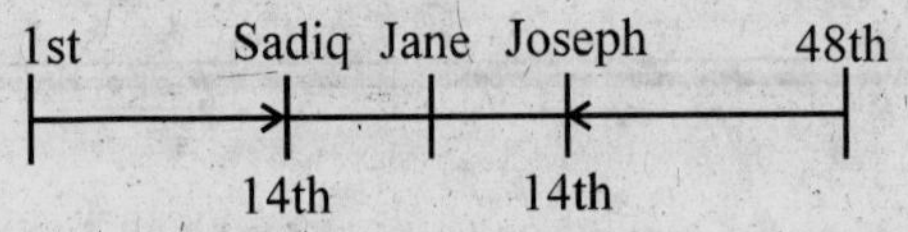

Sadiq's position from last is :
(48 – 14) + 1 = 35th
Number of persons between Sadiq and Joseph are (35 – 17) – 1 = 17
Jane is in-between Sadiq and Joseph *i.e.,* she's at 9th position from both the boys.
∴ there are 8 persons between Sadiq and Jane.
Note : (8 + 8) – 1 = 17

9. 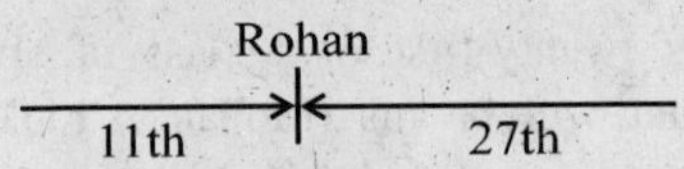

Number of students who passed the examination (11+ 27) – 1 = 37
Those who failed = 12
Total number of students who appeared in the examination = 37 + 12 = 49.

10. 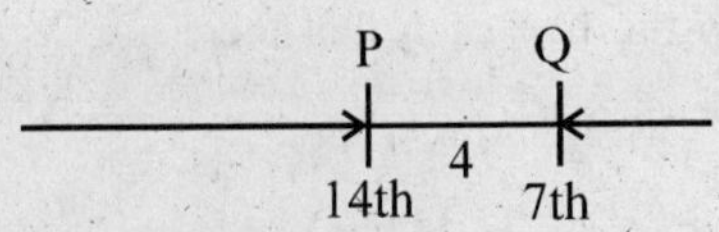

The number of boys in the row are :
(14 + 4 + 7) = 25

NUMBER PROBLEMS

1. How many 6's are there in the following series of numbers which are preceded by 7 but not immediately followed by 9?
6 7 9 5 6 9 7 6 8 7 6 7 8 6 9 4 6 7 7 6 9 5 7 6 3

A. One B. Two
C. Three D. Four

2. In a chess tournament each of six players will play every other player exactly once. How many matches will be played during the tournament?

A. 12 B. 15
C. 30 D. 36

3. How many 4's are there in the following series which are preceded by 7, but are not preceded by 8?
3 4 5 7 4 3 7 4 8 5 4 3 7 4 9 8 4 7 2 7 4 1 3 6

A. 1 B. 2
C. 3 D. 4

4. How many even numbers are there in the following series of numbers, each of which is immediately preceded by an odd number, but not immediately followed by an even number?
5 3 4 8 9 7 1 6 5 3 2 9 8 4 3 5

A. Nil B. 1
C. 2 D. 3

5. If all the numbers from 1 to 51 which are exactly divisible by 3 are arranged in descending order, which of the following numbers will come at the seventh and tenth places from the top?

A. 33 & 27 B. 33 & 21
C. 21 & 30 D. 33 & 24

ANSWERS

1	2	3	4	5
C	B	D	C	D

EXPLANATORY ANSWERS

1. $6795697\underset{1}{\underline{768}}\underset{2}{\underline{767}}86946776957\underset{3}{\underline{763}}$

2. When all the players have to play with each other then the method of calculating the number of matches to be played is $\frac{n(n-1)}{2}$ where '*n*' is the number of players playing the match. So, the number of matches played will be :
$(6 \times 5) \div 2 = 30 \div 2 = 15$

3. $345\underset{1}{\underline{74}}3\underset{2}{\underline{74}}8543\underset{3}{\underline{74}}98472\underset{4}{\underline{74}}136$

4. $534897\underset{1}{\underline{165}}\underset{2}{\underline{329}}8435$

5. The numbers divisible by 3 in descending order are :
51, 48, 45, 42, 39, 36, 33, $\underset{7th}{\underline{30}}$, 27, $\underset{10th}{\underline{24}}$, 21, 18, 15, 12, 9, 6, 3.

SYMBOL SUBSTITUTION

1. If "+" means "–"; "–" means "×"; "×"means "÷" and "÷" means "+", then
$15 \times 5 \div 10 + 5 - 3 = ?$
A. 9.5 B. 0
C. – 2 D. 24

2. If "+" means "–"; "–" means "×"; "×"means "÷" and "÷" means "+", then
$15 \times 3 \div 15 + 5 - 2 = ?$
A. 0 B. 10
C. 20 D. 6

3. If "+" means "÷"; "×" means "–"; "÷"means "+" and "–" means "×", then
$16 \div 8 \times 6 - 2 + 12 = ?$
A. 22 B. 24
C. 23 D. 20

4. If "+" means "×"; "–" means "÷"; "÷"means "+" and "×" means "–", then what will be the value of $20 \div 40 - 4 \times 5 + 6 = ?$
A. 60 B. 1.67
C. 150 D. 0

5. If "+" means "×"; "–" means "÷"; "×"means "–" and "÷" means "+", then
$5 + 8 - 4 \times 2 \div 9 = ?$
A. 15 B. 13
C. 17 D. 11

ANSWERS

1	2	3	4	5
C	B	C	D	C

EXPLANATORY ANSWERS

1. $15 \div 5 + 10 - 5 \times 3$
$3 + 10 - 15 = -2$

2. $15 \div 3 + 15 - 5 \times 2$
$5 + 15 - 10 = 10$

3. $16 + 8 - 6 \times 2 \div 12$
$16 + 8 - 1 = 23$

4. $20 + 40 \div 4 - 5 \times 6$
$20 + 10 - 30 = 0$

5. $5 \times 8 \div 4 - 2 + 9$
$10 - 2 + 9 = 17$

MISSING NUMBERS

Directions: *In each question given below which one number can be placed at the sign of interrogation?*

1. 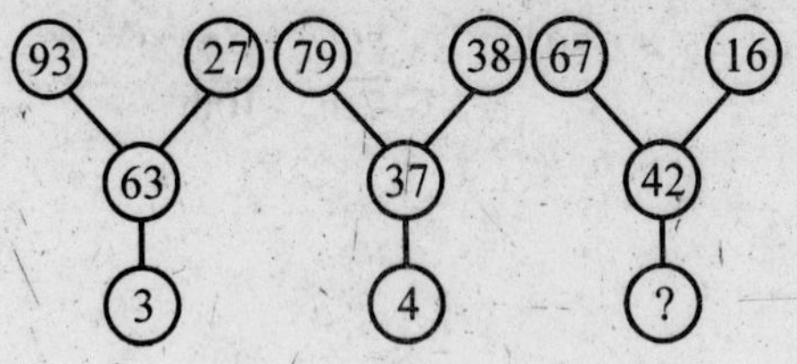

A. 5 B. 6
C. 8 D. 9

2. 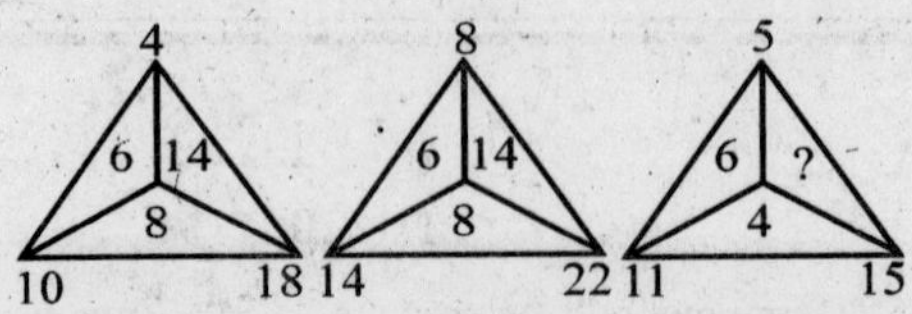

A. 8 B. 14
C. 10 D. 6

3. 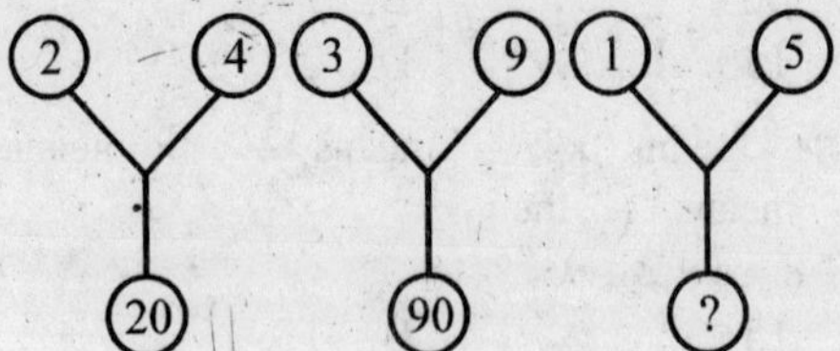

A. 20 B. 25
C. 26 D. 75

4.

27	22	50
13	12	26
9	2	?

A. 12 B. 39
C. 18 D. 24

5. 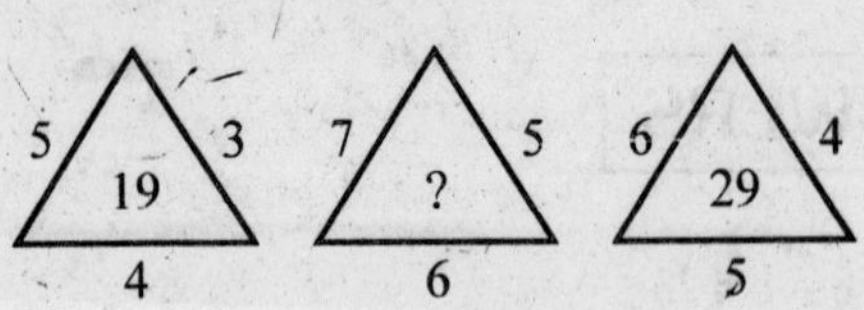

A. 25 B. 47
C. 37 D. 41

6. 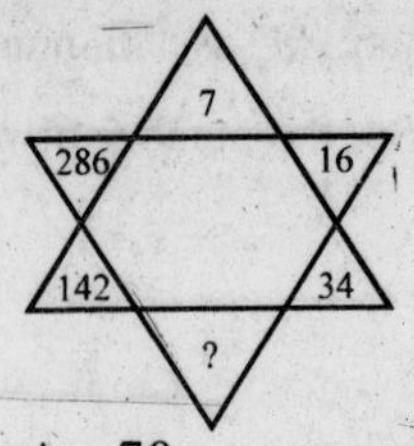

A. 70 B. 68
C. 56 D. 92

7. 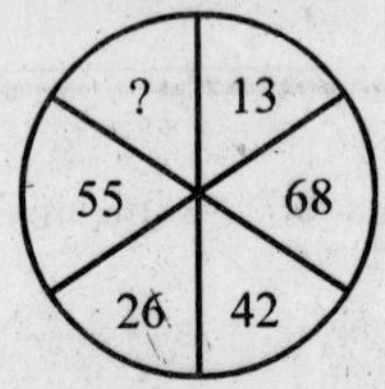

A. 41 B. 37
C. 29 D. 25

8. 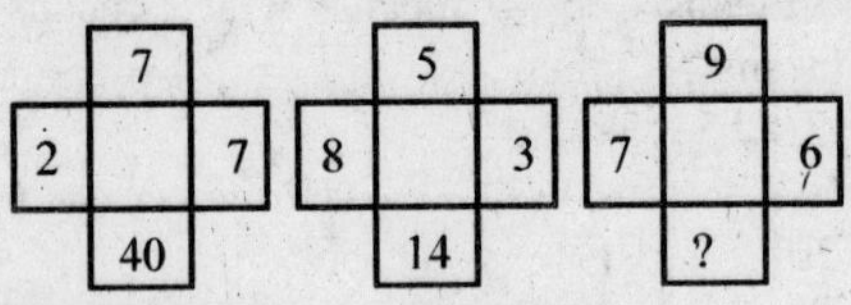

A. 72 B. 68
C. 82 D. 96

9.

42	(21)	22
78	(?)	84
162	(18)	99

A. 12 B. 13
C. 60 D. 72

10. 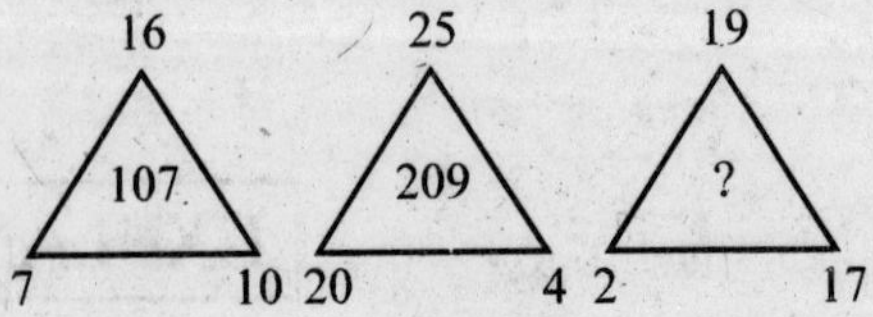

A. 68 B. 93
C. 175 D. 217

ANSWERS

1	2	3	4	5	6	7	8	9	10
D	C	C	A	D	A	C	B	B	A

EXPLANATORY ANSWERS

1. The sum of numbers on right and centre subtracted from the number on the left gives the number at the bottom, *i.e.*,

$93 - (27 + 63) = 3$

$79 - (38 + 37) = 4$

Similarly,
$67 - (16 + 42) = 9$

2. The number inside each triangle is the difference of the numbers at its base *i.e.*
$10 - 4 = 6$, $18 - 4 = 14$ and $18 - 10 = 8$
$14 - 8 = 6$, $22 - 8 = 14$ and $22 - 14 = 8$, similarly
$11 - 5 = 6$, $15 - 5 = 10$ and $15 - 11 = 4$.

3. The sum of squares of two numbers at the top gives the third number below, *i.e.*,
$2^2 + 4^2 = 20$
$3^2 + 9^2 = 90$, similarly
$1^2 + 5^2 = 26$

4. The sum of numbers in 1st and 2nd column plus 1 is the number in the 3rd column, *i.e.*,
$27 + 22 + 1 = 50$
$13 + 12 + 1 = 26$, similarly
$9 + 2 + 1 = 12$

5. The product of numbers on either side of the triangle plus the number at the base is the number inside the triangle, *i.e.*,
$(5 \times 3) + 4 = 19$
$(6 \times 4) + 5 = 29$, similarly
$(7 \times 5) + 6 = 41$

6. Clockwise starting from number 7, the next number is obtained by doubling the number and adding 2, *i.e.*,
$(7 \times 2) + 2 = 16$
$(16 \times 2) + 2 = 34 \ldots$, similarly
$(34 \times 2) + 2 = 70$
$(70 \times 2) + 2 = 142$
$(142 \times 2) + 2 = 286$

7. The difference between the numbers in opposite sectors is 13, *i.e.*,
$26 - 13 = 13$
$68 - 55 = 13$, similarly
The missing number is $42 - 13 = 29$
($42 + 13 = 55$ is not given as option)

8. The number at the bottom is obtained by subtracting the sum of two numbers in the centre grid line from the square of the number at the top, *i.e.*,
$7^2 - (2 + 7) = 40$
$5^2 - (8 + 3) = 14$, similarly
$9^2 - (7 + 6) = 68$

9. The number inside the brackets is obtained by multiplying the number on the left by 2 and then dividing the product by the sum of digits of number on the right, *i.e.*,
$(42 \times 2) \div (2 + 2) = 21$
$(162 \times 2) \div (9 + 9) = 18$, similarly
$(78 \times 2) \div (8 + 4) = 13$

10. Subtracting the sum of squares of two numbers at the base from the square of number at the apex gives the number inside the triangle, *i.e.*,
$16^2 - (7^2 + 10^2) = 107$
$25^2 - (20^2 + 4^2) = 209$, similarly
$19^2 - (2^2 + 17^2) = 68$

ALPHABET PROBLEMS

Directions : *The following questions are based on alphabet series in natural or reverse order and the combinations that can be made by changing the position of alphabet in given words.*

1. Which alphabet comes immediately before the sixth alphabet from the left extreme in alphabetical series?
   A. U B. E
   C. F D. V

2. Which letter is midway between G and S?
   A. L B. N
   C. M D. No letter

3. Which letter should be ninth letter to the left of ninth letter from the right if the first half of the alphabet is reversed?
   A. I B. D
   C. F D. E

4. If the alphabet is in reverse order, which letter will be eighth letter to the left of the seventh letter counting from the right end?
   A. O B. P
   C. N D. Q

5. What will be the fifth letter to the right of the thirteenth letter from the right?
   A. R B. S
   C. I D. O

ANSWERS

1	2	3	4	5
B	C	D	A	B

EXPLANATORY ANSWERS

1. 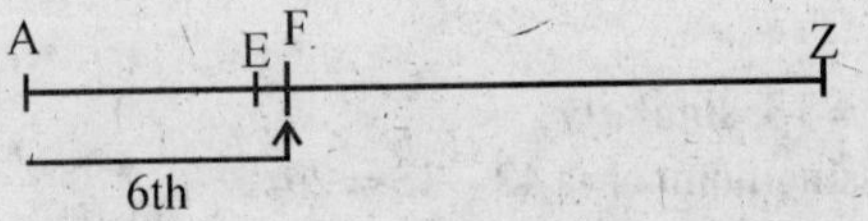

Sixth letter from left is 'F' and letter immediately before 'F' is 'E'.

2. 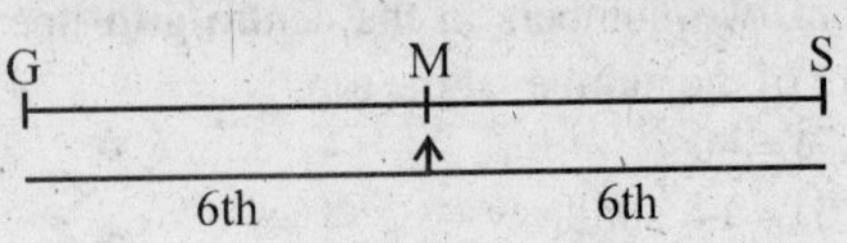

'M' is midway between G and S.

3. MLKJIHGFEDCBANOPQRSTUVWXYZ

9th 9th

4. ZYXWVUTSRQPONMLKJIHGFEDCBA

8th 7th

5. 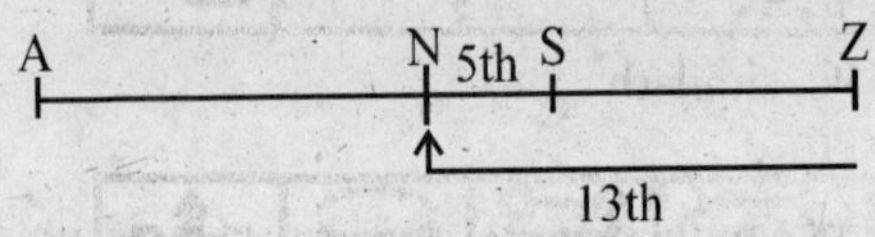

13th letter from right is 'N' and 5th letter to the right of 'N' is 'S'.

NON-VERBAL SERIES

Directions (Q. 1–10) : *In each of the following questions which one of the five answer figures given below should come after the problem figures if the sequence are continued?*

Problem Figures | **Answer Figures**

1. 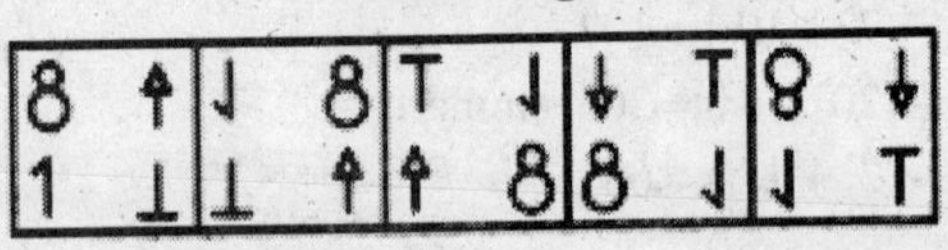 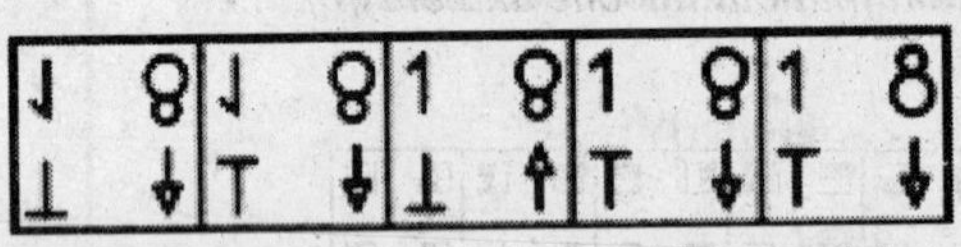

(a) (b) (c) (d) (e)

2. 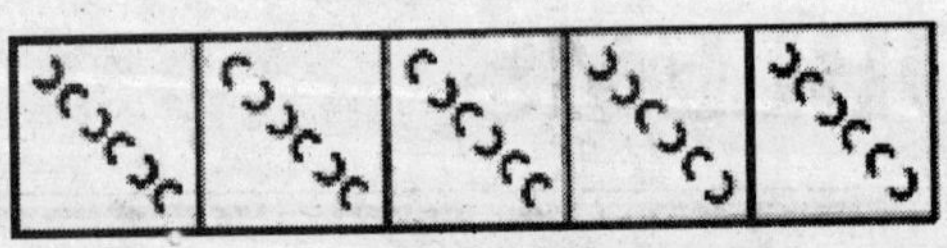 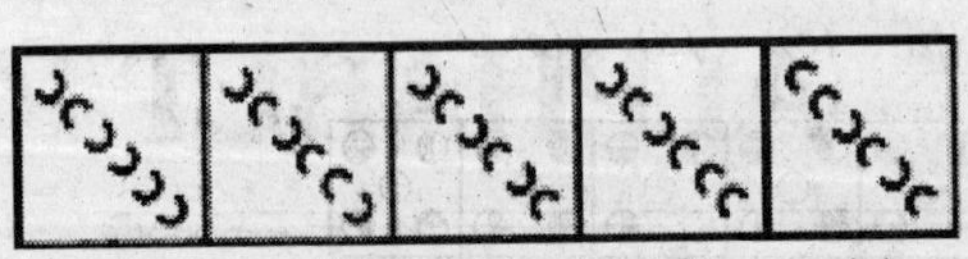

(a) (b) (c) (d) (e)

3. 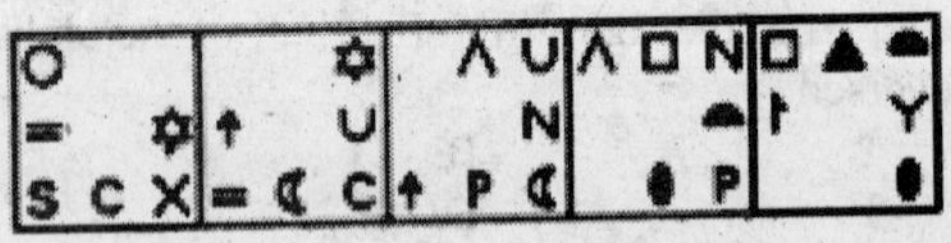 

(a) (b) (c) (d) (e)

4.  

(a) (b) (c) (d) (e)

5. 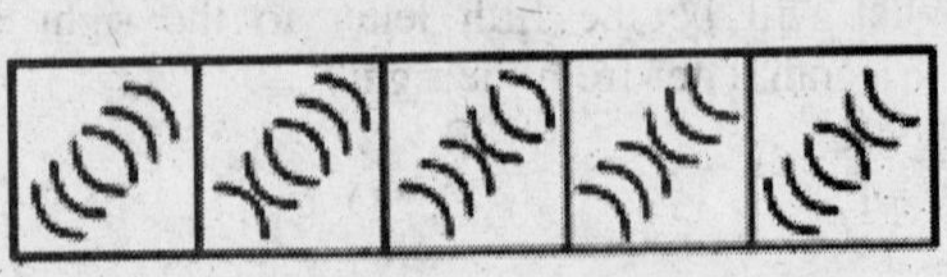 

(a) (b) (c) (d) (e)

6. 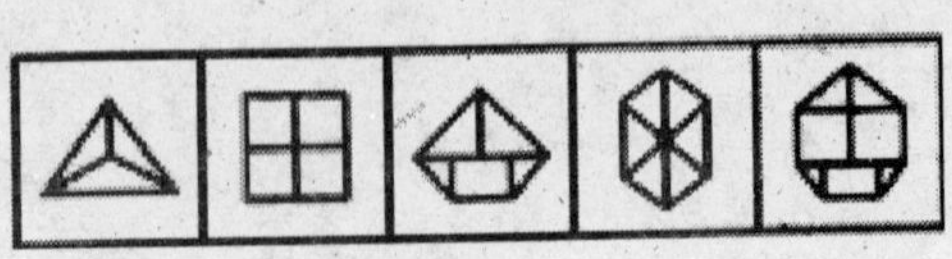 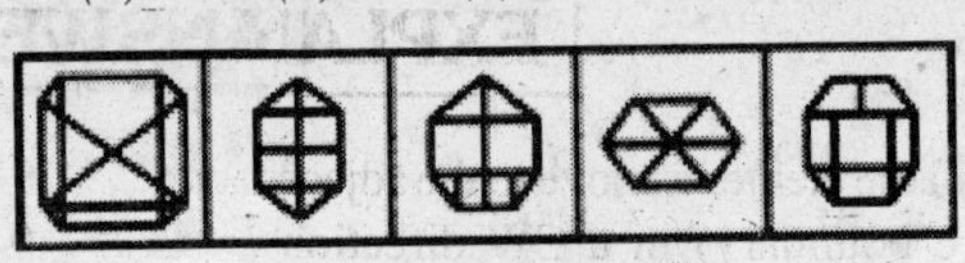

(a) (b) (c) (d) (e)

7. 

(a) (b) (c) (d) (e)

Problem Figures **Answer Figures**

8. 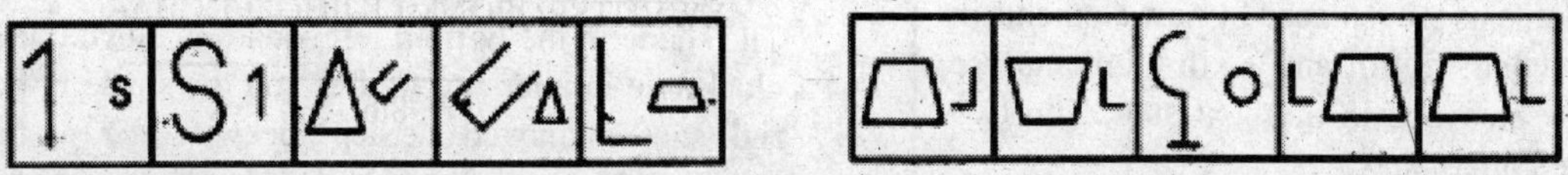

(a) (b) (c) (d) (e)

9. 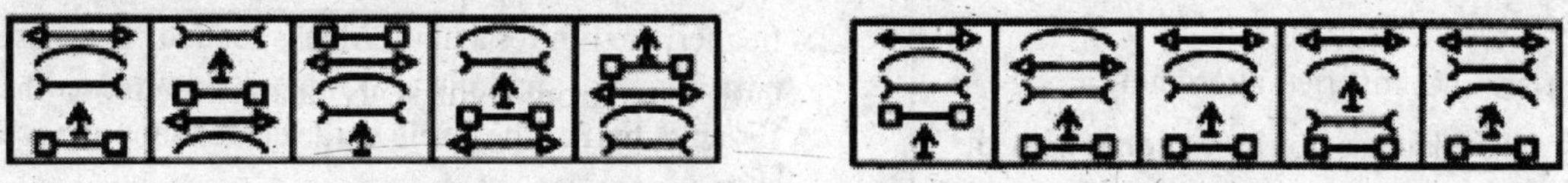

(a) (b) (c) (d) (e)

10. 

(a) (b) (c) (d) (e)

Directions (Q. 11-20) : *In each of these questions, a series begins with an unmarked figure on the extreme left in the row of figures. One and only one of the five lettered figures in the series does not fit into the series. The two unmarked figures, one on the extreme left and the other on the extreme right fit into the series. Take as many aspects into account as possible of the figures in the series and find out the one and only of the five marked figures which does not fit into the series. The letter of that figure is the answer.*

11. 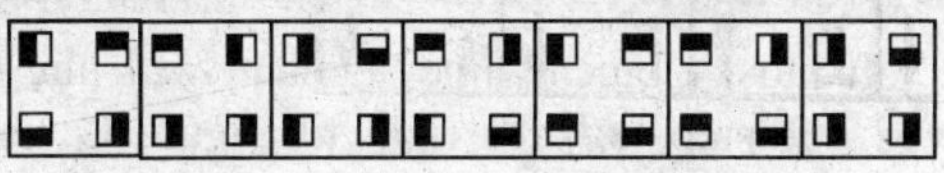

(a) (b) (c) (d) (e)

12. 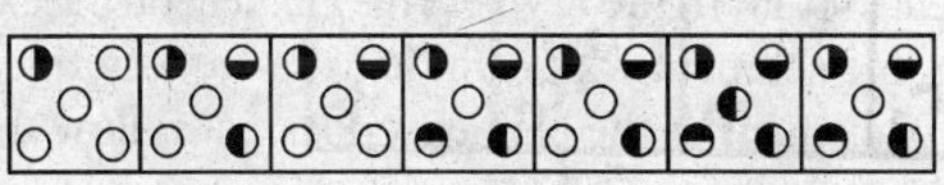

(a) (b) (c) (d) (e)

13. 

(a) (b) (c) (d) (e)

14. 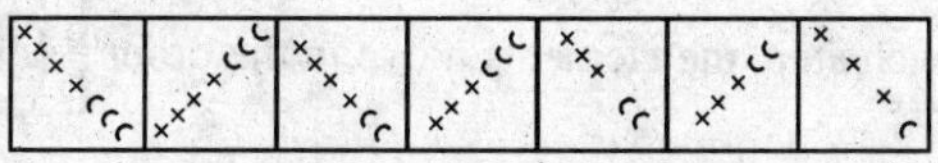

(a) (b) (c) (d) (e)

15. 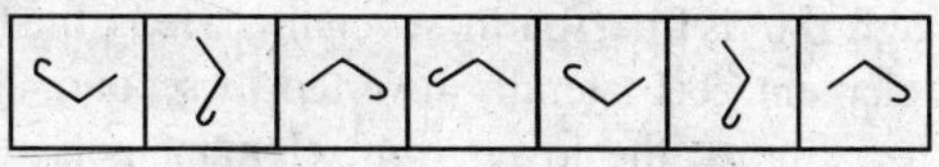

(a) (b) (c) (d) (e)

16. 

(a) (b) (c) (d) (e)

ANSWERS

1	2	3	4	5	6	7	8	9	10
D	C	D	A	C	E	C	E	C	B
11	**12**	**13**	**14**	**15**	**16**				
A	E	A	C	C	E				

EXPLANATORY ANSWERS

1. In each step, all the elements move to the adjacent corner (of the square boundary) in a CW direction and the element that reaches the upper-left corner gets vertically inverted.

2. We can label the arcs as shown  . The arcs get inverted in the sequence (1 & 2), (3, 4 & 5), (6 & 1), (2, 3 & 4), (5 & 6), ...

3. All the elements move half-a-side of the square boundary in ACW direction in each step. Also, first, third and fifth elements are replaced by new elements in one step and second, fourth and sixth elements are replaced by new elements in the next step. The two steps are repeated alternately.

4. In each step, the dot moves one space CW and the arrow moves two spaces CW.

5. One arc and four arcs get inverted alternately.

6. The number of parts increases by one along with the number of sides in the figure.

7. The pin rotates 45°CW and 90°CW alternately and moves one space (each space is equal to half-a-side of the square) and two spaces CW alternately. The arrow rotates 90°ACW and 45°ACW alternately and moves two spaces and one space.

8. In one step, the two elements interchange positions and the smaller element gets enlarged while the larger element gets reduced in size. In the next step, the smaller element is replaced by a new small element and the larger element is replaced by a new large element.

9. In each step, the elements move in the order .

10. The upper-left element gets laterally inverted in first, third, fifth. .... steps; the upper-right element gets rotated through 180° is first, fourth, seventh,.... steps; the lower-left element gets laterally inverted in second, fourth, sixth, ... steps; the lower-right element gets rotated through 180° in third, sixth,... steps and the pin at the middle-right position gets laterally inverted in every second step.

11. The shade in the top left square is moved one step clockwise till figure B and then reversed, the process is repeated. The shade in the top right square is moved one step anticlockwise till figure D and then reversed. The shade in the bottom left square is moved one step clockwise in alternate figures and the shade in bottom right square is moved one step clockwise after two figures. In figure 'A' the rule is isolated by the shade in the bottom left square.

12. In alternate figures a new circle is shaded clockwise. The pattern of the shade is also moved clockwise. In figure 'E' right half of the circle in the centre should have been shaded.

13. The three elements are placed either horizontally or vertically. In option 'A' neither of the placements can be applied.

14. The placement of elements is same in alternate figures. The number and type of elements is same in two subsequent figures. In this manner, figure 'C' should have four crosses and two C shapes.

15. *(c)* : The element is moved one step anticlockwise and the arc at one end is turned outside and inside alternately. In figure 'C' the element should be on the right side with the arc turned outside on the top side.

16. The left most element, line segment with the dot is moved one step towards right till figure C where it reaches the extreme right position. This process is repeated from figure D where the element on the extreme left, line segment with a circle, is moved. In figure 'E' the placement of the elements does not follow the rule of the series.

VENN DIAGRAMS

1. What is the number which is common to only two geometrical figures?

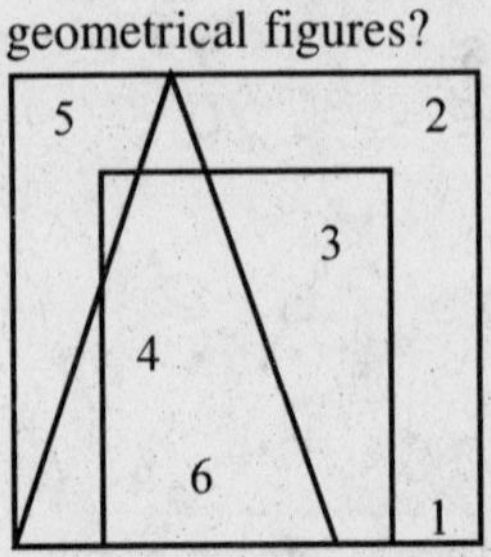

A. 4 B. 3

C. 5 D. 2

Directions (Qs. 2 and 3) : *In the following diagram, rectangle represents Hindi Announcers, circle represents English Announcers, square represents French Announcers, and triangle represents German Announcers.*

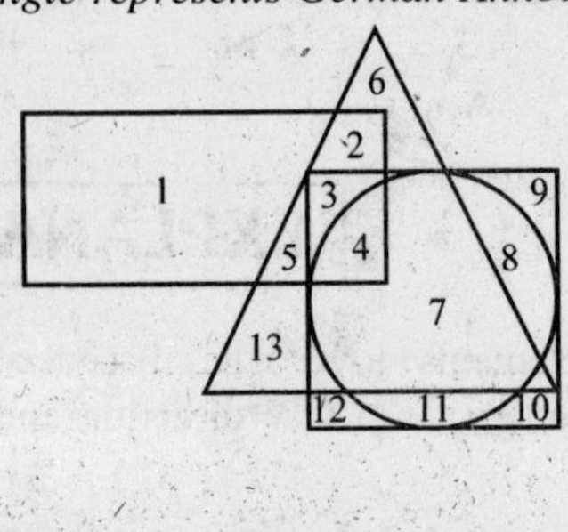

2. Which area represents those announcers who can present programmes in Hindi, French and German only?

A. 1 B. 2
C. 3 D. 4

3 Which area represents those announcers who can present programmes in French and English only?

A. 7 B. 9
C. 11 D. 13

Directions (Qs. 4 and 5) : *Study the diagram to answer these questions.*

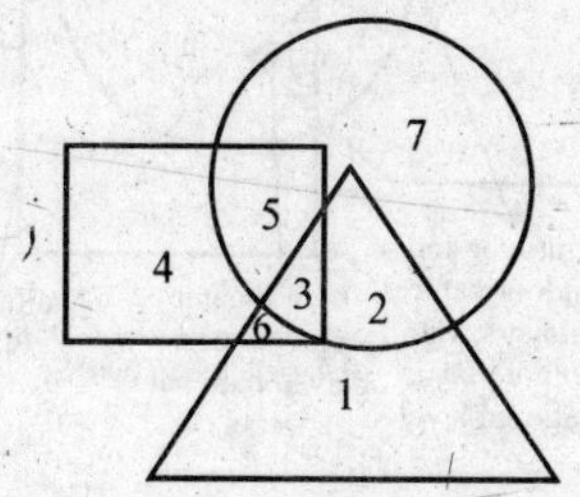

4. Which number is in all the geometrical figures?

A. 5 B. 6
C. 2 D. 3

5. Number 6 is in :

A. Rectangle and triangle
B. Circle and traingle
C. Rectangle and circle
D. Rectangle only

Directions (Qs. 6 to 9) : *In the following diagram*

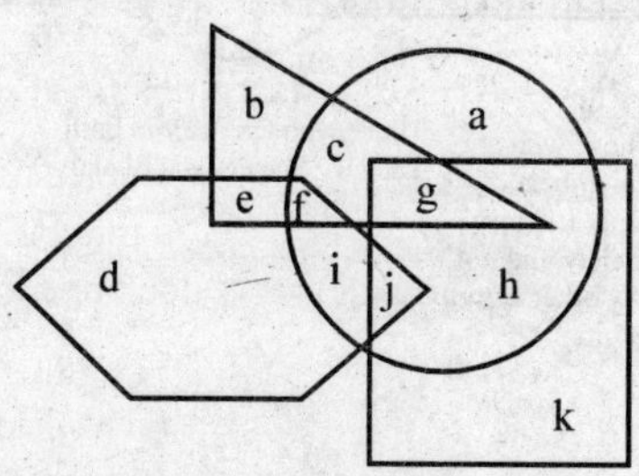

The Circle represents players
The Triangle represents outdoor games
The Hexagon represents indoor games and
The Square represents national level players
Study the diagram and answer the questions given below :

6. The letter in the section representing the players who play indoor games at national level is :

A. f B. i
C. j D. g

7. The letter representing the section of outdoor as well as indoor game players who do not play at the national level is :

A. c B. f
C. e D. i

8. The section representing national level players who do not play either outdoor or indoor games but still come under the category of players is :

A. k B. g
C. c D. h

9. Persons who play outdoor games but do not come under the category of players are represented in the section marked :

A. b B. c
C. a D. d

Directions (Qs. 10 to 13) : *Study the diagram given below.*

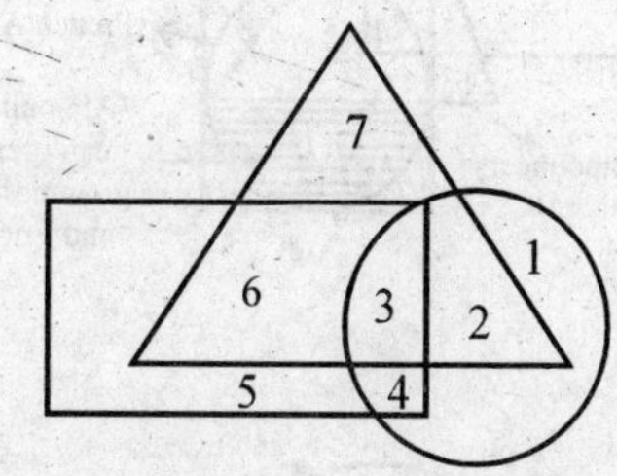

A college provides three different activities, students union represented by triangle, literary society represented by rectangle and social service league represented by circle.

10. Those who take part in both literary society and social service league but not in students union are represented by :

A. 3 & 4 B. 5 & 6
C. 5 & 1 D. 4

11. Those who take part in students union but not in social service league are represented by:

A. 2 & 7 B. 6 & 7
C. 6 D. 7

12. Those students who are members of literary society only and not of any other activity are represented by:

A. 2 B. 5
C. 3 & 4 D. 3

13. Those students who are members of all three groups are represented by :

A. 2 B. 3
C. 4 D. 6

ANSWERS

1	2	3	4	5	6	7	8	9	10
B	C	C	D	A	C	B	D	A	D
11	**12**	**13**							
B	B	B							

EXPLANATORY ANSWERS

1.

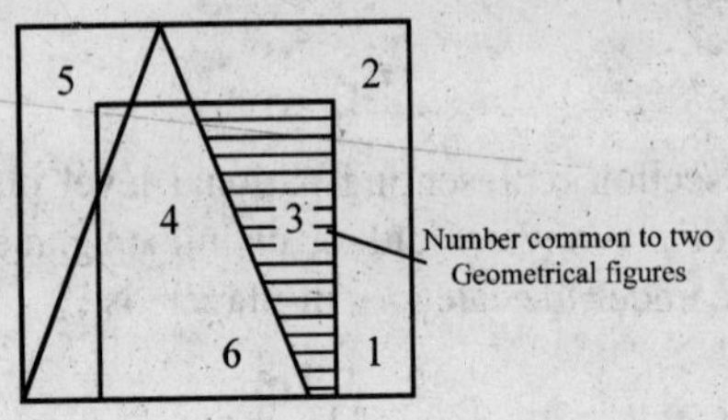

Note : Numbers 4 and 6 are common to all three geometrical figures.

Qs. 2 and 3.

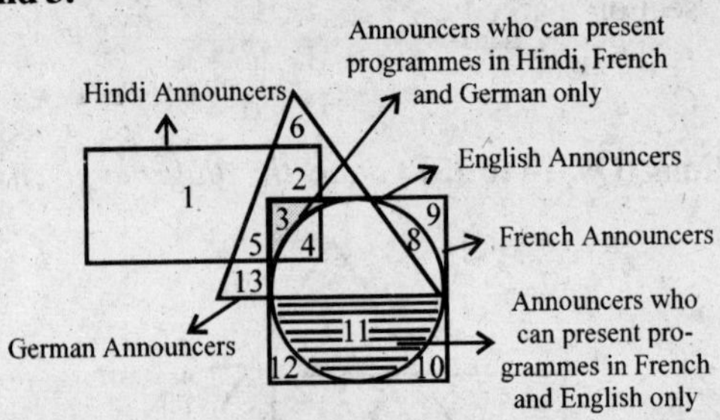

Qs. 4 and 5.

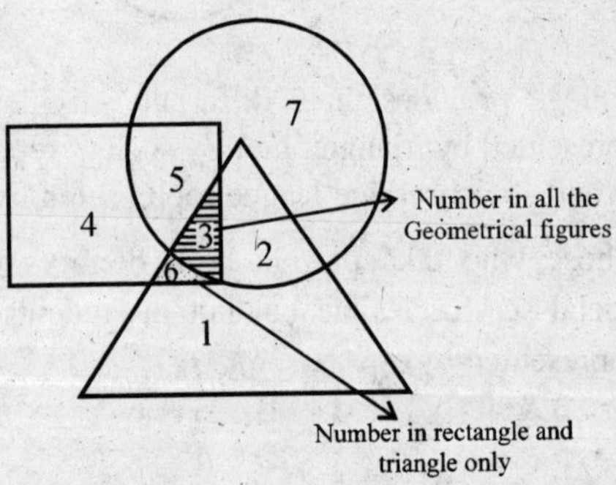

Qs. 6 to 9.

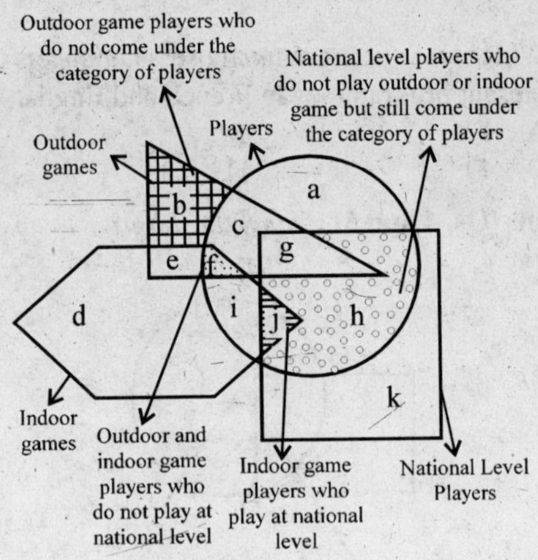

Qs. 10 to 13.

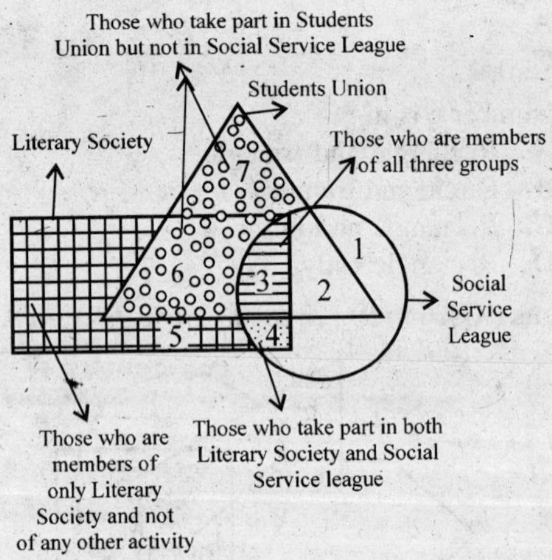

QUANTITATIVE APTITUDE

NUMBER SYSTEM

1. There are four numbers A, B, C and D. Average of the first three *i.e.*, A, B and C is 15 and that of B, C and D is 16. If the last number, *i.e.*, D is 19, then the first number is—
   A. 15 B. 16
   C. 17 D. 18

2. Of the three numbers, the first is twice the second and thrice the third. If the average of three is 22, the three numbers are—
   A. 12, 18, 36
   B. 18, 12, 36
   C. 36, 12, 18
   D. 36, 18, 12

3. If a person is standing on the sixth number in the queue from both the ends, the total persons in the queue are—
   A. 9 B. 11
   C. 12 D. 13

4. A number 'x' when multiplied by 5 and added to three times its own gives 64, the number is—
   A. 8 B. 12
   C. 14 D. 18

5. A number which when multiplied by 11 is as much above 180 as it was originally below it. The number is—
   A. 25 B. 30
   C. 40 D. 45

6. The sum of a number and its reciprocal is thrice the difference of the number and its reciprocal. Find the number.
   A. $\sqrt{2}$ B. $\sqrt{3}$
   C. $\sqrt{5}$ D. $\sqrt{7}$

7. A boy was asked to find $\frac{7}{9}$ of a fraction. He made a mistake of dividing the fraction by $\frac{7}{9}$ and so got an answer which exceeded the correct answer by $\frac{8}{21}$. Find the correct answer.
   A. $\frac{2}{3}$ B. $\frac{5}{7}$
   C. $\frac{7}{12}$ D. $\frac{7}{15}$

8. There are 408 boys and 312 girls in a school, which are to be divided into equal sections of either boys or girls alone. Find the maximum number of boys or girls that can be placed in a section. Also find the total number of sections thus formed.
   A. 10, 20 B. 24, 30
   C. 24, 40 D. 30, 30

9. The sum of all possible two-digit number formed from three different one-digit natural numbers, when divided by the sum of the original three numbers is equal to—
   A. 11 B. 18
   C. 22 D. 36

10. There are four prime numbers written in ascending order. The product of the first three is 385 and that of the last three is 1001. The last number is—
   A. 19 B. 17
   C. 13 D. 11

11. If the number 357 ★ 25 ★ is divisible by both 3 and 5, then the missing digits in the unit's place and thousandth place respectively are—
   A. 0, 4 B. 5, 4
   C. 5, 6 D. 0, 6

12. The difference between two numbers is 1365. When the larger number is divided by the smaller one, the quotient is 6 and the remainder is 15. The smaller number is:
   A. 360 B. 295
   C. 270 D. 240

13. When a number is divided by 31, the remainder is 29. When the same number is divided by 16, what will be the remainder?
   A. 15 B. 13
   C. 11 D. Data inadequate

14. In dividing a number by 585, a student applied the method of short division. He divided the number successively by 5, 9 and 13 (factor of 585) and got the remainders 4, 8 and 12. If he had divided the number by 585, the remainder would have been:
   A. 584 B. 292
   C. 144 D. 24

15. When a number divided by 6 leaves a remainder 3. When the square of the same number is divided by 6, the remainder is:
   A. 3 B. 2
   C. 1 D. zero

ANSWERS

1	2	3	4	5	6	7	8	9	10
B	D	B	A	B	A	C	B	C	C
11	**12**	**13**	**14**	**15**					
C	C	D	A	A					

EXPLANATORY ANSWERS

1. $\dfrac{A+B+C}{3} = 15,$

or, $A + B + C = 15 \times 3 = 45$ ... (*i*)

$\dfrac{B+C+D}{3} = 16,$

or $B + C + D = 48$ ... (*ii*)

$D = 19$

$\therefore\ B + C + 19 = 48$ or, B +

$C = 48 - 19 = 29$

But, $A + B + C = 45$

Putting the value of $B + C = 29$ in the above equation (*i*), we get $A + 29 = 45$

$\therefore\ A = 45 - 29 = 16.$

2. Let the third number $= x$

$\therefore$ First number $= 3x$

Second number $= \dfrac{3x}{2}$

$\therefore\ \dfrac{1}{3}\left[x+3x+\dfrac{3x}{2}\right] = 22 \Rightarrow \dfrac{11}{2}x = 66$

$\Rightarrow x = \dfrac{66\times 2}{11} = 12 =$ Third number,

$12 \times 3 = 36 =$ First number,

$\dfrac{12\times 3}{2} = 18 =$ Second number.

3. If the person is standing at sixth number in the queue from both sides, that means there are five persons ahead and five persons behind him. Hence, total number of persons in the queue is $5 + 1 + 5 = 11$.

4. $5 \times x + 3x = 64 \quad \Rightarrow 8x = 64$

$\therefore \quad x = \dfrac{64}{8} = 8.$

5. Let the number is x

$\therefore \quad 180 - x = 11x - 180$

$\Rightarrow \quad 180 + 180 = 11x + x$

$\Rightarrow \quad 360 = 12x,$

$\Rightarrow \quad x = \dfrac{360}{12} = 30.$

6. Let the no. $= x$ then its reciprocal $= \dfrac{1}{x}$

By the question, $\left(x+\dfrac{1}{x}\right) = 3\left(x-\dfrac{1}{x}\right)$

$\Rightarrow \quad \dfrac{x^2+1}{x} = \dfrac{3(x^2-1)}{x}$

$\Rightarrow \quad x^2 + 1 = 3x^2 - 3$

$\Rightarrow \quad 3x^2 - x^2 = 3 + 1$

$\therefore \quad x = \sqrt{2}.$

7. Let the required fraction $= x$

then, by the question $x\div\dfrac{7}{9} - x\times\dfrac{7}{9} = \dfrac{8}{21}$

$\Rightarrow \quad x\times\dfrac{9}{7} - \dfrac{7x}{9} = \dfrac{8}{21}$

$\Rightarrow \quad \dfrac{32x}{63} = \dfrac{8}{21}$

$\Rightarrow \quad x = \dfrac{8}{21}\times\dfrac{63}{32} = \dfrac{3}{4}$

Hence, the correct answer $= \dfrac{3}{4}\times\dfrac{7}{9} = \dfrac{7}{12}.$

8.

```
312) 408(1
     312
     ---
      96) 312 (3
          288
          ---
           24) 96 (4
               96
               --
                ×
```

$\therefore$ Maximum number of girls or boys that can be placed in a section = 24 and total number of such

section $= \dfrac{408}{24} + \dfrac{312}{24}$

$= 17 + 13 = 30$

9. Let three different one digit natural numbers be x, y and z.

Then, sum of all possible two digits numbers

$= (10x + y) + (10y + x) + (10x + z) + (10z + x) + (10y + z) + (10z + y)$

$= 22x + 22y + 22z = 22(x + y + z)$

Hence, required number = 22.

10. Let four prime numbers be a, b, c and d respectively.

Now, $\frac{abc}{bcd} = \frac{385}{1001}$

$\Rightarrow \frac{c}{d} = \frac{5}{13}$

Hence, $a = 5$ and $d = 13$

11. 357 ★ 25 ★

For divisible by 5, the last digit must be either 0 or 5.

If last digit is 0, then other required digit will be 2 or 5 or 8

Hence, the numbers are (0, 2) or (0, 5) or (0, 8)

If last digit is 5, then other required digit will be 0 or 3 or 6 or 9

Hence, the numbers are (5, 0) or (5, 3) or (5, 6) or (5, 9)

So, correct option is (c).

12. Here, $(x + 1365) = 6x + 15$

$\Rightarrow 5x = 1350$

$\therefore x = \frac{1350}{5} = 270$

Hence, the smaller number = 270.

13. The number = $31x + 29$.

Here, given data is inadequate.

14.

5	a
9	$b - 4$
13	$c - 8$
	$1 - 12$

Now, $c = 13 \times 1 + 12 = 25$

$b = 9c + 8 = 9 \times 25 + 8 = 233$

$a = 5b + 4 = 5 \times 233 + 4$

$= 1165 + 4 = 1169$

$1169 = 585 \times 1 + 584$

Hence, required remainder = 584.

15. The number = $6x + 3$

Now, $(6x + 3)^2 = 36x^2 + 36x + 9$

$= (36x^2 + 36x + 6) + 3$

$= 6(6x^2 + 6x + 1) + 3$

Hence, required remainder = 3.

LCM AND HCF

1. The L.C.M. and H.C.F. of two numbers are 4284 and 32 respectively. If one of the numbers is 204, the other is

A. 672 B. 576
C. 676 D. 572

2. Two numbers are in the ratio of 8 : 15. If their H.C.F. is 4, the numbers are

A. 32 and 60 B. 16 and 30
C. 80 and 150 D. 64 and 120

3. The greatest number that will divide 366, 513 and 324 leaving the same remainder in each case is

A. 21 B. 18
C. 27 D. 42

4. The L.C.M. of two numbers is 45 times their H.C.F. If the sum of the L.C.M. and the H.C.F. of these two numbers is 1150 and one of the numbers is 125, then the other number is

A. 256 B. 225
C. 250 D. 255

5. The H.C.F. and the L.C.M. of two numbers are 50 and 250 respectively. On dividing one of these numbers by 2, 50 is obtained as quotient. The numbrs are

A. 100, 125 B. 80, 100
C. 125, 100 D. 200, 250

6. Three bells ring respectively at an interval of 15 seconds, 20 seconds and 24 seconds. If they ring continuously for 12 minutes then how many times, during this period, will they ring together?

A. 2 times B. 6 times
C. 5 times D. 3 times

7. If the sum of two numbers is 55 and the H.C.F. and L.C.M. of these numbers are 5 and 120 respectively. Find the sum of their reciprocals.

A. $\frac{120}{11}$ B. $\frac{11}{120}$

C. $\frac{601}{55}$ D. $\frac{55}{601}$

8. The LCM of two numbers is 48. The numbers are in the ratio of 2 : 3. The sum of the numbers is

A. 64 B. 40
C. 32 D. 28

9. Find the greatest number that will divide 43, 91 and 183 so as to leave the same remainder in each case.

A. 13 B. 9
C. 7 D. 4

10. The greatest possible length which can be used to measure exactly the length 7m, 3m 85cm, 12m 95 cm is

A. 42 cm B. 35 cm
C. 25 cm D. 15 cm

11. A, B and C start at the same time in the same direction to run around a circular park. A completes a round in 252 seconds, B in 308 seconds and C in 198 seconds, all starting at the same point. After what time will they meet again at the starting point?
A. 46 minutes 12 seconds
B. 45 minutes
C. 42 minutes 36 seconds
D. 26 minutes 18 seconds

12. Which of the following has most numbers of divisors?
A. 182 B. 176
C. 101 D. 99

13. Which is of the following is a co-primes?
A. (23, 92) B. (21, 35)
C. (18, 25) D. (16, 62)

14. Let N be the greatest number that will divide 1305, 4665 and 6905, leaving the same remainder in each case. Then find the sum of the digits in N.
A. 8 B. 6
C. 5 D. 4

15. The greatest number which one dividing 1657 and 2037 leaves remainder 6 and 5 respectively, is:
A. 305 B. 235
C. 127 D. 123

ANSWERS

1	2	3	4	5	6	7	8	9	10
A	A	A	B	A	B	B	B	D	B
11	**12**	**13**	**14**	**15**					
A	B	C	D	C					

EXPLANATORY ANSWERS

1. 1st number × 2nd number = LCM × HCF

$\therefore$ 204 × 2nd number = 4284 × 32

$\therefore$ 2nd number $= \frac{4284 \times 32}{204} = 672$

$\therefore$ 2nd number = 672

2. Let the numbers be $8x$ and $15x$

$8x = 2 \times 2 \times 2 \times x$

$15x = 3 \times 5 \times x$

$\therefore$ LCM of $8x$ and $15x = 2 \times 2 \times 2 \times x \times 3 \times 5$
$= 120x$

Now, 1st number × 2nd number = HCF × LCM

$\Rightarrow \quad 8x \times 15x = 4 \times 120x$

$\Rightarrow \quad 120x^2 = 4 \times 120x$

$\Rightarrow \quad x = 4$

$\therefore$ Numbers are $8 \times 4 = 32$ and $15 \times 4 = 60$

3. Difference between 366 and 513 = 513 − 366
= 147

and difference between 513 and 324
= 513 − 324 = 189

$\therefore$ HCF of 147 and 189

```
147) 189 (1
     147
     ×42) 147 (3
          126
          ×21) 42 (2
               42
               ×
```

$\therefore$ The required largest number is 21.

4. LCM of the two numbers = 45 × HCF

and LCM + HCF = 1150

$\Rightarrow \quad 45 \times \text{HCF} + \text{HCF} = 1150$

$\Rightarrow \quad \text{HCF}(45 + 1) = 1150$

$\Rightarrow \quad \text{HCF} = \frac{1150}{46} = 25$

$\therefore \quad \text{LCM} = 45 \times 25 = 1125$

$\because$ 1st number × 2nd number = LCM × HCF

$\therefore$ 125 × 2nd number = 1125 × 25

$\therefore$ 2nd number $= \frac{1125 \times 25}{125} = 225.$

5. According to the condition of the problem, 50 is obtained on dividing one of the numbers by 2

$\therefore$ One of the numbers = 50 × 2 = 100

Now, 1st number × 2nd number = LCM × HCF

$\therefore$ 100 × 2nd number = 250 × 50

$\therefore$ 2nd number $= \frac{250 \times 50}{100} = 125$

Hence, numbers are 100 and 125.

6. LCM of 15, 20 and 24

5	15, 20, 24
4	3, 4, 24
3	3, 1, 6
	1, 1, 2

LCM = 5 × 4 × 3 × 2 = 120

$\because$ 12 minutes = 12 × 60 = 720 seconds

$\therefore$ Number of times the bells will ring together during 12 minutes

$= \frac{720}{120} = 6$ times.

7. Let the number be x and y.
Then, $x + y = 55$;
$xy = \text{HCF} \times \text{LCM} = 5 \times 120$
$\therefore$ Sum of their reciprocals

$$= \frac{1}{x} + \frac{1}{y} = \frac{x+y}{xy} = \frac{55}{5\times120} = \frac{11}{120}.$$

8. Let the two numbers be $2x$ and $3x$;
their LCM = $6x$
Now, $6x = 48$ $\therefore$ $x = 8$
Hence, the numbers are $2 \times 8,\ 3 \times 8 = 16, 24$
Their sum = 16 + 24 = 40.

9.

```
2240) 3360 (1        1120) 5600 (5
      2240                 5600
      ----                 ----
      1120 ) 2240 (2         ×
             2240
             ----
               ×
```

Hence, N = HCF of 3360,
2240 and 5600 = 1120
Sum of digits in N = 1 + 1 + 2 + 0 = 4.

10. 7m = 700 cm;
3m 85 = 385 cm;
12m 95cm = 1295 cm

```
385) 700 (1
     385
     ---
     315) 385 (1
          315
          ---
           70) 315 (4
               280
               ---
                35 ) 70 (2
                     70
                     --
                      ×

35) 1295 (37
    105
    ---
     245
     245
     ---
      ×
```

Hence, required length = HCF of 700 cm, 385 cm, 1295 cm = 35 cm.

11.

2	252,	308,	198
2	126,	154,	99
3	63,	77,	99
3	21,	77,	33
7	7,	77,	11
11	1,	11,	11
	1,	1,	1

Hence, LCM = 2 × 2 × 3 × 3 × 7 × 11 = 2772
Hence, A, B, C will meet again at the starting point after 2772 sec. = 46 min 12 sec.

12.

Numbers	***Their divisors***
182	→ 1, 2, 7, 13, 14, 26, 91 and 182
176	→ 1, 2, 4, 8, 16, 22, 44, 88 and 176
101	→ 1 and 101
99	→ 1, 3, 9, 11, 33 and 99

Therefore, 176 has the most number of divisors.

13. HCF of 23 and 92 = 23
HCF of 21 and 35 = 7
HCF of 18 and 25 = 1
HCF of 16 and 62 = 2
Hence, 18 and 25 are co-prime numbers.

14. N = HCF of (4665 – 1305),
(6905 – 4665) and (6905 – 1305)
= HCF of 3360, 2240 and 5600 = 112
Sum of digit of 1 + 1 + 2 = 4.

15. Required number = HCF of (1657 – 6) and (2037 – 5)
= HCF of 1651 and 2032 = 127.

```
1651) 2032 (1
      1651
      ----
      381) 1651 (4
           1524
           ----
           127) 381 (3
                381
                ---
                 ×
```

AVERAGE

1. One-third of a certain journey was covered at the rate of 25 km per hour, one-fourth at the rate of 30 km per hour and the rest at the 50 km per hour. What is the average speed per hour for whole journey?

A. $33\frac{1}{3}$ kmph   B. $44\frac{1}{4}$ kmph
C. $22\frac{1}{2}$ kmph   D. 33 kmph

2. A batsman has a certain average of runs for 16 innings. In the 17th innings, he makes a score of 85 runs thereby increasing his average by 3. What is the average after the 17th inning?
A. 33 runs   B. 34 runs
C. 37 runs   D. 36 runs

3. The average of 6 observations is 12. A new seventh observation is included and the new average is decreased by 1. The seventh observation is

A. 1 B. 3
C. 5 D. 6

4. The average age of 30 students in a class is 12 years. The average age of a group of 5 of the students is 10 years and that of another group of 5 of them is 14 years. The average age of the remaining students is
A. 8 years B. 10 years
C. 12 years D. 14 years

5. Out of the three given numbers, the first number is twice the second and thrice the third. If the average of three numbers is 121, what is the difference between the first and third number?
A. 144 B. 77
C. 99 D. 132

6. If the average marks of three batches of 55, 60 and 45 students is 50, 55 and 60, then average marks of all the students is:
A. 55 B. 54
C. 54.68 D. 55.68

7. The average of 8 numbers is 20. The average of first two numbers is $15\frac{1}{2}$ and that of the next three is $21\frac{1}{3}$. If the sixth number is less than the seventh and eighth numbers by 4 and 7 respectively, then the eighth number is:
A. 27 B. 25
C. 22 D. 18

8. A pupil's marks were wrongly entered as 83 instead of 63. Due to that the average marks for the class got increased by half. What is the number of pupils in the class?
A. 73 B. 40
C. 40 D. 10

9. A cricketer whose bowling average is 12.4 runs per wicket takes 5 wickets for 26 runs and thereby decreases his average by 0.4. The number of wickets taken by him till the last match was:
A. 85 B. 80
C. 72 D. 64

10. The average weight of a class of 24 students is 35 kg. If the weight of the teacher is included, the average rises by 400 g. What is the weight of the teacher?
A. 55 kg B. 53 kg
C. 50 kg D. 45 kg

11. Nine men went to a hotel. Eight of them spent Rs. 3 for each over their meals and the ninth spent Rs. 2 more than the average expenditure of all the nine. What is the total money spent by them?
A. Rs. 29.25 B. Rs. 29.50
C. Rs. 29 D. Rs. 30

12. The average age of 24 students in a class is 10. If the teacher's age is included, the average increases by one. The age of the teacher is
A. 25 B. 30
C. 35 D. 40

13. The average of 5 consecutive even numbers A, B, C, D and E is 34. What is the product of B and D?
A. 1152 B. 1368
C. 1224 D. 1088

14. The average of 50 numbers is 30. If two numbers, 35 and 40 are discarded, then the average of the remaining numbers is nearly:
A. 29.68 B. 29.27
C. 28.78 D. 28.32

15. The average monthly salary of 20 employees of an organisation is Rs. 1500. If the manager's salary is added, then the average salary increases by Rs. 100. Find the manager's monthly salary?
A. Rs. 4800 B. Rs. 3600
C. Rs. 2400 D. Rs. 2000

ANSWERS

1	2	3	4	5	6	7	8	9	10
A	C	C	C	D	C	B	B	A	D
11	**12**	**13**	**14**	**15**					
A	C	A	A	B					

EXPLANATORY ANSWERS

1. Let the total distance covered during journey = 60 km

$\frac{1}{3}$ of the distance covered during journey

$= 60 \times \frac{1}{3} = 20$ km

$\frac{1}{4}$ of the distance covered during journey

$= \frac{1}{4} \times 60 = 15$ km

∴ The distance covered during the rest of journey = 60 – (20 + 15) = 25 km

Time taken to cover 20 km at 25 km/h

$= \frac{20}{25}$ hours $= \frac{4}{5}$ hour

Time taken to cover 15 km at 30 km/h

$= \frac{15}{30}$ hours $= \frac{1}{2}$ hour

Time taken to cover 25 km at 50 km/h

$= \frac{25}{50}$ hours $= \frac{1}{2}$ hour

Total time taken $= \frac{4}{5} + \frac{1}{2} + \frac{1}{2}$

$= \frac{9}{5}$ hours

Hence average speed per hour $= 60 \div \frac{9}{5}$

$= \frac{60 \times 5}{9} = \frac{100}{3}$ km/h

$= 33\frac{1}{3}$ km/h

2. Average increase in the score of 17 innings
= 3 runs
Total increase in the score of 17 innings
= 3 × 17 = 51 runs
∴ His average of 16 innings = 85 – 51
= 34 runs
Hence, average after the 17th innings
= 34 + 3 = 37 runs

3. Seventh observation = (7 × 11 – 6 × 12) = 5

4. Let, the required average age be x
Then, 5 × 10 + 5 × 14 + 20 × x = 30 × 12
⇒ $20x = 360 - 120$
⇒ $20x = 240$
⇒ $x = 12$

5. Let the three numbers be x, $\frac{x}{2}$ and $\frac{x}{3}$ respectively,

Now, $\frac{1}{3}\left(x + \frac{x}{2} + \frac{x}{3}\right) = 121$

⇒ $\frac{11x}{6} = 121 \times 3$

∴ $x = \frac{121 \times 3 \times 6}{11} = 198$

Hence, required difference $= x - \frac{x}{3} = \frac{2x}{3}$

$= \frac{2}{3} \times 198 = 132$

6. Required average Marks

$= \frac{55 \times 50 + 60 \times 55 + 45 \times 60}{55 + 60 + 45} = \frac{8750}{160} = 54.68$

7. Let the sixth, seventh and eighth numbers are x, x + 4 and x + 7.
Sum of last three numbers

$= 8 \times 20 - (2 \times \frac{31}{2} + 3 \times \frac{64}{3})$

⇒ $x + x + 4 + x + 7 = 160 - 95$
⇒ $3x + 11 = 65$
⇒ $3x = 54$ ∴ $x = 18$
New eighth number = x + 7 = 18 + 7 = 25

8. Let the total number of pupils in the class be x; then,

$\frac{83 - 63}{x} = \frac{1}{2}$ ⇒ $\frac{20}{x} = \frac{1}{2}$ ∴ $x = 40$

9. Let the number of wickets taken by him be x till the last match.

Then, $\frac{x \times 12.4 + 26}{x + 5} = 12$

⇒ $12.4x + 26 = 12x + 60$

⇒ $0.4x = 34$ ∴ $x = \frac{340}{4} = 85$

10. Let the weight of the teacher be x kgs, then

$\frac{24 \times 35 + x}{25} = 35.4$

⇒ $840 + x = 885$ ∴ $x = 45$ kgs

12. Age of the teacher = (25 × 11 – 24 × 10) years
= 35 years

13. Let 5 consecutive even numbers A, B, C, D and E be x, $x + 2$, $x + 4$, $x + 6$ and $x + 8$ respectively.

Now, $\frac{x + x + 2 + x + 4 + x + 6 + x + 8}{5} = 34$

⇒ $5x + 20 = 170$
⇒ $5x = 150$ ∴ $x = 30$
Then, B = x + 2 = 30 + 2 = 32;
D = x + 6 = 30 + 6 = 36
Hence, their product = 32 × 36 = 1152

14. The average of remaining 48 numbers

$= \frac{50 \times 30 - (35 + 40)}{48} = \frac{1500 - 75}{48}$

$= \frac{1425}{48} = 29.68$

15. Let manager's salary be Rs. x, then

$\frac{20 \times 1500 + x}{21} = 1600$

⇒ $30{,}000 + x = 33600$
∴ x = Rs. 3600

PROBLEMS BASED ON AGES

1. The ratio of ages of A and B is 3 : 11. After 3 years the ratio becomes 1 : 3. What are the ages of A and B?

A. 9 years, 33 years
B. 10 years, 40 years
C. 9 years, 27 years
D. None of these

2. Two years ago, the ratio of Ram's and Mohan's age was 3 : 2 and at present 7 : 5. What are their present ages?

A. 14 years, 10 years B. 15 years, 10 years
C. 13 years, 9 years D. None of these

3. The ages of Samir and Saurabh are in the ratio of 8 : 15 respectively. After 9 years the ratio of their ages will be 11 : 18. What is the difference between their ages in years?

A. 20 years B. 21 years
C. 22 years D. 24 years

4. The present age of father is 34 years more than that of his son. 12 years ago, father's age was 18 times the age of his son. The present age of son in years is:

A. 12 B. 14
C. 16 D. 18

5. A mother is 25 years older than her daughter. Five years ago, the age of the mother was 6 times the age of the daughter. What is the present age of mother?

A. 25 years B. 29 years
C. 32 years D. 35 years

6. The difference between the present ages of P and Q is 4 years. The ratio of their ages after 5 years will be 9 : 8. The present age of P is:

A. 24 years B. 30 years
C. 32 years D. None of these

7. Ten years ago, the age of Divya was half of the age of Namrata. If the ratio of present ages of both is 3 : 4, the sum of their present ages is:

A. 35 years B. 30 years
C. 25 years D. 18 years

8. The ratio between the present ages of A and B is 5 : 3 respectively. The ratio between A's age 4 years ago and B's age 4 years hence is 1 : 1. The ratio between A's age 4 years hence and B's age 4 years ago is:

A. 4 : 1 B. 3 : 1
C. 2 : 1 D. 1 : 3

9. Ram got married 8 years ago. His present age is $\frac{6}{5}$ times his age at the time of marriage. Ram's sister was 10 years younger to him at the time of his marriage. What is the present age of Ram's sister?

A. 40 years B. 38 years
C. 36 years D. 32 years

10. A father said to his son, "I was as old as you are at present at the time of your birth." If the father's age is 38 years now. Five years ago the age of son was:

A. 38 years B. 33 years
C. 19 years D. 14 years

ANSWERS

1	2	3	4	5	6	7	8	9	10
A	A	B	B	D	D	A	B	B	D

EXPLANATORY ANSWERS

1. Let the ages of A and B be $3x$ and $11x$ years; then

$$\frac{3x+3}{11x+3}=\frac{1}{3} \Rightarrow 9x+9=11x+3$$

$\Rightarrow 2x = 6 \therefore x = 3$

Hence, their present age, $3x = 3 \times 3 = 9$ years; $11x = 11 \times 3 = 33$ years

2. Let the present ages of Ram and Mohan are $7x$ and $5x$ years; then

$$\frac{7x-2}{5x-2}=\frac{3}{2} \Rightarrow 14x-4=15x-6 \therefore x=2$$

Hence, their present ages : $7 \times 2 = 14$ years and $5 \times 2 = 10$ years

3. Let the present ages of Samir and Saurabh are $8x$ and $15x$ years respectively; then

$$\frac{8x+9}{15x+9}=\frac{11}{18} \Rightarrow 144x+162=165x+99$$

$\Rightarrow 21x = 63 \quad \therefore x = 3$

Hence, difference of their ages $= 15x - 8x = 7x = 7 \times 3 = 21$ years

4. Let the present ages of father and his son be $x + 34$ and x years respectively; then

$18(x - 12) = x + 34 - 12$

$\Rightarrow 18x - 216 = x + 22$

$\Rightarrow 17x = 238 \quad \therefore x = 14$

Hence, present age of his son = 14 years

5. Let the present ages of mother and her daughter are $(x + 25)$ and x years respectively; then

$6(x - 5) = x + 25 - 5$

$\Rightarrow 6x - 30 = x + 20$

$\Rightarrow 5x = 50 \quad \therefore x = 10$

Hence, the age of the mother = 10 + 25 = 35 years

6. Let the present ages of P and Q be $(x + 4)$ and x years;

then, $\frac{x+4+5}{x+5} = \frac{9}{8} \quad \Rightarrow \quad 8x + 72 = 9x + 45 \quad \therefore x = 27$

Hence, present age of P = 27 + 4 = 31 years

7. Let the present ages of Divya and Namrata are $3x$ and $4x$ years respectively; then

$\frac{3x-10}{4x-10} = \frac{1}{2}$

$\Rightarrow 6x - 20 = 4x - 10$

$\Rightarrow 2x = 10 \quad \therefore x = 5$

Hence, sum of their ages $= 3x + 4x = 7x$
$= 7 \times 5 = 35$ years

8. Let the present ages of A and B are $5x$ and $3x$ years respectively; then,

$\frac{5x-4}{3x+4} = 1 \quad \Rightarrow 5x - 4 = 3x + 4$

$\Rightarrow 2x = 8 \quad \therefore x = 4$

Hence, their present ages are 20 years and 12 years.

So, required ratio = (20 + 4) : (12 – 4)
= 24 : 8 = 3 : 1

9. Let the present age of Ram be x years; then

$\frac{x}{x-8} = \frac{6}{5} \quad \Rightarrow \quad 5x = 6x - 48$

$\therefore x = 48$

Hence, present age of Ram's sister
= 48 – 10 = 38 years.

10. Let the age of father was x years at the time of his son's birth, then present age of father and his son will be $2x$ and x years,

Now, $2x = 38 \quad \therefore x = 19$ years

Hence, 5 years ago the age of son was
19 – 5 = 14 years

CHAIN RULE

1. A fort has provision for 50 days. After 15 days a reinforce ment of 150 men arrives and the provision now lasts 25 days. How many men were there in the fort?

A. 300 B. 225
C. 275 D. 200

2. In a fort there is provisions for 40 days for 275 persons. If after 16 days 125 persons leave the fort for how many more days the provisions will last?

A. 35 days B. 44 days
C. 45 days D. 53 days

3. 60 men could complete a work in 250 days. They worked together for 200 days. After that the work had to be stopped for 10 days due to bad weather. How many more men should be engaged to complete the work in time?

A. 20 B. 18
C. 15 D. 10

4. A contractor undertook to complete a project in 90 days and employed 60 men on it. After 60 days, he found that $\frac{3}{4}$ of the work has already been completed. How many men can he discharge so that the project may completed exactly on time?

A. 15 B. 20
C. 30 D. 40

5. A flagstaff 17.5 m high casts a shadow of length 40.25 m. The height of the building, which casts a shadow of length 28.75m under similar condition will be:

A. 21.25 m B. 17.5 m
C. 12.5 m D. 10 m

6. If 5 men or 9 women can do a piece of work in 19 days, then 3 men and 6 women will do the same work in how many days?

A. 21 B. 18
C. 15 D. 12

7. A certain number of men can finish a piece of work in 100 days. If there were 10 men less, it will take 10 days more for the work to be finished. How many men were there originally?

A. 110 B. 100
C. 82 D. 75

8. Some persons can do a piece of work in 12 days. Two times the number of such persons will do half of that work in:

A. 12 days B. 3 days
C. 6 days D. 4 days

9. 2 men and 7 boys can do a piece of work in 14 days; 3 men and 8 boys can do the same in 11 days. Then 8 men and 6 boys can do three times of this work in
A. 30 days B. 4 days
C. 21 days D. 18 days

10. If 3 men or 6 boys, working 7 hours a day can do a piece of work in 10 days; how many days will it take to complete a piece of work twice as large with 6 men and 2 boys working together for 8 hours a day?
A. 9 B. $8\frac{1}{2}$
C. $7\frac{1}{2}$ D. $6\frac{1}{2}$

11. If 15 men can do a certain amount of work in 20 days working 8 hours a day, in how many days will 10 men do three times the work working 6 hours a day?
A. 120 days B. 70 days
C. 100 days D. None of these

12. 40 men consume 60 kgs of rice in 15 days, then in how many days will 30 men consume 12 kgs of rice?
A. 9 days B. $6\frac{1}{4}$ days
C. 4 days D. $3\frac{1}{4}$ days

13. 56 men can complete a piece of work in 24 days. In how many days can 42 men complete the same piece of work?
A. 48 B. 32
C. 20 D. 16

14. Running at the same constant rate, 6 identical machines can produce a total of 270 bottles per minute. At this rate, how many bottles could 10 such machines produce in 4 minutes?
A. 1400 B. 1600
C. 1800 D. 2000

15. 400 persons, working 9 hours a day complete $\frac{1}{4}th$ of the work in 10 days. The number of additional persons, working 8 hours a day, required to complete the remaining work in 20 days, is:
A. 275 B. 250
C. 675 D. 200

ANSWERS

1	2	3	4	5	6	7	8	9	10
B	B	C	B	C	C	A	B	C	C
11	**12**	**13**	**14**	**15**					
A	C	B	C	C					

EXPLANATORY ANSWERS

1. Days Men
35↑ x
25 $x + 150$↓

$$\Rightarrow \frac{x+150}{x} = \frac{35}{25} \quad \Rightarrow 1 + \frac{150}{x} = \frac{35}{25}$$

$$\Rightarrow \frac{150}{x} = \frac{10}{25}$$

$$\therefore x = \frac{25}{10} \times 150 = 375$$

Required number of men = 375 – 150 = 225

2. Persons Days
275↑ 24
150 x↓

$$\Rightarrow \frac{x}{24} = \frac{275}{150} \quad \therefore \quad x = \frac{275}{150} \times 24 = 44 \text{ days}$$

3. Days Men
50↑ 60
40 x↓

$$\Rightarrow \frac{x}{60} = \frac{50}{40} \quad \therefore \quad x = \frac{50}{40} \times 60 = 75 \text{ men}$$

Hence, number of additional men = 75 – 60
= 15

4. Work Days Men
$\frac{3}{4}$↓ 60↑ 60↓
$\frac{1}{4}$ 30 x

$$\Rightarrow \frac{x}{60} = \frac{60}{30} \times \frac{1/4}{3/4}$$

$$\therefore \quad x = \frac{60}{30} \times \frac{1}{3} \times 60 = 40 \text{ days}$$

Hence, number of men to be discharged
$= 60 - 40 = 20$

5. Shadow (m) Object (m)

40.25 ↓ 17.5 ↓

28.75 x

$$\Rightarrow \frac{x}{17.5} = \frac{28.75}{40.25}$$

$$\therefore x = \frac{28.75 \times 17.5}{40.25} = 12.5 \text{ m}$$

6. 5 men $\equiv$ 9 women

$$\therefore 3 \text{ men} = \frac{9}{5} \times 3 = \frac{27}{5} \text{ women}$$

Hence, 3 men and 6 women $= \frac{27}{5} + 6$

$$= \frac{57}{5} \text{ women}$$

Women ↑ Days ↓

9 19

$\frac{57}{5}$ x

$$\Rightarrow \frac{x}{19} = \frac{9 \times 5}{57}$$

$$\therefore x = \frac{9 \times 5}{57} \times 19$$

$= 15$ days

7. Days ↑ Men ↓

100 x

110 $x - 10$

$$\Rightarrow \frac{x-10}{x} = \frac{100}{110}$$

$\Rightarrow 110x - 1100 = 100x$

$\Rightarrow 10x = 1100 \quad \therefore x = 110$

Hence, initially the number of men = 110

8. Work ↓ Persons ↑ Days ↓

1 x 12

$\frac{1}{2}$ $2x$ a

$$\Rightarrow \frac{a}{12} = \frac{x}{2x} \times \frac{1}{2} \quad \therefore \quad a = \frac{1}{4} \times 12 = 3 \text{ days}$$

9. Here, 14×2 men + 14×7 boys $\equiv 11 \times 3$ men + 11×8 boys

$\Rightarrow$ 28 men + 98 boys $\equiv$ 33 men + 88 boys

$\Rightarrow$ 5 men = 10 boys

$\therefore$ 1 man = 2 boys

Then, 2 men and 7 boys $\equiv$ 4 boys + 7 boys
= 11 boys

& also, 8 men and 6 boys $\equiv$ 16 boys + 6 boys
= 22 boys

Work ↓ Boys ↑ Days ↓

1 11 14

3 22 x

$$\Rightarrow \frac{x}{14} = \frac{11}{22} \times \frac{3}{1}$$

$$\therefore \quad x = \frac{1}{2} \times 3 \times 14$$

$= 21$ days

12. Men ↑ Rice (kgs) ↓ Days ↓

40 60 15

30 12 x

$$\Rightarrow \frac{x}{15} = \frac{12}{60} \times \frac{40}{30}$$

$$\therefore \quad x = \frac{12}{60} \times \frac{40}{30} \times 15 = 4 \text{ days}$$

14. Machines ↓ Time (minutes) ↓ Bottles ↓

6 1 270

10 4 x

$$\Rightarrow \frac{x}{270} = \frac{4}{1} \times \frac{10}{6}$$

$$\therefore \quad x = \frac{4 \times 10}{6} \times 270$$

$= 1800$ bottles

15. Work ↓ Hours ↑ Days ↑ Persons ↓

$\frac{1}{4}$ 9 10 400

$\frac{3}{4}$ 8 20 x

$$\Rightarrow \frac{x}{400} = \frac{10}{20} \times \frac{9}{8} \times \frac{3/4}{1/4}$$

$$\therefore \quad x = \frac{1}{2} \times \frac{9}{8} \times 3 \times 400 = 675$$

Hence, number of additional persons
$= 675 - 400 = 275$

TIME AND DISTANCE

1. Starting from a point at a speed of 4 km/hr a man reaches at a cerain place and returns back to the point from where he had started journey on bicycle at the speed of 16 km/hr. His average speed during the entire journey will be :
   A. 6.4 km/h B. 8.4 km/h
   C. 5.4 km/h D. 10 km/h
2. A motorist covers a certain distance at a average speed of 48 km/h in 45 minutes. What speed in km/h he must maintain to cover the same distance in 30 minutes?
   A. 66 km/h B. 79 km/h
   C. 80 km/h D. 72 km/h
3. A policeman saw a thief at a distance of 200 m. The policeman and the thief started running at the same time. If the policeman runs at a speed of $4\frac{1}{6}$ m per second and the thief at a speed of $3\frac{1}{3}$ m per second, after what time the policeman will catch the thief?
   A. 12 min B. 10 min
   C. 9 min D. 4 min
4. A monkey wants to climb up a glazed pole. He climbs 12 metres in 1 minute and then he slips back 3 metres in the next minute. If the pole is 63 metre high, how long does he take to climb at the top of the pole?
   A. $11\frac{1}{4}$ min B. $12\frac{1}{2}$ min
   C. $12\frac{3}{4}$ min D. $14\frac{3}{4}$ min
5. The distance between two stations A and B is 300 km. A train leaves the station A with a speed of 40 km/hr. At the same time another train departs from the station B with a speed of 50 km/hr. How much time will these two trains take to cross each other?
   A. 3 hrs 40 min B. 3 hrs 20 min
   C. 2 hrs 20 min D. 3 hrs 45 min
6. Nilesh goes to school from his village at the speed of 4 km/hr and returns from school to village at the speed of 2 km/hr. If he takes 6 hours in all, then what is the distance between the village and the school?
   A. 8 km B. 6 km
   C. 5 km D. 4 km
7. By increasing the speed of the bus by 10 km/hr the time of journey for 72 km is reduced by 36 minutes. What was the original speed of the bus?
   A. 30 km/hr B. 35 km/hr
   C. 40 km/hr D. 45 km/hr
8. A train covers a distance in 50 minutes, if it runs at a speed of 48 km/hr on an average. The speed at which the train must run to reduce the time of journey to 40 minutes will be:
   A. 70 km/hr B. 60 km/hr
   C. 55 km/hr D. 50 km/hr
9. A certain distance is covered by a vehicle at a certain speed. If half of this distance is covered by another vehicle in double the time, the ratio of the speeds of the two vehicles is:
   A. 4 : 1 B. 1 : 4
   C. 2 : 1 D. 1 : 2
10. A is faster than B. A and B each walk 24 km. The sum of their speeds is 7 km/hr and sum of times taken by them is 14 hours. What is the speed of A?
    A. 7 km/hr B. 5 km/hr
    C. 4 km/hr D. 3 km/hr

ANSWERS

1	2	3	4	5	6	7	8	9	10
A	D	D	C	B	A	A	B	A	C

EXPLANATORY ANSWERS

1. Average speed during the entire journey

$$= \frac{2xy}{x+y} = \frac{2\times4\times16}{4+16} = \frac{8\times16}{20} = 6.4 \text{ km/hr.}$$

2. Let required speed be x km/hr; then

$$x \times \frac{1}{2} = 48 \times \frac{3}{4} \quad \therefore \quad x = 48 \times \frac{3}{4} \times 2$$

$$= 72 \text{ km/hr}$$

3. Suppose the policeman will catch the thief after t seconds

then, $\left(\frac{25}{6}-\frac{10}{3}\right)t = 200 \Rightarrow \frac{5}{6}t = 200$

$\therefore\ t = \frac{200\times 6}{5} = 240$ sec = 4 min.

4. The monkey climbs 12 metres in 1 minute and then he slips back 3 metres in the next minute

$\therefore$ The monkey climbs in the first 2 minutes
= 12 – 3 = 9 metres

$\therefore$ In the first 12 minutes the monkey climbs
= 9 × 6 = 54 metres

Remaining height of the pole to be covered by the monkey = 63 – 54 = 9 metre

$\therefore$ The monkey will climb the height of 9 metres in the 13th minute

$\because$ The monkey climbs 12 metres in 1 minute

$\therefore$ The monkey will climb 9 metres in $\frac{1}{12}\times 9$

$= \frac{3}{4}$ minute

$\therefore$ Time spent in climbing at the top of the pole

$= \left(12+\frac{3}{4}\right)$ minutes $= 12\frac{3}{4}$ minutes

5. The two trains are moving in the opposite directions

$\therefore$ Relative speed = 40 + 50 = 90 km/hr.

$\therefore$ Time taken to cross each other $= \frac{300}{90} = 3\frac{1}{3}$ hours

or, 3 hours 20 minutes.

6. Let x km be the distance between village and the school; then

$\frac{x}{4}+\frac{x}{2}=6 \qquad \Rightarrow \frac{3x}{4}=6$

$\therefore\ x = \frac{6\times 4}{3} = 8$ km

8. Let x km/hr be the required speed of the train; then

$x\times\frac{40}{60} = 48\times\frac{50}{60}$

$\therefore\ x = \frac{48\times 50}{40} = 60$ km/hr

9. Let x km/hr and t hr be the certain speed and certain time.

Then, ratio of their speeds $= \frac{x}{t}:\frac{x}{2\times 2t} = 1:\frac{1}{4} = 4:1$

10. Let speeds of A and B are x_1 and x_2 km/hr and times taken by them are t_1 and t_2 hrs, then

$x_1 + x_2 = 7$ km/hr ...(i)

$t_1 + t_2 = 14$ hrs ...(ii)

Now, $\frac{24}{x_1}+\frac{24}{x_2} = 14 \Rightarrow \frac{24(x_1+x_2)}{x_1x_2} = 14$

$\therefore\ x_1x_2 = \frac{24\times 7}{14} = 12$

Then, $x_1 - x_2 = \sqrt{(x_1+x_2)^2 - 4x_1x_2}$

$= \sqrt{(7)^2 - 4\times 12} = 1$ ...(iii)

Solving *(i)* and *(iii)* we get $x_1 = 4$ km/hr

TIME AND WORK

1. A and B working together complete a work in 35 days. If A takes 60 days to complete it, how long would B alone take to complete it?

A. 64 days B. 72 days
C. 81 days D. 84 days

2. A few children working together can do a piece of work in 18 days. If the number of children employed on the work is made double, how long would they take to complete half of the work?

A. $4\frac{1}{2}$ days B. $2\frac{1}{3}$ days
C. $8\frac{3}{4}$ days D. $6\frac{1}{2}$ days

3. 10 men or 18 boys can do a piece of work in 15 days. In how many days would 25 men and 15 boys complete the same work working together?

A. $5\frac{1}{2}$ days B. $4\frac{1}{2}$ days
C. $6\frac{2}{3}$ days D. $2\frac{1}{3}$ days

4. A cistern is filled by a tap in $3\frac{1}{2}$ hours. Due to a leak in the bottom of the cistern, it takes half an hour longer to fill the cistern. If the cistern is full, how long will it take the leak to empty it?

A. 28 hours B. 29 hours
C. $31\frac{1}{3}$ hours D. 38 hours

5. A is twice as good a workman as B and thrice as good a workman as C. If C alone can do a piece of work in 24 days, how long would the three persons take to finish the work working together?

A. $3\frac{3}{11}$ days B. $4\frac{4}{7}$ days

C. $4\frac{4}{11}$ days D. $3\frac{4}{11}$ days

6. If 3 men and 5 women can do a piece of work in 8 days and 2 men and 7 boys can do the same work in 12 days. Find the number of boys, the work done by whom can equate the work done by 10 women.

A. 19 boys B. 21 boys
C. 23 boys D. 15 boys

7. 8 men alone can complete a piece of work in 12 days. 4 women alone can complete the same piece of work in 48 days and 10 children alone can complete the piece of work in 24 days. In how many days can 10 men, 4 women and 10 children together complete the piece of work?

A. 6 B. 8
C. 10 D. 15

8. A works twice as fast as B. If B can complete a piece of work independently in 12 days. Find in how many days A and B together can complete the work?

A. 8 days B. 6 days
C. 4 days D. 18 days

9. A contractor undertook to complete a project in 90 days and employed 60 men on it. After 60 days, he found that $\frac{3}{4}$ of the work has already been completed. How many men can he discharge so that the project may be completed exactly on time?

A. 15 B. 20
C. 30 D. 40

10. A can do a piece of work in 25 days and B can do it in 20 days. They work together for 5 days and then A goes away. In how many days will B finish the remaining work?

A. 33 days B. 20 days
C. 11 days D. 10 days

ANSWERS

1	2	3	4	5	6	7	8	9	10
D	A	B	A	C	B	A	C	B	C

EXPLANATORY ANSWERS

1. (A + B)'s 1 day's work = $\frac{1}{35}$

and also, A's 1 day's work = $\frac{1}{60}$

Hence, B's 1 day's work = $\frac{1}{35}-\frac{1}{60}=\frac{5}{420}=\frac{1}{84}$

So, B will do the whole work in 84 days.

3. 10 men ≡ 18 boys

25 men ≡ $\frac{18}{10}\times 25 = 45$ boys

Hence, 25 men + 15 boys = 45 + 15 = 60 boys

Now, 18 boys can do a piece of work in 15 days.

Hence, 60 boys will do a piece of work in $\frac{15\times 18}{60}=\frac{9}{2}$ days = $4\frac{1}{2}$ days.

4. In 1 hour $\frac{2}{7}$ cistern is filled by the tap.

Hence, in $\frac{1}{2}$ hour $\frac{2}{14}=\frac{1}{7}$ cistern is filled by the tap.

So, $\frac{1}{7}$ cistern is emptied by the leakage in 4 hours.

So, 1 cistern will be emptied by the leakage in 28 hours.

6. Here, (3 men + 5 women) × 8

≡ (2 men + 7 boys) × 12

⇒ 40 women ≡ 84 boys

∴ 10 women ≡ $\frac{84}{40}\times 10$ = 21 boys

Hence, work done by 10 women

= work done of 21 boys.

7. B's 1 day's work = $\frac{1}{4}-\frac{1}{12}=\frac{2}{12}=\frac{1}{6}$

Hence, B alone will complete the work in 6 days.

8. Ratio of efficiency of A and B = 2 : 1

Then, ratio of their time taking = 1 : 2

Hence, if B can complete the work in 12 days, then A in 6 days.

Now, (A + B)'s 1 day's work = $\frac{1}{6}+\frac{1}{12}=\frac{3}{12}=\frac{1}{4}$

So, A and B together can complete the work in 4 days.

9. After 60 days remaining work $= 1 - \frac{3}{4} = \frac{1}{4}$

In 60 days $\frac{3}{4}$ work has been done by 60 men

In 30 days $\frac{1}{4}$ work will be done by $60 \times \frac{4}{3} \times \frac{1}{4} \times \frac{60}{30}$

= 40 men.

Hence, required number of men = 60 – 40 = 20 (which are to be discharged).

BOATS AND STREAMS

1. A boat goes 6 km upstream and back to the starting point in 2 hours. If the current of the stream runs at the rate of 4 km/hr, find the speed of the boat in still water.

A. 6 km/hr B. 8 km/hr
C. 10 km/hr D. 12 km/hr

2. A boat covers 24 km upstream and 36 km downstream in 6 hours, while it covers 36 km upstream and 24 km downstream in 6½ horus. Find the speed of the current.

A. 2 km/hr B. 4 km/hr
C. 6 km/hr D. 8 km/hr

3. A man can row 5 km/hr in still water and the speed of the stream is 1.5 km/hr. He takes an hour when he travels upstream to a place and back again to the starting point. How far is the place from the starting point?

A. 2.275 km B. 3.5 km
C. 1.5 km D. None of these

4. The speed of a boat in still water is 6 km/hr and the speed of the stream is 1.5 km/hr. A man rows to a place at a distance of 22.5 km and comes back to the starting point. Find the total time taken by him.

A. 8 hours B. 10 hours
C. 12 hours D. 4 hours

5. A boat covers 20 km downstream and 6 km upstream in 3 hours, while it covers 30 km downstream and 12 km upstream in 5 hours. What is the speed of boat in still water?

A. 6 km/hr B. 8 km/hr.
C. 10 km/hr D. 12 km/hr.

6. Samir can travel 12 miles downstream in a certain river in 6 hours less than it takes him to travel the same distance upstream. But when he could double his rowing rate for his 24-mile round trip, the downstream 12 miles would then take only one hour less than the upstream 12 miles. Find the speed of the current in miles/hour.

A. $2\frac{2}{3}$ B. $2\frac{1}{3}$
C. $1\frac{2}{3}$ D. $1\frac{1}{3}$

7. A boat takes 6 hours to travel from place M to N downstream and back from N to M upstream. If the speed of the boat in still water is 4 km/hr; what is the distance between two places?

A. 6 kms B. 8 kms
C. 12 kms D. Data inadequate

8. A man can row upstream at 8 km/hr and downstream at 13 km/hr. The speed of the stream is:

A. 2.5 km/hr B. 4.2 km/hr
C. 5 km/hr D. 10.5 km/hr

9. A man's speed with the current is 15 km/hr and the speed of the current is 2.5 km/hr. The man's speed against the current is:

A. 12.5 km/hr B. 10 km/hr
C. 9 km/hr D. 8.5 km/hr

10. A motorboat, whose speed is 15 km/hr in still water goes 30 km downstream and comes back in a total of 4 hours 30 minutes. What is the speed of the stream (in km/hr)?

A. 10 B. 6
C. 5 D. 4

ANSWERS

1	2	3	4	5	6	7	8	9	10
B	A	A	A	B	B	D	A	B	C

EXPLANATORY ANSWERS

1. Let the speed of a boat in still water = x km/hr; then

$$\frac{6}{x-4}+\frac{6}{x+4}=2 \Rightarrow \frac{2x}{x^2-16}=\frac{1}{3}$$

$\Rightarrow x^2 - 6x - 16 = 0$

$\Rightarrow (x - 8)(x + 2) = 0$

Hence, the speed of the boat = 8 km/hr.

2. Let x km/hr and y km/hr be the speeds of the boat in still water and the speed of the current respectively, then

$$\frac{24}{x-y}+\frac{36}{x+y}=6 \Rightarrow \frac{4}{x-y}+\frac{6}{x+y}=1 \quad ...(i)$$

And, $\frac{36}{x-y}+\frac{24}{x+y}=\frac{13}{2}$ ...(ii)

Solving these two equations, we get

$x + y = 12; x - y = 8$

Hence, $y = \frac{1}{2}(12-8) = 2$ km/hr.

3. Let required distance be x km, then

$$\frac{x}{5-1.5}+\frac{x}{5+1.5}=1 \Rightarrow \frac{x\times 2}{7}+\frac{x\times 2}{13}=1$$

$\Rightarrow 40x = 91 \quad \therefore x = 91/40 = 2.275$ km

4. Required time period = $\frac{22.5}{6+1.5}+\frac{22.5}{6-1.5}$

$= \frac{45}{15}+\frac{45}{9} = 8$ hours.

5. Let x km/hr and y km/hr be the speed of boat in still water and speed of current respectively; then

$\frac{20}{x+y}+\frac{6}{x-y}=3$ ...(i)

and also, $\frac{30}{x+y}+\frac{12}{x-y}=5$

$\Rightarrow \frac{15}{x+y}+\frac{6}{x-y}=\frac{5}{2}$ ...(ii)

Solving equations (*i*) & (*ii*), we get $x + y = 10$ and $x - y = 6$

Since, $x = \frac{1}{2}(10 + 6) = 8$ km/hr.

6. Let x km/hr and y km/hr be the speed of rowing in still water and speed of the current respectively; then

$$\frac{12}{x-y}-\frac{12}{x+y}=6 \Rightarrow \frac{24y}{x^2-y^2}=6$$

$\Rightarrow x^2 = y^2 + 4y$ ...(i)

Again, $\frac{12}{2x-y}-\frac{12}{2x+y}=1$

$\Rightarrow \frac{24y}{4x^2-y^2}=1 \Rightarrow x^2=\frac{y^2+24y}{4}$ ...(ii)

From equations (i) and (ii), we get

$y^2 + 4y = \frac{y^2+24y}{4} \Rightarrow 3y^2 = 8y$

$\therefore y = \frac{8}{3} = 2\frac{1}{3}$ miles/hr.

8. The speed of the stream = $\frac{1}{2}(13 - 8) = \frac{5}{2}$

= 2.5 km/hr.

9. The man's speed in still water

= 15 – 2.5 = 12.5 km/hr

Hence, the men's speed against the current

= 12.5 – 2.5 = 10 km/hr

10. Let speed of the stream be x km/hr, then

$$\frac{30}{15+x}+\frac{30}{15-x}=4\frac{1}{2} \Rightarrow \frac{30\times 30}{225-x^2}=\frac{9}{2}$$

$\Rightarrow \frac{200}{225-x^2}=1 \Rightarrow x^2 = 225 - 200$

$\Rightarrow x^2 = 25 \quad \therefore x = 5$ km/hr.

ALLIGATION OR MIXTURE

1. A shopkeeper buys 26 kgs of milk @ Rs. 16 per kg. He also buys from another source an inferior quality of milk @ Rs. 10 per kg. How much quantity of the latter should he buy to mix it with the former so that he can sell the mixture @ Rs. 14 per kg without making any loss?

A. 13 kgs B. 12 kgs
C. 14 kgs D. 16 kgs

2. Two vessels A and B contain mixture of milk and water in the ratio 4 : 1 and 9 : 11 respectively. They

are mixed in the ratio of 3 : 2. Find the ratio of milk : water in the resulting mixture.

A. 34 : 16 B. 33 : 17
C. 16 : 34 D. 17 : 33

3. A shopkeeper has 50 kgs of rice. He sells a part of it at 20% profit and the rest at 40% profit. If he gains 25% on the whole, find the quantity of each part.

A. 12.5 kgs and 37.5 kgs
B. 37.5 kgs and 12.5 kgs
C. 23.5 kgs and 21.5 kgs
D. 21.5 kgs and 23.5 kgs

4. A man bought a certain quantity of sugar for Rs. 8000. He sells one-fourth of it at 20% loss. At what per cent profit should he sell the remainder stock so as to make an overall profit of 20%?

A. 20% B. 30%
C. 35% D. 40%

5. Rs. 675 was divided among 75 boys and girls. Each boy gets Rs. 20 whereas a girl gets Rs. 5. Find the number of boys and girls.

A. 20, 55 B. 15, 60
C. 25, 50 D. 30, 45

6. A vessel contains mixture of liquids A and B in the ratio 3 : 2. When 20 litres of the mixture is taken out and replaced by 20 litres of liquid B, the ratio changes to 1 : 4. How many litres of liquid A was there initially present in the vessel?

A. 12 litres B. 18 litres
C. 24 litres D. 22 litres

7. A container is full of milk. One-third of milk is taken out of it and replaced by same quantity of water. Then again one-third of the mixture is taken out of it and replaced by the same quantity of water. The process is repeated 4 times. If 16 litres of milk is left in the container at the end of 4th operation, find the capacity of the container.

A. 76 litres B. 81 litres
C. 82 litres D. 85 litres

8. The cost of type-I rice is Rs. 15 per kg and type-II is Rs. 20 per kg. If both type I and type II are mixed in the ratio of 2 : 3, then find the price per kg of the mixed variety.

A. Rs. 19.50 B. Rs. 19
C. Rs. 18.50 D. Rs. 18

9. In what ratio must a grocer mix two varieties of tea worth Rs. 60 a kg and Rs. 65 a kg so that by selling the mixture at Rs. 68.20 a kg he may gain 10%?

A. 4 : 5 B. 3 : 5
C. 3 : 4 D. 3 : 2

10. A vessel contains 80 litres of milk. 16 litres of milk was taken out of the vessel and replaced by water. Then 16 litres of mixture was withdrawn and again replaced by water. The operation was repeated for third time. How much milk is now left in the vessel?

A. 96.40 litres
B. 50.36 litres
C. 40.96 litres
D. 32.76 litres

ANSWERS

1	2	3	4	5	6	7	8	9	10
A	B	B	B	A	B	B	D	D	C

EXPLANATORY ANSWERS

1.

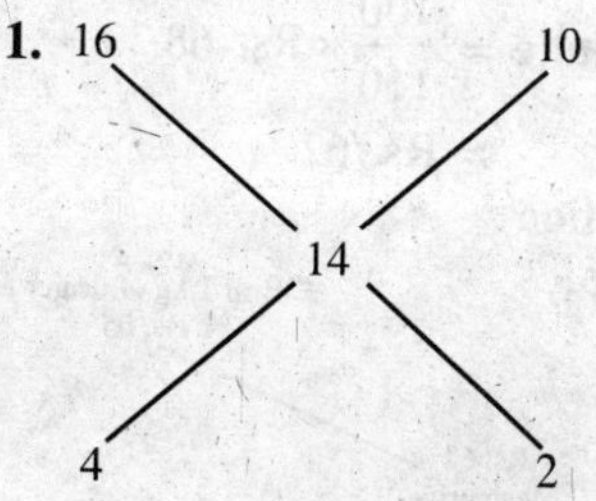

or 2 : 1 $\dfrac{\text{Quantity of milk @ Rs.10 per kg}}{\text{Quantity of milk @ Rs. 16 per kg}} = \dfrac{1}{2}$.

So, quantity of milk @ Rs. 10 per kg. $= \dfrac{26}{2} = 13$ kgs.

2. Fraction is

	Milk	*Water*
A :	$\dfrac{4}{5}$	$\dfrac{1}{5}$
B :	$\dfrac{9}{20}$	$\dfrac{11}{20}$

$(3A + 2B) = A$ and $B : \left(\dfrac{12}{5}+\dfrac{9}{10}\right) \left(\dfrac{3}{5}+\dfrac{11}{10}\right)$

$\dfrac{33}{10}$ $\dfrac{17}{10}$

So, Ratio of milk : water in the resulting mixture = 33 : 17.

3.

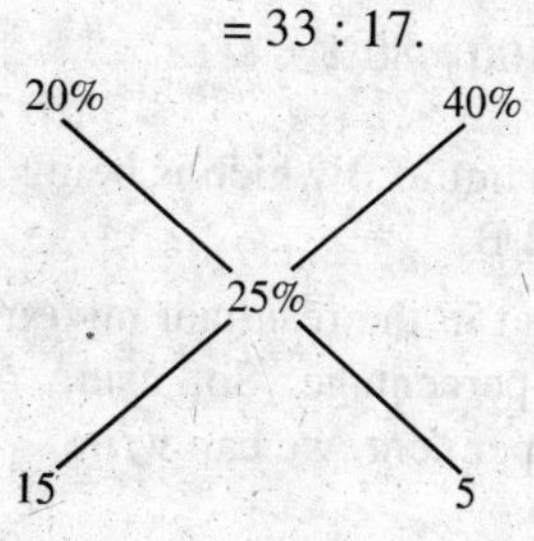

or 3 : 1

Quantity sold at 20% profit = $\frac{3}{3+1} \times 50$

$= 37.5$ kgs.

Quantity sold at 40% profit = $(50 - 37.5)$

$= 12.5$ kgs.

4. Let the remainder stock be sold at $x\%$ profit.

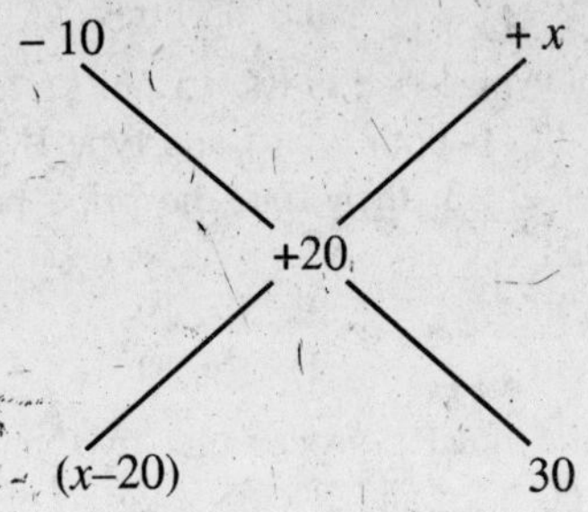

$$\frac{x-20}{30} = \frac{1/4}{3/4}$$

or $\quad x - 20 = 30 \times \frac{1}{3}$

or $\quad x = 20 + 10$

$x = 30\%$ profit.

5. Average money per head (boy or girl)

$= \text{Rs. } \frac{675}{75} = \text{Rs. } 9$

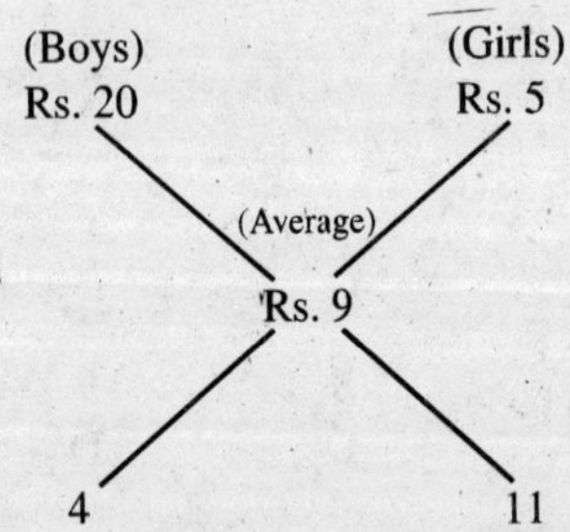

Number of boys = $\frac{4}{4+11} \times 75 = 20$

Number of girls = $\frac{11}{4+11} \times 75 = 55.$

6. % of liquid B initially present in the vessel

$= \frac{2}{3+2} \times 100 = 40\%$

% of liquid B finally present in the vessel

$= \frac{4}{1+4} \times 100 = 80\%$

The second solution is liquid B which is being mixed and it has 100% liquid B.

80% of liquid B present in the resultant mixture may be taken as average percentage. So, using rule of alligation on liquid B per cent, we can write,

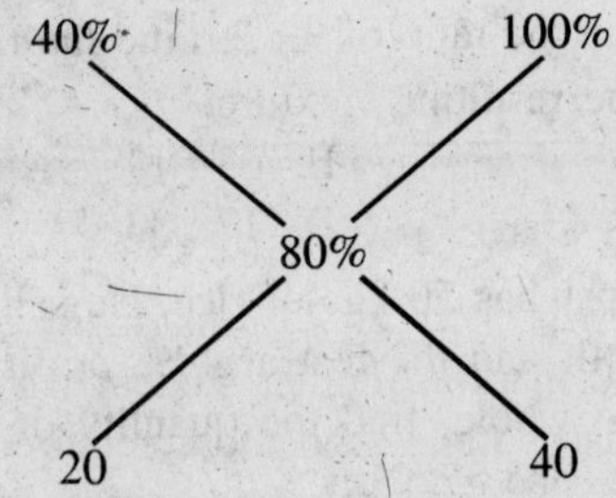

or $\quad 1 : 2$

The ratio of liquid left in the vessel to liquid B being mixed = 1 : 2

Since the quantity of liquid B being mixed is 20 litres, the quantity of liquid left in the vessel is 10 litres. Therefore, the total quantity of liquid initially present in the vessel

$= 10 + 20 = 30$ litres

Quantity of liquid A = $\frac{3}{2+3} \times 30 = 18$ litres.

7. Let capacity of the container be x litre; then

$x(1 - 1/3)^4 = 16 \Rightarrow x\left(\frac{2}{3}\right)^4 = 16$

$\Rightarrow x \times \frac{16}{81} = 16 \qquad \therefore\ x = 81$ litres

8. Let the price per kg of mixed variety be Rs. x; then

By the rule of alligation,

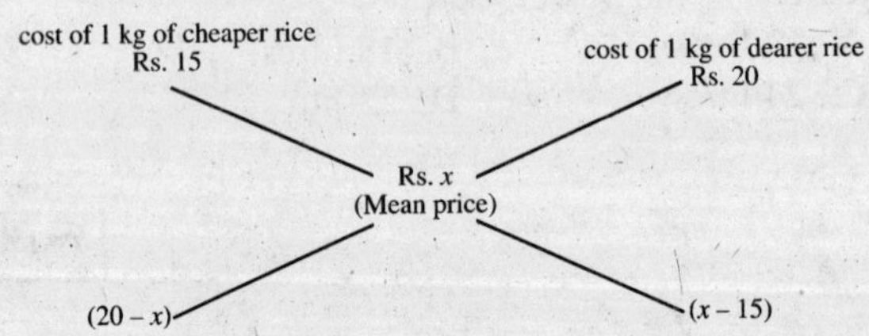

Now, $\frac{20-x}{x-15} = \frac{2}{3} \Rightarrow 60 - 3x = 2x - 30$

$\Rightarrow 5x = 90 \qquad \therefore\ x = \text{Rs. } 18$

9. S.P. of 1 kg mixture = Rs. 68.20, Gain % = 10%

Hence, C.P. of 1 kg mixture = $\frac{100}{110} \times \text{Rs. } 68.20$

= Rs. 62

By the rule of alligation

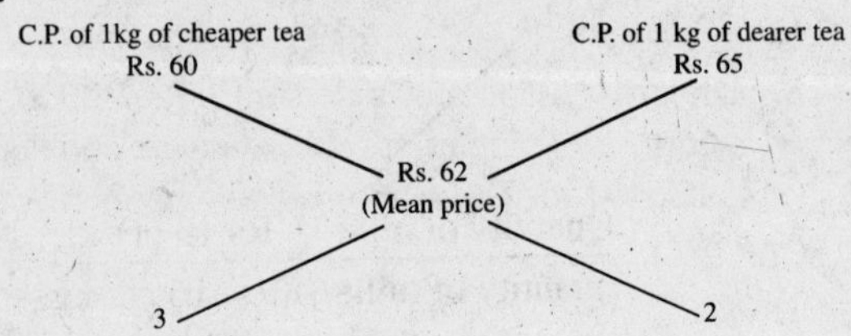

Hence, required ratio = 3 : 2

10. Amount of milk left = $80\left(1 - \frac{16}{80}\right)^3 = 80\left(\frac{4}{5}\right)^3$

$80 \times \frac{64}{125} = 40.96$ litres.

PERCENTAGE

1. A student who secures 20% marks in an examination fails by 30 marks. Another student who secures 32% gets 42 marks more than those required to pass. The percentage of marks required to pass is:
   A. 20 B. 25
   C. 28 D. 30
2. In a college election, a candidate secured 62% of the votes and is elected by a majority of 144 votes. The total number of votes polled is:
   A. 600 B. 800
   C. 925 D. 1200
3. In an organisation, 40% of the employees are matriculates, 50% of the remaining are graduates and the remaining 180 are postgraduates. How many employees are graduates?
   A. 360 B. 240
   C. 300 D. 180
4. The population of a village is 4500. $\frac{5}{9}$th of them are males and rest females. If 40% of the males are married, then the percentage of married female is :
   A. 35 B. 40
   C. 50 D. 60
5. A's income is 10% more than B's. How much per cent is B's income is less than A's?
   A. 10% B. 7%
   C. $9\frac{1}{11}\%$ D. $6\frac{1}{2}\%$
6. If the price of a television set is increased by 25%, then by what percentage should the new price be reduced to bring the price back to original level?
   A. 15% B. 20%
   C. 25% D. 30%
7. In an election one of the two candidates gets 40% votes and loses by 100 votes. Total number of votes is :
   A. 500 B. 400
   C. 600 D. 1000
8. The gross income of a person is Rs. 20000. 10% of his income is exempted from income tax and his net income is Rs. 19100. The rate of income tax is :
   A. 3% B. 2%
   C. 4% D. 5%
9. The owner of a cell phone shop charges his customer 32% more than the cost price. If a customer paid Rs. 6600 for the cell phone, then what was the cost price of the cell phone?
   A. Rs. 5000 B. Rs. 5500
   C. Rs. 5800 D. Rs. 6100
10. If the cost of pins reduced by Rs. 4 per dozen, 12 more pins can be purchased for Rs. 48. The cost of pins per dozen after reduction is:
    A. Rs. 8 B. Rs. 12
    C. Rs. 16 D. Rs. 20
11. In an examination 80% of the students passed in Mathematics and 70% passed in English, while 10% students failed in both the subjects. If 360 students passed in both the subjects, find the total number of students who appeared in the examination.
    A. 400 B. 600
    C. 630 D. 640
12. Electric tax is increased by 20% and its consumption is decreased by 20%. The change in the expenditure is:
    A. 4% decrease B. 4% increase
    C. 5% decrease D. 5% increase
13. The selling price of certain commodity was reduced by 25%. As a result of it, the sales increased by 30%. What was the effect of it on cash collected by daily sales?
    A. 2.5% decrease B. 2.5% increase
    C. 5% decrease D. 5% increase
14. The wheat sold by a grocer contained 10% low quality wheat. What quantity of good quality wheat should be added to 150 kgs of wheat so that the percentage of low quality wheat becomes 5%?
    A. 50 kgs B. 85 kgs
    C. 135 kgs D. 150 kgs
15. Nilam spends 15% of her monthly income on household expenses. She spends 17% of the monthly income in travelling and 6% on medical expenses and saves the rest Rs. 15,500. What is her monthly income?
    A. Rs. 20,000 B. Rs. 25,000
    C. Rs. 30,000 D. Rs. 35,000

ANSWERS

1	2	3	4	5	6	7	8	9	10
B	A	D	C	C	B	A	D	A	B
11	**12**	**13**	**14**	**15**					
B	A	A	D	B					

EXPLANATORY ANSWERS

1. 20% of $x + 30 = 32\%$ of $x - 42$

$\Rightarrow$ 12% of $x = 72$

$\Rightarrow$ $x = \dfrac{72 \times 100}{12} = 600$

Pass Mark $= 20\%$ of $600 + 30 = 150$

Pass percentage $= \left(\dfrac{150}{600} \times 100\right)\% = 25\%$

2. (62% of $x - 38\%$ of x) $= 144$

$\Rightarrow 24\%$ of $x = 144 \quad \Rightarrow x = \dfrac{144 \times 100}{24} = 600$

3. Matriculates $= \dfrac{40}{100}x = \dfrac{2x}{5}$

Remaining $= \left(x - \dfrac{2x}{5}\right) = \dfrac{3x}{5}$

Graduates $= \dfrac{50}{100} \times \dfrac{3x}{5} = \dfrac{3x}{10}$

Remaining $= \dfrac{3x}{5} - \dfrac{3x}{10} = \dfrac{3x}{10}$

Now, $\dfrac{3x}{10} = 180 \quad \therefore x = \dfrac{10 \times 180}{3} = 600$

$\therefore$ Graduates $= \dfrac{3 \times 600}{10} = 180$.

4. Males $= \left(\dfrac{5}{9} \times 4500\right) = 2500$

Females $= 2000$

$\therefore$ Married males $= \dfrac{40}{100} \times 2500 = 1000$

and married females $= 1000$

$\therefore$ Percentage of married females

$= \left(\dfrac{1000}{2000} \times 100\right)\% = 50\%$.

5. Required percentage $= \left[\dfrac{10}{(100+10)} \times 100\right]\% = 9\dfrac{1}{11}\%$.

6. Required reduction $= \dfrac{25}{100+25} \times 100 = 20\%$.

7. Out of 100, difference in votes $= (60 - 40) = 20$

20% of $x = 100$

$\therefore x = \dfrac{100 \times 100}{20} = 500$.

8. Gross income = Rs. 20000

Income exempted from income tax = 10% of gross income

$\therefore$ Income on which income tax is chargeable $= (100 - 10\%) = 90\%$ of gross income

$= 20000 \times \dfrac{90}{100} =$ Rs. 18000

$\therefore$ Total income tax paid on

= Rs. 20000 – Rs. 19100 = Rs. 900

$\therefore$ Rate per cent of income tax $= \dfrac{900}{18000} \times 100 = 5\%$.

9. Let cost price of the cell phone be Rs. x; then

$x + \dfrac{32}{100} \times x = 6600 \quad \Rightarrow \dfrac{132x}{100} = 6600$

$\therefore x = \dfrac{100 \times 6600}{132} =$ Rs. 5000.

10. Let reduced price by Rs. x per dozen, then

$\dfrac{48}{x} - \dfrac{48}{x+4} = 1 \quad \Rightarrow \dfrac{48 \times 4}{x^2 + 4x} = 1$

$\Rightarrow x^2 + 4x - 192 = 0$

$\Rightarrow (x + 16)(x - 12) = 0$

$\therefore$ $x =$ Rs. 12.

11. Here, percentage of students failed in Mathematics and English be 30% and 20% respectively.

Percentage of students failed either one or both subjects $= 30 + 20 - 10 = 40\%$

Hence, percentage of pass students $= 100 - 40 = 60\%$

Now, $60\% = 360$

$\therefore 100\% = \dfrac{360}{60} \times 100 = 600$.

12. Let initially electric tax is Rs. 100 and consumption = 100 units

Decrease in consumption

$= 100 \times 100 - 120 \times 80 =$ Rs. 400

Hence, decrease percentage $= \dfrac{400 \times 100}{100 \times 100} = 4\%$.

13. Let the selling price of a commodity be Rs. 100 and number of sales = 100 units

Decrease in daily cash $= 100 \times 100 - 75 \times 130$

= Rs. 250

Hence, decrease percentage $= \dfrac{250 \times 100}{100 \times 100} = 2.5\%$.

14. Let x kg of good wheat be added; then

$\dfrac{10}{100} \times 150 = \dfrac{5}{100}(150 + x)$

$\Rightarrow 150 + x = 300 \quad \therefore x = 150$ kg.

15. Let her monthly income be Rs. x; then

$x - \left(\dfrac{15}{100} \times x + \dfrac{17}{100} \times x + \dfrac{6}{100} \times x\right) = 15{,}500$

$\Rightarrow x - \dfrac{38x}{100} = 15500 \quad \Rightarrow \dfrac{62x}{100} = 15500$

$\therefore x = \dfrac{15500 \times 100}{62} =$ Rs. 25000.

PROFIT AND LOSS

1. Ashok bought 25 kg of rice at the rate of Rs. 6 per kg and 35 kg of rice at the rate of Rs. 7 per kg. He mixed the two and sold the mixture at the rate of Rs. 6.75 per kg. What was his gain or loss in the transaction?

A. Rs. 16 gain B. Rs. 16 loss
C. Rs. 10 gain D. None of these

2. Profit after selling a commodity for Rs. 425 is same as loss after selling it for Rs. 355. The cost of the commodity is :

A. Rs. 285 B. Rs. 390
C. Rs. 295 D. Rs. 400

3. Ram bought 4 dozen apples at Rs. 12 per dozen and 2 dozen at Rs. 16 per dozen. He sold all of them to earn 20%. At what price per dozen did he sell the apples?

A. Rs. 14.40 B. Rs. 16.00
C. Rs. 16.80 D. Rs. 16.20

4. At what price must Kantilal sell a mixture of 80 kg sugar at Rs. 6.75 per kg with 120 kg at Rs. 8 per kg to gain 20%?

A. Rs. 7.50 per kg B. Rs. 8.20 per kg
C. Rs. 8.35 per kg D. Rs. 9 per kg

5. A person bought an article and sold it at a loss of 10%. If he had bought it for 20% less and sold it for Rs. 55 more, he would have had a profit of 40%. The C.P. of the article is :

A. Rs. 200 B. Rs. 225
C. Rs. 250 D. None of these

6. A dealer sold a machine to a shopkeeper at 20% profit. The shopkeeper sold the machine to a customer so as to get 25% profit for himself. The difference between the selling price of the dealer and that of the shopkeeper was found to be Rs. 129. What is the initial price of the machine?

A. Rs. 410 B. Rs. 420
C. Rs. 430 D. Rs. 440

7. A man bought a horse and cart. If he sold the horse at 10% loss and the cart at 20% gain he would not loss anything. If he sold the horse at 5% loss and the cart at 5% gain he would lose Rs. 10 in the bargain. What did he pay for each?

A. Rs. 400, Rs. 200 B. Rs. 300, Rs. 300
C. Rs. 250, Rs. 350 D. Rs. 350, Rs. 250

8. The marked price of a radio is 20% more than its cost price. If a discount of 10% is given on the marked price, the gain percentage is:

A. 8 B. 10
C. 12 D. 15

9. A dishonest dealer sells his goods at the cost price and still earns a profit of 60% by underweight. What weight does he use for a kg?

A. 625 gms B. 750 gms
C. 800 gms D. 850 gms

10. A man sells two horses for Rs. 990 each. On one he gains 10% and the other he loses 10%. What is his total percentage of gain or loss in the transaction?

A. 1% gain B. 1% loss
C. 2% gain D. 2% loss

ANSWERS

1	2	3	4	5	6	7	8	9	10
C	B	B	D	C	C	A	A	A	B

EXPLANATORY ANSWERS

1. C.P. of 60 kg mixture = Rs. $(25 \times 6 + 35 \times 7)$
= Rs. 395

S.P. of 60 kg mixtire = Rs. (60×6.75)
= Rs. 405

$\therefore$ Gain = Rs. $(405 - 395)$
= Rs. 10

2. Let C.P. = Rs. x

Then, $425 - x = x - 355 \Rightarrow 2x = 780$

$\therefore$ $x =$ Rs. 390

3. C.P. of 6 dozen apples = Rs. $(12 \times 4 + 16 \times 2)$
= Rs. 80

$\therefore$ S.P. = Rs. $\left(\frac{120}{100} \times 80\right)$
= Rs. 96

$\therefore$ S.P. per dozen = Rs. $\left(\frac{96}{6}\right)$ = Rs. 16

4. C.P. of 1 kg sugar $= \frac{80 \times 6.75 + 120 \times 8}{200}$

$= \text{Rs. } 7.50$

$\therefore$ S.P. of 1 kg $= \text{Rs.}\left(\frac{120}{100} \times 7.50\right)$

$= \text{Rs. } 9$ per kg

5. Let, C.P. = Rs. x,

then, S.P. $= \frac{90}{100} \times x = \text{Rs. } \frac{9x}{10}$

Now, when C.P. = Rs. $\frac{80x}{100} = \text{Rs. } \frac{4x}{5}$;

then, S.P. $= \frac{140}{100} \times \frac{4x}{5} = \text{Rs. } \frac{28x}{25}$

But, $\frac{28x}{25} - \frac{9x}{10} = 55 \Rightarrow \frac{11x}{50} = 55$

$\therefore x = \text{Rs. } 250$

6. Let the initial price = Rs. x; then C.P. for dealer

$= \frac{120}{100} \times x = \text{Rs. } \frac{6x}{5}$

Again, C.P. for shopkeeper $= \frac{125}{100} \times \frac{6x}{5}$

$= \text{Rs. } \frac{3x}{2}$

Now, $\frac{3x}{2} - \frac{6x}{5} = 129 \Rightarrow \frac{3x}{10} = 129$

$\therefore x = \frac{10 \times 129}{3} = \text{Rs. } 430$

7. Here, 10% C.P. of horse = 20% C.P. of cart; Hence, C.P. of horse = 2 × C.P. of cart;
Let C.P. of cart and horse be Rs. x and Rs. $2x$ respectively; then,

$\frac{5}{100} \times 2x - \frac{5}{100} \times x = 10 \Rightarrow \frac{1}{20}x = 10$

$\therefore x = 200$

Hence, C.P. of a cart = Rs. 200 and C.P. of a horse = 2 × 200 = Rs. 400

8. Let C.P. be Rs. 100; then marked price = Rs. 120

Since, S.P. $= \frac{90}{100} \times 120 = \text{Rs. } 108$

$\therefore$ Profit = 108 – 100 = Rs. 8, Hence, gain = 8%.

9. Required weight $= \frac{100}{160} \times 1000 = 625$ gms.

10. Here, loss % $= \left(\frac{10}{10}\right)^2 = 1\%$.

SIMPLE INTEREST

1. A lent a sum of Rs. 1250 to B at a certain rate of interest for 3 years and a sum of Rs. 1500 to C at the same rate of interest for 2 years. If he was paid total Rs. 258.75 as interest in both cases, find the rate of interest at which money was lent by him.
   A. $4\frac{1}{6}\%$ B. $6\frac{1}{4}\%$
   C. $2\frac{1}{7}\%$ D. $3\frac{5}{6}\%$
2. A invested Rs. 5000 at a certain rate of simple interest and Rs. 4000 for the same period at 1% higher rate of interest. If the interest in both cases is same, the former rate of interest is :
   A. 3% B. 4%
   C. 6% D. 5%
3. If a certain sum of money at simple interest amounts to Rs. 1900 in 3 years and to Rs. 2050 in 5 years, the rate per cent per annum is :
   A. 4½% B. 3½%
   C. 2½% D. 5¼%
4. A certain sum of money lent out on simple interest amounts to Rs. 1760 in 2 years and to Rs. 2000 in 5 years. Find the sum.
   A. Rs. 1650 B. Rs. 1500
   C. Rs. 1580 D. Rs. 1600
5. Out of the sum of Rs. 1550, a part was lent out at 5% p.a. simple interest and the remaining at 8% p.a. simple interest. If the total interest in both cases after 3 years is Rs. 300, the sum of money lent out at 8% p.a. simple interest was:
   A. Rs. 760 B. Rs. 775
   C. Rs. 750 D. Rs. 780
6. If simple interest on a certain sum of money for 4 years at 5% p.a. is same as the simple interest on Rs. 840 for 10 years at the rate of 4% p.a., the sum of money is:
   A. Rs. 1780 B. Rs. 1660
   C. Rs. 1680 D. Rs. 1620
7. What equal instalment of annual payment will discharge a debt which is due as Rs. 848 at the end of 4 years at 4% per annum simple interest?

A. Rs. 200 B. Rs. 212
C. Rs. 225 D. Rs. 250

8. Madhavi lent Rs. 5000 to Kamla for 5 years and Rs. 3000 to Vimla for 4 years. Find the rate of interest, if Madhavi gets an interest of Rs. 600 in the end.
A. 1.62% B. 2.5%
C. 3% D. 4%

9. A sum of money doubles itself in 7 years at simple interest. In how many years it will become four fold?
A. 10 years B. 14 years
C. 21 years D. 35 years

10. An amount doubles itself at the end of 8 years with a certain rate of simple interest. What will be the total simple interest on Rs. 8000 at that rate at the end of 4 years?
A. Rs. 2000 B. Rs. 4000
C. Rs. 6000 D. None of these

ANSWERS

1	2	3	4	5	6	7	8	9	10
D	B	A	D	C	C	A	A	C	B

EXPLANATORY ANSWERS

1. $\frac{1250 \times R \times 3}{100} + \frac{1500 \times R \times 2}{100} = 258.75$

$\Rightarrow 6750\ R = 25875$

$\therefore \quad R = \frac{25875}{6750} = \frac{23}{6} = 3\frac{5}{6}\%$

2. Here, $\frac{5000 \times R \times T}{100} = \frac{4000 \times (R+1) \times T}{100}$

$\Rightarrow 5R = 4R + 4 \quad \therefore \ R = 4\%$

3. Simple interest for 2 years
= Rs. 2050 – Rs. 1900 = Rs. 150

$\therefore$ Simple interest for 1 year = Rs. $\frac{150}{2}$ = Rs. 75

Since simple interest for 3 years = Rs. 75 × 3
= Rs. 225

$\therefore$ Principal = Rs. 1900 – Rs. 225 = Rs. 1675

Hence, Rate = $\frac{75 \times 100}{1675 \times 1} = 4½\%$

4. Interest for 3 years = Rs. 2000 – Rs. 1760
= Rs. 240

$\therefore$ Interest for 1 year = Rs. $\frac{240}{3}$ = Rs. 80

And interest for 2 years = Rs. 80 × 2 = Rs. 160
$\therefore$ Principal = Rs. 1760 – Rs. 160 = Rs. 1600

5. Let Rs. x and Rs $(1550 - x)$ were lent out at 8% and 5% respectively; then

$\frac{x \times 8 \times 3}{100} + \frac{(1550 - x) \times 5 \times 3}{100} = 300$

$\Rightarrow 24x + 23250 - 15x = 30000$

$\Rightarrow 9x = 6750 \quad \therefore \ x = \frac{6750}{9}$ = Rs. 750

6. Here, $\frac{P \times 5 \times 4}{100} = \frac{840 \times 4 \times 10}{100} \Rightarrow 5P = 8400$

$\therefore \ P = \frac{8400}{5}$ = Rs. 1680

7. Let equal instalment be Rs. x; then

$x + \frac{x \times 4 \times 3}{100} + x + \frac{x \times 4 \times 2}{100} + x + \frac{x \times 4 \times 1}{100} + x = 848$

$\Rightarrow 4x + \frac{24x}{100} = 848 \quad \Rightarrow \quad \frac{106x}{25} = 848$

$\therefore \ x = \frac{848 \times 25}{106}$ = Rs. 200

8. $\frac{5000 \times R \times 5}{100} + \frac{3000 \times R \times 4}{100} = 600$

$\Rightarrow \quad 250\ R + 120\ R = 600$

$\Rightarrow \quad 370R = 600$

$\therefore \quad R = \frac{600}{370} = 1.62\%$

9. Let principal be Rs. x; then amount = Rs. $2x$, Hence, I = $2x - x$ = Rs. x.

$R = \frac{x \times 100}{x \times 7} = \frac{100}{7}\%$ p.a.

Now, amount = Rs. $4x$; then I = $4x - x$ = Rs. $3x$

Hence, $T = \frac{3x \times 100}{x \times \frac{100}{7}} = \frac{3 \times 100 \times 7}{100} = 21$ years

10. Let principal = Rs. x; then amount = Rs. $2x$; I
= $2x - x$ = Rs. x

$R = \frac{x \times 100}{x \times 8} = \frac{25}{2}\%$

Again, $I = \frac{8000 \times 25 \times 4}{100 \times 2}$ = Rs. 4000

COMPOUND INTEREST

1. The compound interest on a certain sum of money invested for 3 years at 5% per annum is Rs. 1891.50. What will be the simple interest on the same sum at the same rate for 2 years?
A. Rs. 1700 B. Rs. 1200
C. Rs. 1500 D. Rs. 2100

2. A sum of money lent out at a certain rate of simple interest amounts to Rs. 6600 in 2 years and to Rs. 6900 in 3 years. What will be the compound interest on the same sum of money if lent out at the same rate for 2 years?
A. Rs. 605 B. Rs. 715
C. Rs. 615 D. Rs. 595

3. A man deposits Rs. 1200 in a bank on the 1st day of each year. If the bank pays 5% per annum compound interest on deposited sum of money, what will be the amount to his credit on the 10th day of the second year?
A. Rs. 2560 B. Rs. 2460
C. Rs. 2370 D. Rs. 2860

4. If the difference between compound and simple interest on a certain sum of money for 3 years at 5% per annum is Rs. 244, the sum is :
A. Rs. 40000 B. Rs. 25000
C. Rs. 30000 D. Rs. 32000

5. A man purchased a sewing machine for Rs. 5000. If due to sustained use value of this sewing machine depreciates by 6% annually, find its value after 3 years.
A. Rs. 3775.67 B. Rs. 4152.92
C. Rs. 4250.25 D. Rs. 4356.25

6. Find the sum on which the difference between compound and simple interest for 3 years at 10% per annum will be Rs. 868.
A. Rs. 29500 B. Rs. 27625
C. Rs. 28500 D. Rs. 28000

7. Samir invested Rs. 15000 at the rate of interest 10% p.a. for 1 year. If the interest compound six months. What amount will Samir get at the end of the year?
A. Rs. 16,500 B. Rs. 16525.50
C. Rs. 16537.50 D. Rs. 18,150

8. The compound interest on a certain sum for 2 years at 10% per annum is Rs. 525. The simple interest on the same sum for double the time at half the rate per cent per annum is:
A. Rs. 800 B. Rs. 600
C. Rs. 500 D. Rs. 400

9. The least number of complete years in which a sum of money put at 20% compound interest will be more than doubled is:
A. 6 B. 5
C. 4 D. 3

10. On a sum of money, the simple interest for 2 years is Rs. 660, while the compound interest is Rs. 696.30, the rate of interest being the same in both cases. Find the rate of interest.
A. Rs. 12% B. 11%
C. 10% D. 9%

ANSWERS

1	2	3	4	5	6	7	8	9	10
B	C	B	D	B	D	C	C	C	B

EXPLANATORY ANSWERS

1. Here, $1891.50 = P\left[\left(1+\frac{5}{100}\right)^3 - 1\right]$

$\Rightarrow \quad 1891.50 = P\left[\left(\frac{21}{20}\right)^3 - 1\right]$

$\Rightarrow \quad 1891.50 = P\left(\frac{1261}{8000}\right)$

$\therefore P = \frac{1891.50 \times 8000}{1261} = \text{Rs. } 12000$

Now, $\quad \text{S.I.} = \frac{12000 \times 5 \times 2}{100} = \text{Rs. } 1200$

2. Here, 1 year's S.I. = Rs. 6900 – Rs. 6600
= Rs. 300

$\therefore$ 2 year's S.I. = 300 × 2 = Rs. 600

$\therefore$ Principal = Rs. 6600 – Rs. 600
= Rs. 6000

Hence, $\quad \text{Rate} = \frac{600 \times 100}{6000 \times 2} = 5\%$

$\therefore$ C.I. $= 6000\left[\left(1+\frac{5}{100}\right)^2-1\right]$

$= 6000\left[\left(\frac{21}{20}\right)^2-1\right] = \frac{6000\times 41}{400} =$ Rs. 615

3. Required amount $= 1200\left(1+\frac{5}{100}\right) + 1200$

$= 1200 \times \frac{21}{20} + 1200 = 1260 + 1200 =$ Rs. 2460

4. Here, $P\left[\left(1+\frac{5}{100}\right)^3-1\right]-\frac{P\times5\times3}{100} = 244$

$\Rightarrow P\times\frac{1261}{8000}-\frac{3P}{20} = 244 \Rightarrow P\times\frac{61}{8000} = 244$

$\therefore P = \frac{244\times8000}{61} =$ Rs. 32000

5. Here, value of the machine after 3 years

$= 5000\left(1-\frac{6}{100}\right)^3 = 5000\times\frac{47}{50}\times\frac{47}{50}\times\frac{47}{50}$

= Rs. 4152.92.

6. Here, $P\left[\left(1+\frac{10}{100}\right)^3-1\right]-\frac{P\times10\times3}{100} = 868$

$\Rightarrow P\times\frac{331}{1000}-\frac{3P}{10} = 868$

$\Rightarrow P\times\frac{31}{1000} = 868 \therefore P = \frac{868\times1000}{31}$

= Rs. 28000

7. $A = 15000\left(1+\frac{5}{100}\right)^2 = 15000\times\frac{441}{400}$

= Rs. 16537.50

8. Here, $P\left[\left(1+\frac{10}{100}\right)^2-1\right] = 525$

$\Rightarrow P\left[\frac{121}{100}-1\right] = 525 \Rightarrow P\times\frac{21}{100} = 525$

$\therefore P = \frac{525\times100}{21} =$ Rs. 2500

Hence, required S.I. $= \frac{2500\times5\times4}{100} =$ Rs. 500

9. Here, $P\left(1+\frac{20}{100}\right)^n > 2P \Rightarrow \left(\frac{6}{5}\right)^n > 2$

Hence, if $n = 4$ then, $\left(\frac{6}{5}\right)^4 = \frac{1296}{625} > 2$

So, $n = 4$ years

10. Here, S.I. for 1 year = Rs. 330
Since, simple interest of Rs. 330 for 1 year
= 696.30 – 660 = Rs. 36.30

Hence, required rate $= \frac{36.30\times100}{330\times1} = \frac{3630}{330} = 11\%$

AREA AND PERIMETER

1. If side of a square is reduced by 50%, its area will be reduced by
A. 50% B. 75%
C. 80% D. 60%

2. If each side of a square is doubled, its area will become
A. double B. four times
C. three times D. eight times

3. Three sides of a triangle are in the ratio of 17 : 15 : 8. If the perimeter of this triangle is 40 m, find its area
A. 50 sq. m. B. 49 sq. m.
C. 60 sq. m. D. 69 sq. m.

4. If the length of a rectangle is increased by 20% and width is decreased by 15%, then its area
A. decreases by 4% B. increases by 2%
C. decreases by 2% D. increases by 3%

5. If the length of a rectangle is increased by 20%, then by how much per cent its breadth must be decreased so as to keep its area unaltered?
A. 25% B. $8\frac{1}{3}\%$
C. $16\frac{2}{3}\%$ D. 20%

6. The ratio of length and breadth of a rectangular plot is 71 : 61 respectively. The area of the plot is 17324 m^2. What is perimeter of the plot?
A. 264 m B. 284 m
C. 528 m D. 614 m

7. If the length and breadth of a rectangular field are increased, the area increases by 50%. If the increase in length was 20%, by what percentage was the breadth increased?

A. 20% B. 25%
C. 30% D. 40%

8. The length and breadth of a varandah is 40 m and 15 m respectively. How many stone slabs of size 6 decimetre × 5 decimetre each are needed in flooring it:
A. 1000 B. 2000
C. 3000 D. 4000

9. The circumference of a circular plot is 396 m. What is the area of the circular plot?
A. 9,446 m^2 B. 9,856 m^2
C. 12,474 m^2 D. 18,634 m^2

10. If the sides of an equilateral triangle are increased by 20%, 30% and 50% respectively to form a new triangle, the increase in the perimeter of the equilateral triangle is:
A. 25% B. $33\frac{1}{3}\%$
C. 50% D. 100%

ANSWERS

1	2	3	4	5	6	7	8	9	10
B	B	C	B	C	C	B	B	C	B

EXPLANATORY ANSWERS

1. Area of the square = x^2 sq. m.

Side of the new square = $x - 50\%$ of $x = \frac{x}{2}$ m

$\therefore$ Area of the new square = $\left(\frac{x}{2}\right)^2 = \frac{x^2}{4}$ sq. m.

$\therefore$ Reduction in area of the square = $x^2 - \frac{x^2}{4}$

$= \frac{3x^2}{4}$ sq. m.

$\therefore$ Percentage reduction = $\frac{3x^2/4}{x^2} \times 100 = 75\%$

2. Area of the square = x^2 sq. m
Now, area of the new square = $(2x)^2 = 4x^2$ sq. m
Hence, it is clear that if side of a square is doubled, its area becomes four times.

3. Suppose sides of the triangle are $17x$ m, $15x$ m and $8x$ metres

$\therefore$ Perimeter = $17x + 15x + 8x = 40x$

Now, $40x = 40$

$\Rightarrow$ $x = 1$ m

Therefore, the sides are $17 \times 1 = 17$ m, $15 \times 1 = 15$ m and $8 \times 1 = 8$ m

$\because$ $(17)^2 = (15)^2 + (8)^2$,

i.e., it is a right angled triangle

$\therefore$ Area of the right angled triangle

$= \frac{1}{2} \times 8 \times 15 = 60$ sq.m.

4. Area of the rectangle = xy sq. metre

Area of the new rectangle = $\frac{120}{100}x \times \frac{85}{100}y$

$= 1.020\ xy$ sq. metre

$\therefore$ Increase in the area = $1.02\ xy - xy = .02\ xy$ sq. m.

$\therefore$ Percentage increase = $\frac{.02xy}{xy} \times 100 = 2\%$

5. Area of the rectangle = xy
On reducing the breadth by A% and increasing the length by 20%

Length of the new rectangle = $\frac{120x}{100}$ $x = 1.2x$

Breadth of the new rectangle = $y - $ A% of $y = y\left(1 - \frac{A}{100}\right)$

$\therefore$ Area of the new rectangle = $1.2x \times y\left(1 - \frac{A}{100}\right)$

Now, $xy = 1.2\ xy\left(1 - \frac{A}{100}\right) \Rightarrow 1 = 1.2\frac{(100 - A)}{100}$

$\Rightarrow$ $1.2\ A = 120 - 100$

$\therefore$ $A = \frac{20}{1.2} = 16\frac{2}{3}\%$

6. Let length and breadth of a rectangle be $71x$ and $61x$ m; then

$71x \times 61x = 17324 \Rightarrow x^2 = \frac{17324}{71 \times 61} = 4$

$\therefore$ $x = 2$

Hence, length = $71 \times 2 = 142$ m; breadth $= 61 \times 2 = 122$ m

Since, perimeter = $2(142 + 122) = 2 \times 264 = 528$ m

7. Here, $20 + x + \frac{20 \times x}{100} = 50 \Rightarrow x + \frac{x}{5} = 30$

$\Rightarrow \frac{6x}{5} = 30$ $\therefore x = \frac{5 \times 30}{6} = 25$

Hence, breadth was increased by 25%

8. Required number of stone slabs = $\frac{40 \times 15}{\frac{6}{10} \times \frac{5}{10}}$

$= \frac{40 \times 15 \times 100}{6 \times 5} = 2000$

VOLUME AND SURFACE AREA

1. If a solid sphere of 3 cm radius is melted and recast into a right circular cone whose base radius is same as that of the sphere, the height of the cone will be
A. 8 cm B. 12 cm
C. 6 cm D. 5 cm

2. Diameter of a roller is 2.4 m and it is 1.68 m long. If it takes 1000 complete revolutions once over to level a field, the area of the field is
A. 12672 sq. m B. 12671 sq. m
C. 12762 sq. m D. 11768 sq. m

3. If each edge of a cube is increased by 10%, then by how much per cent will the surface area of this cube be increased?
A. 21% B. 18%
C. 15% D. 20%

4. Height and base radius of a solid cylinder are 14 m and 4 m respectively. It is melted and recast into a solid cone of the same base radius as that of the cylinder, what will be the height of the cone?
A. 21 m B. 42 m
C. 48 m D. 54 m

5. A room is in the form of a cube of side 10 m. How many bales of cotton can be kept in it if each bale covers 5 cu m space?
A. 100 B. 175
C. 200 D. 225

6. Three cubes having side 2 cm, 3 cm and 4 cm respectively are melted together to form a new cube. The side of the new cube will be
A. 3.526 cm B. 4.628 cm
C. 4.626 cm D. 4.528 cm

7. If base diameter of a cylinder is increased by 50%, then by how much per cent its height must be decreased so as to keep its volume unaltered?
A. 45.56% B. 55.56%
C. 50.16% D. 62.33%

8. The surface area of a cube is 600 sq. m. Its diagonal is
A. $10\sqrt{3}$ cm B. $5\sqrt{3}$ cm
C. $4\sqrt{2}$ cm D. $10\sqrt{2}$ cm

9. The base diameter of a conical tomb is 28 m and its slant height is 50 m. Find the cost of white washing its curved surface at the rate of 80 paise per sq. m?
A. Rs. 1860 B. Rs. 1760
C. Rs. 1950 D. Rs. 1875

10. The volume of a cuboid is 1120 cu cm and its height is 5 cm while the length and the breadth of the cuboid are in the ratio 8 : 7. The length of this cylinder exceeds the breadth by
A. 4 cm B. 2 cm
C. 7 cm D. 5 cm

ANSWERS

1	2	3	4	5	6	7	8	9	10
B	A	A	B	C	C	B	A	B	B

EXPLANATORY ANSWERS

1. Volume of the cone = Volume of the sphere

$$\therefore \quad \frac{1}{3}\pi(3)^2 \times h = \frac{4}{3}\pi \times 3^3 \Rightarrow h = 12 \text{ cm}$$

Hence, height of the cone = 12 cm.

2. Surface area of the roller = $2\pi rh$

$$= 2\times\frac{22}{7}\times 1.2\times 1.68 = 12.672 \text{ sq. m}$$

In one complete revolution, the roller covers 12.672 sq. m.

∴ It will cover in 1000 revolutions

= 12.672 × 1000 = 12672 sq. m

Hence, area of the field = 12672 sq. m.

3. Percentage increase in the surface area of the cube

$$= \left(x+y+\frac{xy}{100}\right)\%$$

$$= \left(10+10+\frac{10\times 10}{100}\right)\% = 21\%.$$

4. Here,

volume of the cone = Volume of the cylinder

$$\Rightarrow \quad \frac{1}{3}\pi r^2 \times \text{height} = \pi r^2 \times 14$$

$\therefore$ Height = 14 × 3 = 42 m

Thus, height of the cone = 42 m.

5. Volume of the cubical room $= (10)^3$
$= 1000$ cu m

Number of cotton bales which can be placed in the room

$$= \frac{\text{Volume of the room}}{\text{Volume of each cotton bale}} = \frac{1000}{5} = 200.$$

6. Volume of the new cube $= 2^3 + 3^3 + 4^3$
$= 8 + 27 + 64 = 99$cu cm

$\therefore$ Side of the new cube $= \sqrt[3]{99} = 4.626$ cm.

7. Change in the volume of the cylinder

$$= \left(x+y+(-z)+\frac{xy+y(-z)+(-zx)}{100}+\frac{xy(-z)}{100^2}\right)\%$$

Since volume of the cylinder remains unchanged.

$\therefore$ Change $= 0\%$

Now, $\left(50+50+(-z)+\frac{50\times50-50z-50z}{100}+\frac{50\times50\times(-z)}{100^2}\right)=0$

$\therefore\ 100 - z + 25 - z - .25z = 0$

$\Rightarrow 2.25z = 125 \Rightarrow z = \frac{125}{2.25} = 55.56$

$\therefore$ Height of the cylinder should be decreased by 55.56%.

8. Here, $6 \times (\text{side})^2 = 600$

$\Rightarrow$ $\text{side}^2 = 100$

$\Rightarrow$ side $= \sqrt{100} = 10$ cm

$\therefore$ Diagonal of the cube $= \sqrt{3}\times\text{side}$

$= \sqrt{3}\times 10$

$= 10\sqrt{3}$ cm.

9. Area of the curved surface of the cone

$= \frac{22}{7}\times\frac{28}{2}\times 50 = 2200$ sq. m.

$\therefore$ Cost of white washing at 80 paise per sq. m

$= 2200\times\frac{80}{100} = $ Rs. 1760.

10. Suppose the length and the breadth of the cuboid are $8x$ cm and $7x$ cm

$\therefore$ Here, $8x \times 7x \times 5 = 1120$

$\Rightarrow x^2 = \frac{1120}{280} = 4 = (2)^2 \Rightarrow x = 2$

$\therefore$ Length of the cuboid $= 8 \times 2 = 16$ cm

Breadth of the cuboid $= 7 \times 2 = 14$ cm

Hence, it is clear that length of the cuboid exceeds the breadth by 2 cm.

SERIES

Directions (Qs. 1 to 7) : *In the following number series, one of the numbers does not fit into the series. Find the wrong number.*

1. 2, 5, 10, 18, 26, 37, 50
A. 2 B. 5
C. 37 D. 18

2. 3 , 18, 38, 78, 123, 178, 243
A. 123 B. 178
C. 3 D. 38

3. 380, 188, 92, 48, 20, 8, 2
A. 188 B. 92
C. 48 D. 20

4. 5, 11, 23, 47, 96, 191, 383
A. 11 B. 23
C. 47 D. 96

5. 89, 78, 86, 80, 85, 82, 83
A. 78 B. 86
C. 80 D. 85

6. 58, 57, 54, 50, 42, 33, 32
A. 57 B. 54
C. 50 D. 32

7. 2, 20, 27, 44, 64
A. 27 B. 8
C. 20 D. 44

Directions (Qs. 8 to 10) : *Complete the following series.*

8. 1 4 9 16 25 36 49 ....
A. 54 B. 56
C. 64 D. 81

9. 11 13 17 19 23 29 31 37 41 ....
A. 43 B. 47
C. 53 D. 51

10. 3 7 6 5 9 3 12 1 15 ....
A. 18 B. 13
C. –1 D. 3

ANSWERS

1	2	3	4	5	6	7	8	9	10
D	C	C	D	A	C	C	C	A	C

EXPLANATORY ANSWERS

1. 2 5 10 18 26 37 50

↓ ↓ ↓ ↓ ↓ ↓ ↓

1^2+1 2^2+1 3^2+1 4^2+1 5^2+1 6^2+1 7^2+1

Wrong no. = 18, Correct no. = 17.

2. Only 3 is a prime number.

3. Wrong no. = 48, Correct no. = 44
Each term will be four more than two times the next term.

4. 5 11 23 47 [96] 191 383

+6 +12 +24 +48 +96 +192

Wrong no. = 96, Correct no. = 95.

5. If 87 is written in place of 78 then tens digit of each term will be 8.

6. 58 57 54 [50] 42 33 22

−1 −3 −5 −7 −9 −11

Wrong no. = 50, Correct no. = 49.

7. 2 [20] 27 44 64

+11 +14 +17 +20

Wrong no. = 20, Correct no. = 13.

8. Numbers are $1^2, 2^2, 3^2, 4^2, 5^2, 6^2, 7^2$.
So, the next number is $8^2 = 64$.

9. Numbers are all primes. The next prime is 43.

10. There are two series, beginning respectively with 3 and 7. In one 3 is added and in another 2 is subtracted. The next number is $1 - 2 = -1$.

APPROXIMATE VALUES

1. $85432 \div 2106 + 59.5614 = ?$
(*a*) 100 (*b*) 60
(*c*) 80 (*d*) 140

2. $\sqrt{67621} = ?$
(*a*) 320 (*b*) 260
(*c*) 200 (*d*) 280

3. 9.7 % of 5011 + 55.03 % of 4991
(*a*) 5500 (*b*) 7200
(*c*) 6000 (*d*) 4200

4. $730 \times 199 = ?$
(*a*) 350000 (*b*) 335000
(*c*) 300000 (*d*) 34600

5. $.0144 \times 0.36 = ?$
(*a*) 0.5 (*b*) 0.005
(*c*) 0.05 (*d*) 0.005

6. 31% of 1508 + 26% of 2018
(*a*) 1500 (*b*) 2000
(*c*) 1000 (*d*) 1200

7. $3015 + 13594 + 3738 = ?$
(*a*) 40000 (*b*) 36000
(*c*) 42000 (*d*) 46000

8. $6012 \times 119 = ?$
(*a*) 560000 (*b*) 448000
(*c*) 900000 (*d*) 720000

9. $2712.1563 \div 1805.4018 + 3.4982 = ?$
(*a*) 9 (*b*) 8
(*c*) 4 (*d*) 5

10. $4182.365 \div 20.886 = ?$
(*a*) 300 (*b*) 200
(*c*) 150 (*d*) 250

ANSWERS

1	2	3	4	5	6	7	8	9	10
A	B	D	A	B	C	A	D	D	B

EXPLANATORY ANSWERS

1. $85432 \div 2106 + 60 = 40 + 60 = 100$
Therefore, (B) is the correct answer.

2. $\sqrt{67621} = \sqrt{67600} = 260$
Therefore, (B) is the correct answer.

3. 29.7 % of 5011 + 55.03 % of 4991
= 30 % of 5000 + 55 % of 5000

$= \frac{30}{100} \times 5000 + \frac{55}{100} \times 5000$

$= 1500 + 2750 = 4250 \Rightarrow 4200$
Therefore, (D) is the correct answer.

4. $1730 \times 199 = 1730 \times 200$
$= 346000 \Rightarrow 350000$
Therefore, (B) is the correct answer.

5. $0.0144 \times 0.36 = 0.0140 \times 0.36 = .005040$
$\Rightarrow .005$
Therefore, (B) is the correct answer.

6. 31% of 1508 + 26% of 2018
= 30% of 1500 + 25% × 2000

$= \frac{30}{100} \times 1500 + \frac{25}{100} \times 2000$

$= 450 + 500 = 950 \Rightarrow 1000$
Therefore, (C) is the correct answer.

7. $23015 + 13594 + 3738$
$= 23000 + 13600 + 3700$
$= 40300 \Rightarrow 40000$
Therefore, (A) is the correct answer.

8. $6012 \times 119 = 6000 \times 120 = 720000$
Therefore, (D) is the correct answer.

9. $2712.1563 \div 1805.4018 + 3.4982$
$= 2700 \div 1800 + 3.5 = 1.5 + 3.5 = 5$
Therefore, (D) is the correct answer.

10. $4182.365 \div 20.886 = 4200 \div 21 = 200$
Therefore, (B) is the correct answer.

हिंदी

व्याकरण

व्याकरण वह शास्त्र है जिसके द्वारा किसी भी भाषा के शब्दों और वाक्यों के शुद्ध स्वरूपों एवं शुद्ध प्रयोगों का ज्ञान कराया जाता है।

व्याकरण के चार अंग हैं : (i) वर्ण विचार (ii) शब्द विचार (iii) पद विचार और (iv) वाक्य विचार

भाषा : भाषा अभिव्यक्ति का एक ऐसा साधन है जिसके द्वारा मनुष्य अपने विचारों को दूसरों पर प्रकट कर सकता है और दूसरों के विचार जान सकता है। भाषा के दो रूप हैं–(i) मौखिक और (ii) लिखित।

बोली : भाषा का क्षेत्रीय रूप बोली कहलाता है।

लिपि : किसी भी भाषा के लिखने की विधि को लिपि कहते हैं।

वर्ण : हिन्दी भाषा में प्रयुक्त सबसे छोटी ध्वनि वर्ण कहलाती है। जैसे–अ, आ, ई, क्, ख्, आदि

वर्णमाला : वर्णों के समुदाय को वर्णमाला कहते हैं। हिन्दी वर्णमाला में 44 वर्ण हैं। जिनमें 11 स्वर तथा 33 व्यंजन हैं।

स्वरवर्ण : उन वर्णों को कहते हैं, जिनका उच्चारण बिना किसी दूसरे वर्ण की सहायता से होता है। हिन्दी में 11 स्वर हैं–अ, आ, इ, ई, उ, ऊ, ए, ऐ, ओ, औ, ऋ।

व्यंजन वर्ण : उन वर्णों को कहते हैं, जिनका उच्चारण स्वर वर्णों की सहायता के बिना नहीं हो सकता है। इनकी संख्या 33 है–

क ख ग घ ड़ च छ ज झ ञ ट् ठ

ड ढ़ ण त थ द ध न प फ ब भ

म य र ल व श ष स ह।

वर्ण : एक या अधिक वर्णों से बनी हुई स्वतन्त्र सार्थक ध्वनि शब्द कहलाती है।

शब्दों को तत्सम, तद्भव, देशज और विदेशी भागों में बाँटा जाता है।

तत्सम : जो शब्द संस्कृत भाषा से हिन्दी में बिना किसी परिवर्तन के लिए जाते हैं वे तत्सम कहलाते हैं, जैसे– अग्नि, क्षेत्र, मित्र, नासिका आदि।

तद्भव : उन शब्दों को कहते हैं, जो संस्कृत से ही लिए गए हैं, परन्तु हिन्दी में आने पर जिनका रूप बदल गया है। जैसे–आग, खेत, रात आदि।

देशज : उन शब्दों को कहते हैं, जो बोलचाल तथा देश की अन्य भाषाओं से लिए गए हैं। जैसे–कटोरा, झंझत, डिबिया, लोटा आदि।

विदेशज या विदेशी : उन शब्दों को कहते हैं, जो किसी विदेशी भाषा से आए हैं। जैसे–स्कूल, कार, कमरा, खुदा, जोश, सरकार आदि

शब्द सम्पदा

तत्सम शब्दों के तद्भव रूप

तत्सम	तद्भव	तत्सम	तद्भव
अग्नि	आग	अद्य	आज
अष्ट	आठ	अक्षि	आँख
अर्ध	आधा	अस्थि	हड्डी
अश्रु	आँसू	आम्र	आम
ग्राम	गाँव	गर्दभ	गधा
गृघ्र	गीध	गौर	गोरा
गृह	घर	घट	घड़ा
धातु	धात	धृत	घी
लक्ष	लाख	सप्त	सात
त्वम्	तुम	दुग्ध	दूध
रत्न	रतन	वर्ष	बरस
भक्त	भगत	मर्कट	बन्दर
रात्रि	रात	उलूक	उल्लू
अन्धकार	अन्धेरा	क्षीर	खीर
निद्रा	नींद	पृष्ठ	पीठ
ज्येष्ठ	जेठ	स्वर्ण	सोना
श्वास	साँस	काक	काग
कार्य	काज	कर्ण	कान

तत्सम	तद्भव	तत्सम	तद्भव
पाद	पाँव	हस्त	हाथ
नासिका	नाक	कंटक	काँटा
दश	दस	दधि	दही
दीप	दीया	निद्रा	नींद
नव	नौ	पत्र	पत्ता
प्रस्तर	पत्थर	जिह्वा	जीभ
हस्ती	हाथी	दन्त	दाँत
क्षेत्र	खेत	नृत्य	नाच
सूचिका	सूई	स्वर्णकार	सुनार
लोक	लोग	पर्यङ्क	पलंग
स्वप्न	सपना	कातर	कायर
पुत्र	पूत	मानव	मनुष्य
शत	सौ	पुष्प	फूल
पक्व	पक्का	कृषक	किसान
कर्म	कार्य	आम्र	आम
कर्ण	कान	अष्ट	आठ
घंटिका	घंटी	चन्द्र	चन्द
यव	जौ	धूम्र	धुआँ

विराम चिह्न

विराम का अर्थ रुकना। अपने विचारों को ठीक ढंग से प्रकट करने के पढ़ते अथवा लिखते समय हमें कुछ रुकना पड़ता है। इस प्रकार के रुकने को विराम कहते हैं।

प्रत्येक-विराम के लिए अलग-अलग चिह्न हैं–

पूर्ण विराम	[।]
अल्प विराम	[,]
अर्ध विराम	[;]
प्रश्न बोधक	[?]
विस्मयादि बोधक	[!]
योजक	[–]
उद्धरण	[" "]

कारक

कारक शब्द उस रूप को कहते हैं, जिससे संज्ञा या सर्वनाम वाक्य के साथ सम्बन्ध जाना जाता है। जैसे–शीला कलम **से** लिखती है।

यह सीमा **की** पुस्तक है।

कारक के भेद विभक्ति चिह्नों सहित

कारक	**विभक्ति**
कर्त्ता	ने
कर्म	को
करण	से
सम्प्रदान	के लिए
अपादान	से
सम्बन्ध	का, के, की
अधिकरण	में, पर
सम्बोधन	हे, अरे!

पर्यायवाची शब्द

जिन शब्दों से एक समान अर्थ का बोध होता है, उन्हें पर्यायवाची या समानार्थी शब्द कहते हैं।

कुछ पर्यायवाची शब्दों के उदाहरण निम्नलिखित हैं–

आग – अग्नि, अनल, पावक, हुताशन, ज्वाला।
आकाश – नभ, आसमान, गगन, लोभ।
असुर – राक्षस, दानव, निशाचर, दैत्य।
अमृत – अभिय, पीयूष, सुधा, सोम।
अन्धकार – अन्धेरा, तिमिर, तम, तमिस्त्र।
आँख – नेत्र, नयन, लोचन, चक्षु, दृग।
कमल – जलज, पंकज, नीरज, राजीव।
इन्द्र – सुरपति, देवेन्द्र, सुरेन्द्र, देवेश।
ईश्वर – प्रभु, भगवान, जगदीश, दीनबन्धु।
पक्षी – खग, विहग, चिड़िया, नभचर।
बादल – घन, जलधर, वारिद, नीरद।
गंगा – सुरसरि, जाह्नवी, त्रिपथगा, देवनदी, विष्णुपदी।
चन्द्रमा – शशि, मयंक, निशाकर, सुधाकर, सुधांशु, सोम हिमांशु, राकेश।
जल – पानी, नीर, लोभ, अम्बु, सलिल, क्षीर, वारि।
फूल – पुष्प, कुसुम, सुमन, प्रसून, सारंग।
पृथ्वी – भू, भूमि, धरा, वसुन्धरा, वसुधा, धरती क्षमी, लोक।
कपड़ा – पट, वस्त्र, चीर, अम्बर, दुकूल।
घर – गृह, गेह, निकेतन, आलय, निलय, भवन, शाला, धाम, सदन।
जंगल – वन, कानन, अरण्य, विपिन।
तालाब – सरोवर, ताल, जलाशय, तड़ाग।
दिन – दिवस, वासर, वार।
पहाड़ – गिरि, पर्वत, गूधर, नग, महीधर, मेरू।
पत्थर – पहाड़, प्रस्तर, पाहन।
पवन – वायु, समीर, हवा, मारुत, अनिल।
पुत्र – सुत, तनय, पूत, आत्मज।
बिजली – तड़ित, चपला, दामिनी।
वृक्ष – तरू, रूख, विटप, पेड़।
मनुष्य – नर, मानव, मनुज, आद्रमी।
हाथी – करि, हस्ती, गज।
मित्र – सखा, मीत, सहचर, दोस्त।
राजा – नरेश, नृप, महीप, भूप।
समुद्र – सागर, सिन्धु, जलधि, नीरधि।
सरस्वती – शारदा, वागेश्वरी, भारती, महाश्वेता।
साँप – पन्नग, सर्प, विषधर, अहि, व्याल।
सूर्य – दिनकर, दिवाकर, रवि, भानु, भास्कर।
स्त्री – नारी, महिला, दारा, वामा।
शरीर – देह, तन, काया, गात, बदन।
गणेश – गजानन, गणपति, विनायक, एकदन्त, गजवदन लम्बोदर, विघ्न नाशक।
घोड़ा – तुरंग, बाजि, हय, अश्व, घोटक।
युद्ध – समर, रण, संग्राम।
सिंह – केसरी, मृगराज, केहरी।
शत्रु – अरि, रिपु, बैरी।
विष्णु – हरि, कमलेश, रमापति, चक्रपाणि, केशव, माधव पीताम्बर।
कोष – खजाना, भण्डार, निधि।
धन – दौलत, द्रव्य, मुद्रा।

तलवार – कृपाण, असि, खड्ग।
अंग – भाग, हिस्सा, अवयव।
चोर – तस्कर, दस्यु, रजनीचर।
पत्नी – भार्या, दारा, गृहिणी।
पुत्र – तनय, सुत, लड़का, बेटा।
पुत्री – तनया, सुता, लड़की, बेटी।
माता – जननी, अम्बा, अम्बिका, अम्मा, माँ, धात्री।
मोर – शिखी, नीलकण्ठ, मयूर।
मृत्यु – मौत, काल, देहान्त।
रक्त – रुधिर, शोणित, खून, लहू।
विष – जहर, हलाहल, गरल।
सोना – कंचन, स्वर्ण, कनक।
हृदय – उर, छाती, वक्ष, वक्षस्थल, हिय, हिया।
सभा – अधिवेशन, परिषद्, बैठक, महासभा, समागम, समिति, सम्मेलन।
यमुना – कालिन्दी, कृष्णा, जमुना, रविसुता तरणि-तनुजा।

विलोम-शब्द

शब्दों के अपने निश्चित अर्थ होते हैं। उन अर्थों के विपरीत अर्थ ने वाले शब्द को विलोम-शब्द कहते हैं।

शब्द	विलोम	शब्द	विलोम
अमृत	विष	उदार	संकीर्ण
अनुकूल	प्रतिकूल	अनुराग	विराग
आदि	अन्त	उत्थान	पतन
इच्छा	अनिच्छा	उचित	अनुचित
अल्पायु	दीर्घायु	अनुज	अग्रज
उन्नति	अवनति	आकाश	पाताल
अधिक	न्यून	आयात	निर्यात
एक	अनेक	अन्धकार	प्रकाश
अर्थ	अनर्थ	उदय	अस्त
परकीया	स्वकीया	जड़	चेतन
जय	पराजय	अनिवार्य	वैकल्पिक
नकद	उधार	अपेक्षा	उपेक्षा
उपस्थित	अनुपस्थित	आदर	अनादर
अन्धेरा	उजाला	अपना	पराया
उत्तम	अधम	आय	व्यय
सुपुत्र	कुपुत्र	स्वाधीन	पराधीन
आहार	निराहार	कठोर	कोमल
दाता	याचक	दोषी	निर्दोषि
खेद	प्रसन्नता	धनी	निर्धन
निकट	दूर	चर	अचर
देव	दानव	खरा	खोटा
गरीब	अमीर	प्रेम	घृणा
जीवन	मृत्यु	बुरा	भला
सजीव	निर्जीव	मित्र	शत्रु
सुगन्ध	दुर्गन्ध	मौखिक	लिखित
संक्षेप	विस्तार	कटु	मधुर
आरम्भ	अन्त	कड़वा	मीठा
कृतज्ञ	कृतघ्न	दिन	रात
साक्षर	निरक्षर	पवित्र	अपवित्र
पाप	पुण्य	जल	थल
धीर	अधीर	निर्मल	मलिन

शब्द	विलोम	शब्द	विलोम
गुण	अवगुण	नश्वर	अनश्वर
निन्दा	स्तुति	भारी	हल्का
मनुष्यता	पशुता	सरस	नीरस
मान	अपमान	क्रय	विक्रय
धर्म	अधर्म	गहरा	उथला
गुरु	शिष्य	पक्ष	विपक्ष
जन्म	मृत्यु	बन्धन	मुक्ति
यश	अपयश	ज्ञान	अज्ञान
आदर	अनादर	पूर्ण	अपूर्ण
सफल	असफल	शान्त	अशान्त
कीर्ति	अपकीर्ति	वादी	प्रतिवादी
आंस्तिक	नास्तिक	स्वदेश	परदेश
सज्जन	दुर्जन	राग	द्वेष
ऊसर	उर्वर	उदार	कृपण
अगला	पिछला	अगम	सुगम
अग्नि	जल	अति	अल्प
अर्थ	अनर्थ	अतल	वितल
अत्यधिक	स्वल्प	अद्यः	उपरि
अधिकतम	न्यूनतम	अतिवृष्टि	अनावृष्टि
अनाथ	सनाथ	ईश्वर	जीव
अनुलोम	विलोम	अर्पण	ग्रहण
अवनि	अम्बर	अस्त	उदय
आकर्षण	विकर्षण	आगे	पीछे
आजाद	गुलाम	आदान	प्रदान
आधुनिक	प्राचीन	आना	जाना
आय	व्यय	आयात	निर्यात
आवश्यक	अनावश्यक	आशा	निराशा
आस्था	अनास्था	इहलोक	परलोक
उच्च	निम्न	उत्थान	पतन
उपकार	अपकार	उपयोग	दुरुपयोग
एकता	अनेकता	कल	आज
कृत्रिम	प्राकृत	कृष्ण	शुक्ल
कपूत	सपूत	कोमल	कठोर
गगन	धरा	ज्ञान	अज्ञान

लिंग

लिंग का अर्थ है 'चिह्न'। लिंग शब्द उस चिह्न को कहते हैं जिससे वस्तु के पुरुष या स्त्री होने की कल्पना हो। लिंग दो प्रकार के होते हैं—(1) पुल्लिंग (2) स्त्रीलिंग

पुल्लिंग—पुल्लिंग संज्ञा के उस रूप को कहते हैं जिससे उसके पुरुष होने का ज्ञान होता है। जैसे—राम, श्याम, घोड़ा, हाथी, कुत्ता आदि।

स्त्रीलिंग—स्त्रीलिंग संज्ञा के उस रूप को कहते हैं जिससे उसके स्त्री होने का ज्ञान हो। जैसे—भैंस, गाय, बकरी, सीता, रमा इत्यादि।

पुल्लिंग	स्त्रीलिंग	पुल्लिंग	स्त्रीलिंग
इन्द्र	इन्द्राणी	मेहतर	मेहतरानी
नौकर	नौकरानी	जेठ	जेठानी
देवर	देवरानी	सेठ	सेठानी
पण्डित	पण्डिताइन	ओझा	ओझाइन
बनिया	बनियाइन	दुबे	दुबाइन
हलवाई	हलवाइन	चौबे	चौबाइन
गुरु	गुरुआइन	लड़का	लड़की
दास	दासी	कबूतर	कबूतरी
हिरण	हिरणी	क्षत्रिय	क्षत्राणी
मुगल	मुगलानी	हिन्दू	हिन्दुआनी
चौधरी	चौधरानी	भव	भवानी
लाला	ललाइन	पण्डा	पण्डाइन
ठाकुर	ठकुराइन	बाबू	बबुआइन
घोड़ा	घोड़ी	गूँगा	गूँगी
बच्चा	बच्ची	चाचा	चाची
बकरा	बकरी	मामा	मामी
मुर्गा	मुर्गी	साला	साली
चींटा	चींटी	रस्सा	रस्सी
देव	देवी	ब्राह्मण	ब्राह्मणी
बेटा	बेटी	बूढ़ा	बुढ़िया
चूहा	चुहिया	डिब्बा	डिबिया
गुड्डा	गुड़िया	कुम्हार	कुम्हारिन
सुनार	सुनारिन	नाती	नातिन
जुलाहा	जुलाहिन	दर्जी	दर्जिन
पापी	पापिन	हाथी	हथिनी

पुल्लिंग	स्त्रीलिंग	पुल्लिंग	स्त्रीलिंग
पिता	माता	बैल	गाय
कवि	कवयित्री	विधुर	विधवा
बाप	माँ	बादशाह	बेगम
नर	मादा	मर्द	औरत
युवक	युवती	वर	वधू
सम्राट्	सम्राज्ञी	साढू	साली
फूफा	बुआ	पुत्र	पुत्री
पहाड़	पहाड़ी	गोप	गोपी
गधा	गधी	तरुण	तरुणी
नर्तक	नर्तकी	बेटा	बिटिया
बछड़ा	बछिया	चिड़ा	चिड़िया
बन्दर	बन्दरिया	कुत्ता	कुतिया
नाई	नाइन	धोबी	धोबिन
ग्वाला	ग्वालिन	भंगी	भंगिन
स्वामी	स्वामिनी	विद्वान्	विदुषी
साधु	साध्वी	पुरुष	स्त्री
पति	पत्नी	वीर	वीरांगना
साहब	मेम	सास	ससुर
मियाँ	बीबी	राजा	रानी
बिलाड़	बिल्ली	अनुज	अनुजा
छात्र	छात्रा	महोदय	महोदया
प्रिय	प्रिया	मामा	मामी
लोटा	लुटिया	मोर	मोरनी
शेर	शेरनी	जाट	जाटिन
डाक्टर	डाक्टरनी	मालिक	मालकिन
माली	मालिन	बाघ	बाघिन
हाथी	हथिनी	स्वामी	स्वामिनी
बालक	बालिका	धनवान	धनवती
धावक	धाविका	नेता	नेत्री
गुणवान	गुणवती	नर	मादा
अभिनेता	अभिनेत्री	प्राचार्य	प्राचार्या
प्रबन्धकर्ता	प्रबन्धकर्ती	दाता	दात्री
ननदोई	ननद	अध्यापक	अध्यापिका

वचन

शब्द के जिस रूप से उसके एक अथवा अनेक होने का बोध हो, उसे वचन कहते हैं।

हिन्दी में दो वचन होते हैं—

(1) एकवचन और (2) बहुवचन

एकवचन—शब्द के जिस रूप से एक ही वस्तु का बोध हो, उसे एकवचन कहते हैं। जैसे—लड़का, गाय, बकरी, घोड़ा, राम, सीता आदि।

बहुवचन—शब्द के जिस रूप से अनेकता का बोध हो उसे बहुवचन कहते हैं। जैसे—लड़के, कपड़े, गायें आदि।

एकवचन	बहुवचन	एकवचन	बहुवचन
लड़का	लड़के	कौवा	कौवे
बेटा	बेटे	कमरा	कमरे
कपड़ा	कपड़े	बहन	बहनें
चीज	चीजें	गधा	गधे
रुपया	रुपये	घोड़ा	घोड़े
नहर	नहरें	रात	रातें
बात	बातें	सड़क	सड़कें
दाना	दाने	लोटा	लोटे
पैसा	पैसे	पुस्तक	पुस्तकें
कन्या	कन्याएँ	वधू	वधुएँ
नारी	नारियाँ	लड़की	लड़कियाँ
मुर्गा	मुर्गे	घण्टा	घण्टे
गद्दा	गद्दे	हीरा	हीरे
बच्चा	बच्चे	प्याला	प्याले
छाता	छाते	गाय	गायें
कथा	कथाएँ	कविता	कविताएँ
बहू	बहुएँ	टोपी	टोपियाँ
नाली	नालियाँ	बेटा	बेटे
ताला	ताले	जूता	जूते

एकवचन	बहुवचन	एकवचन	बहुवचन
डिबिया	डिबियाँ	नाक	नाकें
पूँछ	पूँछें	मूँछ	मूँछें
चिड़िया	चिड़ियाँ	सरिता	सरिताएँ
बालिका	बालिकाएँ	चाभी	चाभियाँ
कहानी	कहानियाँ	दरवाजा	दरवाजे
कलम	कलमें	कुटिया	कुटियाँ
रानी	रानियाँ	नाई	नाइयों
माता	माताएँ	बाल	बालों
हाथ	हाथों	मुख	मुख
कोट	कोट	दाँत	दाँतों
नाखून	नाखूनों	पैर	पैरों
बैल	बैलों	माली	मालियों
राजा	राजाओं	पिता	पिता
चन्द्रमा	चन्द्रमा	कवि	कवियों
मुनि	मुनियों	कौआ	कौए
छात्रा	छात्राएँ	सेना	सेनाएँ
दिशा	दिशाएँ	गुड़िया	गुड़ियाँ
मेज	मेजें	भैंस	भैंसें
अंगूर	अंगूरों	समुद्र	समुद्र

अनेक शब्दों के लिए एक शब्द

जिसकी कोई उपमा न हो	: **अनुपम**
तेज बुद्धि वाला	: **कुशाग्रबुद्धि**
कल्पना से परे हो	: **कल्पनातीत**
जो उपकार नहीं मानता है	: **कृतघ्न**
जो उपकार मानता है	: **कृतज्ञ**
किसी की हँसी उड़ाना	: **उपहास**
ऊपर कहा हुआ	: **उपर्युक्त**
ऊपर लिखा हुआ	: **उपरलिखित**
जिस पर उपकार किया गया हो	: **उपकृत**
इतिहास का ज्ञाता	: **इतिहासज्ञ**
आलोचना करने वाला	: **आलोचक**
ईश्वर में आस्था रखने वाला	: **आस्तिक**
बिना वेतन का	: **अवैतनिक**
जो कहा न जा सके	: **अकथनीय**
जो गिना न जा सके	: **अगणित**
जिसका कोई शत्रु ही न जन्मा हो	: **अजातशत्रु**
जिसके समान कोई दूसरा न हो	: **अद्वितीय**
जो परिचित न हो	: **अपरिचित**
आकाश में उड़ने वाला	: **नभचर**
जो टुकड़े-टुकड़े हो गया हो	: **खण्डित**

मछली की तरह आँखों वाली	: **मीनाक्षी**
मयूर की तरह आँखों वाली	: **मयूराक्षी**
बच्चों के लिए काम की वस्तु	: **बालोपयोगी**
जिसकी बहुत अधिक चर्चा हो	: **बहुचर्चित**
जिस स्त्री को कभी सन्तान न हुई हो	: **बन्ध्या (बाँझ)**
फेन से भरा हुआ	: **फेनिल**
प्रिय बोलने वाली स्त्री	: **प्रियम्वदा**
जिसकी उपमा न हो	: **निरुपम**
जो थोड़ी देर पहले पैदा हुआ हो	: **नवजात**
जिसका कोई आधार न हो	: **निराधार**
नगर में वास करने वाला	: **नागरिक**
रात में घूमने वाला	: **निशाचर**
ईश्वर में विश्वास न रखने वाला	: **नास्तिक**
माँस न खाने वाला	: **निरामिष**
बिल्कुल बर्बाद हो गया	: **ध्वस्त**
जिसकी धर्म में निष्ठा हो	: **धर्मनिष्ठ**
देखने योग्य	: **दर्शनीय**
बहुत तेज चलने वाला	: **द्रुतगामी**
जो किसी पक्ष में न रहे	: **तटस्थ**
तत्त्व को जानने वाला	: **तत्त्वज्ञ**

तप करने वाला : **तपस्वी**
जिसे देखकर डर लगे : **डरावना**
जो जन्म से अन्ध हो : **जन्मान्ध**
जीने की प्रबल इच्छा : **जिजीविषा**
जिसने इन्द्रियों को जीत लिया हो : **जितेन्द्रिय**
चिन्ता में डूबा हुआ : **चिन्तित**
जो बहुत समय तक ठहरे : **चिरस्थायी**
जिसकी चार भुजाएँ हों : **चतुर्भुज**
जिसके हाथ में चक्र हों : **चक्रपाणि**
जिससे घृणा की जाए : **घृणित**
जिसे गुप्त रखा जाए : **गोपनीय**
गणित ज्ञाता : **गणितज्ञ**
आकाश को चूमने वाला : **गगनचुम्बी**
जिसका आदि न हो : **अनादि**
जो कुछ न जानता हो : **अज्ञ**
जो अनुकरण करने योग्य हो : **अनुकरणीय**
जिसका अन्त न हो : **अनन्त**
जो कभी न मरे : **अमर**
जो कम बोलता हो : **अल्पभाषी**
जिसका इलाज न हो : **लाइलाज**
जिसका कोई नाथ न हो : **अनाथ**
कम जानने वाला : **अल्पज्ञ**
जहाँ जाना सम्भव न हो : **अगम**
बड़ा भाई : **अग्रज**
कम खाने वाला : **अल्पाहारी**
जो बात पहले कभी न हुई हो : **अभूतपूर्व**
दूसरों के पीछे चलने वाला : **अनुचर**
जो पहले न पढ़ा हो : **अपठित**
जिसके आर-पार दिखाई देता हो : **पारदर्शी**
आज्ञा पालन करने वाला : **आज्ञाकारी**
काम से जी चुराने वाला : **कामचोर**
प्रतिदिन होने वाला : **दैनिक**
जिसका कोई अर्थ न हो : **निरर्थक**
हाथ से लिखा हुआ : **हस्तलिखित**
आँखों के सामने होने वाला : **प्रत्यक्ष**
जिसका आचरण अच्छा हो : **सदाचारी**
वह पुरुष जिसकी पत्नी मर गई हो : **विधुर**
वह स्त्री जिसका पति मर गया हो : **विधवा**
जिसका रूप अच्छा न हो : **कुरूप**
सदा सत्य बोलने वाला : **सत्यवादी**
बड़ी इमारत के टूटे-फूटे भाग : **खण्डहर**
प्रशंसा के योग्य : **प्रशंसनीय**
जहाँ अनाथ रहते हों : **अनाथालय**
प्रत्येक मास होने वाला : **मासिक**
जहाँ पानी के जहाज आकर रुकते हैं : **बन्दरगाह**
प्रत्येक सप्ताह होने वाला : **साप्ताहिक**
प्रत्येक वर्ष होने वाला : **वार्षिक**
जो कठिनाई से मिले : **दुर्लभ**
जिसका आकार हो : **साकार**
जिसका आकार न हो : **निराकार**
जो कभी बूढ़ा न हो : **अजर**
बहुत बोलने वाला : **वाचाल**
पृथ्वी पर रहने वाला : **थलचर**
जल में रहने वाला : **जलचर**
नभ में विचरण करने वाला : **नभचर**
जल-थल दोनों में रहने वाला : **उभयचर**
जिसमें रस न हो : **नीरस**
पढ़ने वाला : **पाठक**
जो भाषण देता हो : **वक्ता**
जो साथ में पढ़ता हो : **सहपाठी**
जिसके नीचे रेखा खींची हो : **रेखांकित**
जानने की इच्छा रखने वाला : **जिज्ञासु**
जिसकी कोई सन्तान न हो : **निःसन्तान**
जिसका कोई मूल्य न हो : **अमूल्य**
जो वन में घूमता हो : **वनचर**
जो इस लोक के बाहर की बात हो : **अलौकिक**
जो इस लोक की बात हो : **लौकिक**
जिसका सम्बन्ध पश्चिम से हो : **पाश्चात्य**
जो स्थिर रहे : **स्थावर**
दुःखान्त नाटक : **त्रासदी**
ज्ञान देने वाली : **ज्ञानदा**
भूत, वर्तमान भविष्य को देखने वाला : **त्रिकालदर्शी**
जो क्षमा के योग्य हो : **क्षम्य**
हिंसा करने वाला : **हिंसक**
हित चाहने वाला : **हितैषी**
सब कुछ जानने वाला : **सर्वज्ञ**
जो स्वयं पैदा हुआ हो : **स्वयंभू**
जो शरण में आया हो : **शरणागत**
जिसका वर्णन न किया जा सके : **वर्णनातीत**
व्याकरण जानने वाला : **वैयाकरण**
रचना करने वाला : **रचयिता**
खून से रंगा हुआ : **रक्तरंजित**
अत्यन्त सुन्दर स्त्री : **रूपसी**
कीर्तिमान पुरुष : **यशस्वी**

महत्त्वपूर्ण शब्दों की भाववाचक संज्ञा

शब्द	भाववाचक संज्ञा	शब्द	भाववाचक संज्ञा
दास	दासता	क्षत्रिय	क्षत्रियत्व
पशु	पशुता	बालक	बालकपन
बन्धु	बन्धुत्व	मित्र	मित्रता
बूढ़ा	बुढ़ापा	सती	सतीत्व
सेवक	सेवा	शिशु	शैशव
अपना	अपनत्व	पराया	परायापन
पण्डित	पाण्डित्य	पुरुष	पुरुषत्व
ब्राह्मण	ब्राह्मणत्व	बच्चा	बचपन
प्रभु	प्रभुता	नारी	नारीत्व
देव	देवत्व	लड़का	लड़कपन
मनुष्य	मनुष्यता	दानव	दानवता
निज	निजता	स्व	स्वत्व

शब्द	भाववाचक संज्ञा	शब्द	भाववाचक संज्ञा
अहं	अहंकार	अपना	अपनापन
व्यक्ति	व्यक्तित्व	मीठा	मिठास
गरीब	गरीबी	सफल	सफलता
बुरा	बुराई	स्वस्थ	स्वास्थ्य
सरल	सरलता	कंजुस	कंजुसी
कमजोर	कमजोरी	हरा	हरियाली
गर्म	गर्मी	मोटा	मोटाई
चालाक	चालाकी	गम्भीर	गम्भीरता
पढ़ना	पढ़ाई	लिखना	लिखाई
थकना	थकावट	लिखना	लिखावट
लूटना	लूट	लड़ना	लड़ाई
हँसना	हँसी	आप	अपनत्व

महत्त्वपूर्ण शब्दों के विशेषण

शब्द	विशेषण	शब्द	विशेषण
अंक	अंकित	अर्थ	आर्थिक
इतिहास	ऐतिहासिक	उदासी	उदास
कलंक	कलंकित	कुसुम	कुसुमित
जटा	जटिल	भार	भारी
बनारस	बनारसी	बाजार	बाजारू
प्यास	प्यासा	पुराण	पौराणिक
पंक	पंकित	पक्ष	पाक्षिक
धन	धनी	दो	दूसरा
तीन	तीसरा	झगड़ा	झगड़ालू
ठण्ड	ठण्डा	जाति	जातीय
काँटा	कँटीला	विदेश	विदेशी
रोज	रोजाना	भूगोल	भौगोलिक
पीड़ा	पीड़ित	पुत्र	पुत्रवान
आलस्य	आलसी	अंतर	आंतरिक
ईर्ष्या	ईर्ष्यालु	कर्म	कर्मठ
करुणा	कारुणिक	कृपा	कृपालु
गुण	गुणी	जल	जलमय
जीव	जैविक	तट	तटस्थ
तर्क	तार्किक	धर्म	धार्मिक
नमक	नमकीन	पत्थर	पथरीला
पल्लव	पल्लवित	पान	पनवाड़ी
मुख	मुखर	मिठास	मीठा
मास	मासिक	मद	मादक
रक्त	रक्तिम	रस	रसीला

शब्द	विशेषण	शब्द	विशेषण
वन	वन्य	विष्णु	वैष्णव
शहर	शहरी	तप	तपस्वी
जापान	जापानी	तेज	तेजस्वी
तत्त्व	तात्त्विक	दया	दयालु
देव	दैविक	निंदा	निंदक
नव	नवीन	पोषण	पोषक
पेट	पेटू	पाप	पापी
पूजा	पूज्य	भूख	भूखा
फेन	फेनिल	भारत	भारतीय
माया	मायावी	रंग	रंगीन
विष	विषैला	श्री	श्रीमान
सुर	सुरीला	विवाह	वैवाहिक
आदर	आदरणीय	ऋण	ऋणी
किताब	किताबी	क्रम	क्रमिक
ग्राम	ग्रामीण	घर	घरेलू
चतुर	चतुरता	जहर	जहरीला
सप्ताह	साप्ताहिक	अनुभव	अनुभवी
ओज	ओजस्वी	कल्पना	काल्पनिक
कुल	कुलीन	गाँव	गँवार
चमक	चमकीला	चाचा	चचेरा
दीन	दीनता	नगर	नागरिक
नागपुर	नागपुरी	परिवार	पारिवारिक
पुष्प	पुष्पित	पिता	पैतृक
फ्रांस	फ्रांसीसी	बाहर	बाहरी

शब्द	विशेषण	शब्द	विशेषण
भय	भयभीत	मधु	मधुर
मौन	मौनी	मन	मानसिक
मानव	मानवीय	रक्षा	रक्षक
रघु	राघव	रोग	रोगी
वर्ष	वार्षिक	शक्ति	शक्तिशाली
श्रम	श्रमिक	अंत	अंतिम
कागज	कागजी	मर्म	मार्मिक
शब्द	शाब्दिक	अज्ञान	अज्ञानी
गुलाब	गुलाबी	प्रकृति	प्राकृतिक
परिचय	परिचित	पूजा	पुजारी
रोग	रोगी	ग्राम	ग्रामीण
सुगंध	सुगंधित	मैं	मेरा
जो	जैसा	आप	आप-सा
तुम	तुम्हारा	कौन	कैसा
वह	वैसा	पढ़ना	पढ़ाकू

शब्द	विशेषण	शब्द	विशेषण
गाना	गायक	बेचना	बिकाऊ
भागना	भगोड़ा	वन्द	वन्दनीय
चलना	चलती	घूमना	घुमक्कड़
चलना	चालू	मरना	मरियल
भूलना	भुलक्कड़	पीछे	पिछला
भीतर	भीतरी	नीचे	निम्न
अणु	आणविक	अधिकार	आधिकारिक
अनुभव	अनुभवी	अन्याय	अन्यायी
अपमान	अपमानित	अभ्यास	अभ्यासी
अवश्य	आवश्यक	आदि	आदिम
आयु	आयुष्मान्	उदय	उदित
उपज	उपजाऊ	एकता	एक
अंत	अंतिम	कुल	कुलीन
खर्च	खर्चीला	खून	खूनी
गुण	गुणी		

श्रुतिसम भिन्नार्थक शब्द

शब्द	अर्थ	शब्द	अर्थ
आदि	आरम्भ	आदी	अभ्यस्त
कुल	वंश	कूल	किनारा
अरि	शत्रु	अरी	सम्बोधन
अगम	दुर्गम	आगम	शास्त्र
अयश	अपकीर्ति	अयस्क	लोहा
अपेक्षा	चाहना, तुलना में	उपेक्षा	निरादर
अनिल	हवा	अनल	आग
अवधि	काल, समय	अवधी	अवध की भाषा
आयात	बाहर से आना	आयत	एक आकृति
चिर	पुराना	चीर	कपड़ा
तनु	पतला	तनू	पुत्र, गाय
तरंग	लहर	तुरंग	घोड़ा
दारा	स्त्री	द्वार	दरवाजा
दूत	संदेशवाहक	द्यूत	जुआ
जलद	बादल	जलज	कमल
प्रदीप	दीपक	प्रतीप	उल्टा
प्रसाद	कृपा	प्रासाद	महल
पास	निकट	पाश	बन्धन
द्विप	हाथी	द्वीप	टापू
देव	देवता	दैव	भाग्य
नीर	जल	नीड़	घोंसला
पवन	वायु	पावन	पवित्र

शब्द	अर्थ	शब्द	अर्थ
बन्द	खुला नहीं	बंद	बुरा
पथ	रास्ता	पथ्य	रोगी का भोजन
पुर	नगर	पूर	बाढ़
भवन	महल	भुवन	संसार
लक्ष्य	उद्देश्य	लक्ष	लाख
सर	तालाब	शर	बाण
सर्ग	अध्याय	स्वर्ग	एक लोक
कर्म	कार्य	क्रम	सिलसिला
चिता	शव जलाने के लिए लकड़ियों का ढेर	चीता	बाघ
शव	लाश	शब	रात
शस्त्र	हथियार	शास्त्र	ग्रन्थ
श्रवण	सुनना	श्रमण	बौद्ध संन्यासी
मत	विचार	मत्त	मस्त
शोक	दुःख	शौक	चाव
ग्रह	नक्षत्र	गृह	घर
कपट	धोखा	कपाट	दरवाजा
उपयुक्त	ठीक	उपर्युक्त	ऊपर कहा गया
सुत	बेटा	सूत	धागा
शूर	वीर	सूर	अंधा
श्याम	कृष्ण	शाम	संध्या
दिन	वार	दीन	गरीब
कटिबद्ध	तैयार रहना	करबद्ध	हाथ जोड़ना

अनेकार्थक शब्द

शब्द	विभिन्न अर्थ
अंक	संख्या, गोद
अक्षर	वर्ण, ईश्वर
पानी	जल, प्रतिष्ठा
अचल	पवर्त, स्थिर
आम	फल, सामान्य
अंबर	वस्त्र, आकाश
अवस्था	आयु, दशा
उत्तर	दिशा, जबाव
विधि	तरीका, भाग्य
कर	हाथ, टैक्स
कनक	सोना, धतुरा
गुरु	श्रेष्ठ, शिक्षक
हान	भारी हथौड़ा, बादल
जड़	मूर्ख, मूल
कल	मशीन, आनेवाला कल, चैन
सुर	देवता, स्वर

शब्द	विभिन्न अर्थ
द्विज	पक्षी, ब्राह्मण
तीर	किनारा, बाण
प्रकृति	स्वभाव, कुदरत
पत्र	चिट्ठी, पत्र
पद	पैर, उपाधि
फल	परिणाम, फल
तनु	पतला, कोमल
वर्ण	रंग, जाति
हल	समाधान, खेत जोतने का साधन
अशोक	राजा, वृक्ष
आभीर	अहीर, एक राग
एकाक्ष	काना, कौआ
खल	दुष्ट, खलिहान
घट	घड़ा, हृदय
जलज	कमल, मछली
हेम	सोना, जल

सामान्य अशुद्धियाँ

अशुद्ध	शुद्ध	अशुद्ध	शुद्ध
दुनियां	दुनिया	श्रीमति	श्रीमती
सामिग्री	सामग्री	वापिस	वापस
प्रदर्शिनी	प्रदर्शनी	द्वारिका	द्वारका
ऊत्थान	उत्थान	दुसरा	दूसरा
प्रशाद	प्रसाद	अमावश्या	अमावस्या
बसंत	वसंत	बर्ष	वर्ष
विना	बिना	बन	वन
दाइत्व	दायित्व	सम्वाद	संवाद
कुन्डली	कुण्डली	मॉसिक	मानसिक
कन्ठ	कण्ठ	अगामी	आगामी
सप्ताहिक	साप्ताहिक	संसारिक	सांसारिक
आधीन	अधीन	हस्ताक्षेप	हस्तक्षेप
बरात	बारात	क्षत्रीय	क्षत्रिय
तिथी	तिथि	कालीदास	कालिदास
पुर्ती	पूर्ति	अतिथी	अतिथि
नीती	नीति	ग्रहणी	गृहिणी
क्यूँ	क्यों	साधू	साधु
वधु	वधू	रेणू	रेणु
नुपुर	नूपुर	निर्वान	निर्वाण
जादु	जादू	द्रश्य	दृश्य

अशुद्ध	शुद्ध	अशुद्ध	शुद्ध
अनुग्रहीत	अनुगृहीत	बृज	ब्रज
बनस्पति	वनस्पति	श्राप	शाप
सैना	सेना	सेनिक	सैनिक
इतिहासिक	ऐतिहासिक	प्रथक	पृथक
सम्पति	सम्पत्ति	कृतघन	कृतघ्न
बिमारी	बीमारी	व्यक्तिक	वैयक्तिक
वितीत	व्यतीत	निस्वार्थ	निःस्वार्थ
परिस्थित	परिस्थिति	रचियता	रचयिता
मैथिलिशरण	मैथिलीशरण	आर्शिवाद	आशीर्वाद
निरिक्षण	निरीक्षण	पत्नि	पत्नी
शताब्दि	शताब्दी	लड़ायी	लड़ाई
स्थाई	स्थायी	लिखायी	लिखाई
अलोकिक	अलौकिक	कृप्या	कृपया
गंवार	गँवार	असोक	अशोक
दुस्कर	दुष्कर	मूल्यावान	मूल्यवान्
नवम्	नवम	क्षात्र	छात्र
छमा	क्षमा	प्रन्तु	परन्तु
प्रीक्षा	परीक्षा	मरयादा	मर्यादा
दुदर्शा	दुर्दशा	विषेश	विशेष
उज्वल	उज्ज्वल	आल्हाद	आहलाद्

अशुद्ध	शुद्ध	अशुद्ध	शुद्ध
महत्व	महत्त्व	उपलक्ष	उपलक्ष्य
लीये	लिये	पिओ	पियो
हुये	हुए	कवित्री	कवयित्री
प्रमात्मा	परमात्मा	घनिष्ट	घनिष्ठ
यथेष्ठ	यथेष्ट	पियास	प्यास
व्यस्क	वयस्क	त्यौहार	त्योहार
मुसलिम	मुस्लिम	ऐनक	ऐनक
नोकरी	नौकरी	कल्यान	कल्याण
पाणी	पानी	आसा	आशा
ह्रदय	हृदय	घ्रणा	घृणा
श्रंगार	शृंगार	हिन्दुस्थान	हिन्दुस्तान
प्रशन	प्रश्न	ग्यान	ज्ञान
अन्धेरा	अँधेरा	पेड	पेड़
महयान्ह्न	मध्यान्ह	मेंह्दी	मेहंदी
शमशान	श्मशान	चिन्ह	चिह्न
कुंज	कुञ्ज	ग्रहस्थ	गृहस्थ
अजोध्या	अयोध्या	अनधिकार	अनाधिकार
अनिष्ठा	अनिष्ट	अनुकुल	अनुकूल
अनुसंगिक	आनुषंगिक	अनुशरण	अनुसरण
अभिसेक	अभिषेक	अरमाण	अरमान
अहिल्या	अहल्या	आदरनीय	आदरणीय
आविस्कार	आविष्कार	उँचाई	ऊँचाई
उत्तरदाई	उत्तरदायी	उपर	ऊपर
उपरोक्त	उपर्युक्त	उश्रृंखल	उच्छृंखल
कलस	कलश	कल्यान	कल्याण
गनित	गणित	जबाब	जवाब
तत्व	तत्त्व	तलाब	तालाब
तिरष्कार	तिरस्कार	त्रिवार्षिक	त्रैवार्षिक
दिपिका	दीपिका	देहिक	दैहिक
द्वन्द	द्वन्द्व	नरायन	नारायण
निरव	नीरव	निरोग	नीरोग
पुष्टी	पुष्टि	पुस्प	पुष्प
पेत्रिक	पैतृक	प्रनय	प्रणय

अशुद्ध	शुद्ध	अशुद्ध	शुद्ध
प्रनाम	प्रणाम	प्रयाप्त	पर्याप्त
प्रसंशा	प्रशंसा	प्रांगन	प्रांगण
प्रान	प्राण	पृष्ट	पृष्ठ
ब्रत	व्रत	भगीरथी	भागीरथी
भरथ	भरत	भष्म	भस्म
मंत्रीमंडल	मंत्रिमण्डल	रसायण	रसायन
राज्यमहल	राजमहल	रामायन	रामायण
वनोवास	वनवास	वानी	वाणी
वाल्मीकी	वाल्मीकि	वास्प	वाष्प
व्योहार	व्यवहार	सन्यासी	संन्यासी
सम्राज	साम्राज्य	सविनयपूर्वक	सविनय
सिंदुर	सिंदूर	स्त्रवण	श्रवण
हरीश्चन्द्र	हरिश्चन्द्र	हिन्दु	हिन्दू
हिन्दूस्तान	हिन्दुस्तान	बुद्धिवान	बुद्धिमान्
भाग्यमान	भाग्यवान	विद्वान	विद्वान्
श्रीमान	श्रीमान्	आंख	आँख
ऊंट	ऊँट	कंगना	कँगना
गँगा	गंगा	गांधी	गाँधी
जांच	जाँच	तांगा	ताँगा
दांत	दाँत	मंहगा	महँगा
मांस	माँस	मुंह	मुँह
सांप	साँप	सांस	साँस
हुँकार	हुंकार	निर्पेक्ष	निरपेक्ष
भाष्कर	भास्कर	सन्मुख	सम्मुख
माताहीन	मातृहीन	विद्यार्थि	विद्यार्थी
गुणि	गुणी	द्वैवाषिक	द्विवार्षिक
पूज्यनीय	पूजनीय	अकाश	आकाश
इद	ईद	इसलाम	इस्लाम
ऐसा	ऐसा	दोसरा	दूसरा
पुत्रि	पुत्री	प्रस्तूत	प्रस्तुत
हरयाली	हरियाली	दिवाली	दीवाली
राष्ट्रिय	राष्ट्रीय	एकहरा	इकहरा
एतबार	इतबार		

वाक्यगत अशुद्धियाँ

अशुद्ध	शुद्ध
हम अच्छी भाषण दिए थे।	हमने अच्छा भाषण दिया था।
आप खाए कि नहीं?	आपने खाया कि नहीं?
वह मुझे देखा तो घबरा गया।	उसने मुझे देखा तो घबरा गया।
मैं किताब पढ़ा हूँ।	मैंने किताब पढ़ी है।
मैं सारी पुस्तक पढ़ डाली।	मैंने सारी पुस्तक पढ़ डाली।
सीता भात खायी।	सीता ने भात खाया।
राम रोटी खाया।	राम ने रोटी खायी।
लड़की ने दही गिरा दी।	लड़की ने दही गिरा दिया।
शुद्ध गाय की घी दो।	गाय का शुद्ध घी दो।
तुम, मैं और वह चलेगा।	तुम, वह और मैं चलूँगा।
राम और सीता आयी थी।	राम और सीता आए थे।
भाई-बहन जा रही हैं।	भाई-बहन जा रहे हैं।

अशुद्ध	शुद्ध
वह लड़की को बुलाओ।	उस लड़की को बुलाओ।
मेरे लिए पढ़ता हूँ।	अपने लिए पढ़ता हूँ।
सीता राम की आज्ञाकारी पत्नी थी।	सीता राम की आज्ञाकारिणी पत्नी थीं।
देरी न करना।	देर न करना।
उसे मृत्युदण्ड की सजा मिली।	उसे मृत्युदण्ड मिला।
हमारे शिक्षक प्रश्न पूछते हैं।	हमारे शिक्षक प्रश्न करते हैं।
कै बजे? तीन बजा।	कितना बजा? तीन बजे।
उसका प्राण उड़ गया।	उसके प्राण उड़ गये।
मैंने आँख से देखा।	मैंने आँखों से देखा।
अपन को पढ़ना है।	मुझे पढ़ना है।
पुस्तक फट गया।	पुस्तक फट गई है।
घोड़ी तेज़ दौड़ता है।	घोड़ी तेज दौड़ती है।
मेरा प्रणम स्वीकार करो।	मेरा प्रणाम स्वीकार करो।
दो बालक खेलता है।	दो बालक खेलते हैं।

अशुद्ध	शुद्ध
ये सब मेरा पुस्तक है।	ये सब मेरी पुस्तकें हैं।
सूरज पूरब में उगते हैं।	सूरज पूर्व में उगता है।
वह लौट आए।	वे लौट आए।
वहाँ अनेकों लोग थे।	वहाँ अनेक लोग थे।
मेरे को मत मारो।	मुझे मत मारो।
मोहन ने पत्र को पढ़ा।	मोहन ने पत्र पढ़ा।
पुस्तक पर नहीं लिखो।	पुस्तक पर मत लिखो।
वह सज्जन पुरुष है।	वह सज्जन है।
आप हमारे घर आओ।	आप हमारे घर आइए।
हम आपसे कुछ कहे थे।	हमने आपसे कुछ कहा था।
मकान की दायीं ओर सड़क है।	मकान के दायीं ओर सड़क है।
पिताजी घर नहीं हैं।	पिताजी घर पर नहीं हैं।
घर पर सब कुशल हैं।	घर में सब कुशल हैं।
उसे भारी दुःख हुआ।	उसे बहुत दुःख हुआ।
सड़क में मत खेलो।	सड़क पर मत खेलो।

मुहावरे तथा लोकोक्तियाँ

- अँगूठी का नगीना–अत्यन्त महत्त्वपूर्ण।
- अंधा दरबार–न्यायहीन स्थान।
- अंधेर नगरी–न्याय का अभाव।
- अक्ल का दुश्मन–मूर्ख।
- अक्ल का दुम–मूर्ख।
- आँख का तारा–अतिप्रिय।
- ईद का चाँद–बहुत दिनों के बाद दिखाई देना।
- कछुआ चाल–धीमी गति।
- काला नाग–दुष्ट आदमी।
- किताबी कीड़ा–सदैव कुछ-न-कुछ पढ़ना।
- किस्मत का मारा–भाग्य का मन्द।
- कोल्हू का बैल–बहुत कठिन परिश्रम करनेवाला।
- कोड़ी का तीन–तुच्छ।
- खाली हाथ–पैसे का अभाव।
- गाजर-मूली–अशक्त।
- गुलर का फूल–दुर्लभ वस्तु।
- गोबर-गणेश–निरामूर्ख।
- घर का उजाला–कुल-दीपक।
- घड़ियाली आँसू–बनावटी शोक।
- चलता-पुरजा–चालाक।
- चाँद का टुकड़ा–परम सुन्दर वस्तु या व्यक्ति।
- चाँदी का जूता–रिश्वत।
- चार दिन की चाँदनी–थोड़े समय का सुख।
- जलती आँख–क्रोधाभिभूत।
- जीभ का पतला–लालची।
- टेढ़ी खीर–विकट काम।
- ठिकाने की बात–न्यायसंगत बात।
- अढ़ाई दिन की हुकूमत–थोड़े समय का ऐश्वर्य।
- तकदीर का सिकन्दर–भाग्य का बलवान्।
- थाली का बैंगन–मत बदलते रहना।
- दाँत कटी रोटी–घनिष्ठता।
- दाहिना हाथ–सहायक।
- दिल का बादशाह–बहुत बड़ा उदार।
- दूध का दूध और पानी का पानी–उचित न्याय।
- दूध का धोआ–निर्दोष।
- दो दिन का मेहमान–बहुत थोड़े समय ठहरने वाला।
- धरती का फूल–ऐसा व्यक्ति जो हाल में अमीर हुआ है।
- धोबी का कुत्ता–निकम्मा।
- नसीब का मारा–बुरे दिन देखनेवाला।
- निन्यानबे का फेरा–धन बढ़ाने की चिन्ता।
- पत्थर का कलेजा–हर दुःख सहने की शक्ति।
- पत्थर की लकीर–चिरस्थायी सदा सत्य।
- फूलों की सेज–आनन्ददायक कार्य।
- बगुला-भगत–कपटी व्यक्ति।

- बच्चों का खेल–साधारण काम।
- बलि का बकरा–निःसहाय व्यक्ति।
- बरसाती बादल–अस्थायी।
- बात का पक्का–सत्यवादी।
- बायें हाथ का खेल–सरल काम।
- बिन बादल बरसात–असमय लाभ।
- बे-पेंदी का लोटा–बे ठिकाने का आदमी।
- भागीरथ प्रयत्न–अत्यधिक परिश्रम।
- भीष्म प्रतिज्ञा–दृढ़ संकल्प।
- मक्खी चूस–कंजूस।
- मिट्टी के मोल–बहुत सस्ता।
- मोटा असामी–मूर्ख मालदार।
- राम कहानी–आत्मवृतान्त।
- लँगोटिया यार– बचपन का मित्र।
- हवाई महल–कोरी कल्पना।
- आँख लगना–नींद आना।
- आँख खुलना–होश में आना।
- आँखें दिखाना–क्रोध से घूरना।
- आँसू पोंछना–धैर्य बँधाना।
- अन्धे की लकड़ी–एकमात्र सहारा।
- कान भरना–चुगली करना।
- कान पर जूँ न रेंगना–कोई असर न होना।
- नाक कटना–प्रतिष्ठा खत्म होना।
- नाक रगड़ना–दीनता दिखाना।
- नाकों चने चबवाना–खूब सताना।
- मुँह की खाना–बुरी तरह हारना।
- आस्तीन का साँप–विश्वासघाती मित्र।
- कन्धे से कन्धा मिलाना–पूरा सहयोग करना।
- ईंट से ईंट बजाना–पूरी तरह नष्ट कर देना।
- नौ दो ग्यारह होना–भाग जाना।
- दाँत खट्टे करना–बुरी तरह हराना।
- हाथ मलना–पछताना।
- खून का प्यासा–जानी दुश्मन।
- घी के दिए जलाना–खुशी मनाना।
- चार चाँद लगाना–प्रतिष्ठा बढ़ाना।
- तीन तेरह होना–अलग-अलग होना।
- पानी फेर देना–नाश कर देना।
- गाल बजाना–डींगे मारना।
- जान से हाथ धो बैठना–मारा जाना।
- पानी-पानी होना–बहुत लज्जित होना।
- फूला न समाना–बहुत प्रसन्न होना।
- अपना उल्लू सीधा करना–अपना मतलब निकालना।
- आँखें चुरा लेना–अनदेखा कर देना।
- अन्धे की लाठी–एकमात्र सहारा।
- आसमान पर चढ़ना–बहुत अभिमान करना।
- आँखें खुलना–होश आना।
- चोरी और सीना जोरी–दोषी होकर धमकाना।
- आग में घी डालना–क्रोध को भड़काना।
- अँगुली पर नचाना– अच्छी तरह वश में करना।
- एक आँख से देखना–समान दृष्टि से देखना।
- एक ही थैले के चट्टे-बट्टे–एक जैसे।
- ओखली में सिर देना–जान-बूझकर आपत्ति मोल लेना।
- कलेजा मुँह को आना–बहुत दुःखी होना।
- कफन बाँधकर चलना–मौत से न घबराना।
- काँटे बिछाना–बाधा डालना।
- कलेजा ठण्डा होना–सन्तोष होना।
- कमर कसना–तैयार होना।
- खून खौलना–जोश में आना।
- खाक छानना–मारे-मारे फिरना।
- गागर में सागर भरना–थोड़े शब्दों में बहुत कुछ कह देना।
- घाव पर नमक छिड़कना–दुखी को अधिक दुखी करना।
- घी के दिए जलाना–खुशी मनाना।
- घोड़े बेचकर सोना–गहरी नींद में सोना।
- चल बसना–परलोक सिधारना।
- छठी का दूध याद आना–भारी संकट में पड़ना।
- छाती पर साँप लोटना–बहुत ईर्ष्या होना।
- जमीन पर पैर न रखना–अधिक घमण्ड होना।
- झक मारना–व्यर्थ समय खोना।
- टेढ़ी खीर–कठिन काम।
- डींग मारना–अपनी झूठी प्रशंसा करना।
- डूब मरना–बहुत लज्जित होना।
- तलवे चाटना–चापलूसी करना।
- ताक में रहना–मौका ढूँढ़ते रहना।
- दंग रह जाना–आश्चर्य में पड़ जाना।
- दाल न गलना–वश न चलना।
- दाल में काला होना–संदेह होना।
- पीठ दिखाना–हारकर भागना।
- मुँह तोड़ उत्तर देना–खरा उत्तर देना।

वस्तुनिष्ठ प्रश्न

अभ्यास-1

निर्देशः *नीचे प्रत्येक शुद्ध शब्द की वर्तनी के लिए चार विकल्प दिए गए हैं। आपको सही विकल्प का चयन करना है।*

1. A. ऋषि B. ऋषी C. रिषी D. ऋसि

2. A. विषेसन B. विशेषण C. विसेशन D. विशेशन

3. A. दुशासन B. दुसाशन C. दूशाषण D. दुःशासन

4. A. संस्कृति B. संसकृति C. संष्कृति D. संस्कृती

5. A. दूनियां B. दुनियां C. दुनिया D. दूनिआ

6. A. टिपनी B. टिप्पणि C. टिप्पणी D. टिप्पनी

7. A. शाषण B. साशन C. शासन D. शाशन

8. A. किसमस B. किरसमस C. क्रिसमूस D. कृसमस

9. A. अनुग्रहित B. अनुग्रहीत C. अनुगृहीत D. अनुग्रहिति

10. A. पराकम B. प्राक्रम C. पराक्रम D. प्राकर्म

11. A. नायका B. नाइका C. नाइक D. नायिका

12. A. समरिधी B. समद्धी C. समृद्धि D. समरिद्धि

13. A. युधिष्ठर B. यूधिष्ठर C. युधिष्ठिर D. युधिष्टर

14. A. वाल्मीकि B. बाल्मीकि C. बालमीकि D. बाल्मिक

15. A. परलोकिक B. प्रलौकिक C. पारलौकिक D. परलौकिक

16. A. त्रितीय B. तर्तीय C. तृतीय D. तिरतीय

17. A. व्योहार B. व्यौहार C. व्यवहार D. ब्यवहार

18. A. अहिल्या B. अहल्या C. अहिलया D. अहीलया

19. A. आदरनीय B. आदरणीय C. आदरनीया D. आदरणीया

20. A. आर्द B. आद्र C. आर्द्र D. आर्दृ

21. A. आधीन B. अधिन C. अधीन D. अधीम

22. A. आविस्कार B. आविष्कार C. आवीस्कार D. आविश्कार

23. A. आसा B. आषा C. आशा D. अशा

24. A. उज्वल B. उजज्ज्वल C. उजज्वल D. उज्ज्वल

25. A. उन्नती B. उन्नित C. उन्नति D. उन्नती

26. A. कलस B. कलष C. कलश D. कलशा

27. A. गनीत B. गनित C. गणीत D. गणित

28. A. तलाव B. तालाव C. तलाब D. तालाब

29. A. दुष्ट B. दूष्ट C. दुस्त D. दुश्त

30. A. निरोग B. निररोग C. नीरोग D. नीरोगी

उत्तरमाला

1. A	**2.** B	**3.** D	**4.** A	**5.** C
6. C	**7.** C	**8.** C	**9.** C	**10.** C
11. D	**12.** C	**13.** C	**14.** A	**15.** C
16. C	**17.** C	**18.** B	**19.** B	**20.** C
21. C	**22.** B	**23.** C	**24.** D	**25.** C
26. C	**27.** D	**28.** D	**29.** A	**30.** C

अभ्यास-2

निर्देशः *नीचे कुछ शब्द दिए गए हैं। प्रत्येक के पर्यायवाची के चार विकल्प दिए गए हैं। इनमें से एक विकल्प सही पर्यायवाची है, उसका चयन कीजिए :*

1. अग्नि

A. अनिल B. अनल C. गर्म D. ताप

2. अमृत

A. पीयूष B. गरल C. सरस D. जीवनदायनी

3. आँख
A. लोचन B. आस्थि
C. वदन D. जलज

4. आकाश
A. अनन्त B. पाताल
C. वितल D. तल

5. कपड़ा
A. परिधान B. पटिका
C. पीताम्बर D. लँहगा

6. कमल
A. सरोज B. सरोवर
C. पंक D. पुष्प

7. गंगा
A. पाताल नदी B. हिमनदी
C. भागीरथ D. त्रिपथगा

8. चाँद
A. मयंक B. भानु
C. दिनकर D. रवि

9. नदी
A. सरिता B. प्रवाह
C. धारा D. जलधर

10. पर्वत
A. पत्थर B. चट्टान
C. शिखर D. मेरू

11. पवन
A. अनिल B. अनल
C. अग D. विहग

12. पति
A. साजन B. प्रिया
C. भार्या D. दारा

13. पानी
A. मही B. मेदिनी
C. अम्बु D. तरणी

14. पुत्र
A. आत्मज B. तनया
C. सुता D. आत्मजा

15. पुत्री
A. सुता B. सुत
C. आत्मज D. नन्दन

16. फूल
A. बहार B. मधु
C. माधव D. सुमन

17. वृक्ष
A. विटप B. अभ्र
C. प्रसून D. रसा

18. बादल
A. अज B. व्यामोह
C. नीरद D. मधुप

19. बिजली
A. चंचला B. खटका
C. त्रास D. संत्रास

20. माता
A. धात्री B. धरणी
C. धरित्री D. श्यामा

21. घोषणा
A. आवाज B. पुकारना
C. ऐलान D. ललकारना

22. उत्कर्ष
A. आकर्षण B. विकर्षण
C. उन्नति D. निष्कर्ष

23. उदय
A. अन्त B. विकास
C. प्रगट D. व्यस्त

24. दक्ष
A. निपुण B. समर्थ
C. कर्मठ D. मेहनती

25. संवाद
A. विवाद B. झगड़ा
C. सम्बोधन D. वार्तालाप

उत्तरमाला

1. B	**2.** A	**3.** A	**4.** A	**5.** A
6. A	**7.** D	**8.** A	**9.** A	**10.** D
11. A	**12.** A	**13.** C	**14.** A	**15.** A
16. D	**17.** A	**18.** C	**19.** A	**20.** A
21. C	**22.** C	**23.** C	**24.** A	**25.** D

अभ्यास-3

निर्देशः *नीचे चार-चार शब्दों के समूह दिए गए हैं। प्रत्येक समूह में एक शब्द बेमेल है तथा शेष तीन शब्द पर्यायवाची हैं, आपको उस शब्द का चयन करना है, जो बेमेल है :*

1. A. तम B. अंधकार
C. तिमिर D. अंश

2. A. अनल B. आग
C. दहन D. तमिस्त्रा

3. A. अतुल B. अद्वितीय
C. अनुपम D. शुष्मा

4. A. अहं B. अहंकार
C. दर्प D. निराला

5. A. पता B. खोज
C. जाँच D. शोध

6. A. गरल B. पीयूष
C. सुधा D. सोम

7. A. कानन B. जंगल
C. पादप D. वन

8. A. अश्व B. गज
C. घोड़ा D. तुरंग

9. A. दानव B. मानव
C. दैत्य D. राक्षस

10. A. आँख B. चक्षु
C. नयन D. मुख

11. A. अन्तरिक्ष B. वसुन्धरा
C. आसमान D. गगन

12. A. इच्छा B. अभिलाषा
C. कामना D. प्रयोजन

13. A. कपड़ा B. चीर
C. वसन D. पोशाक

14. A. अब्ज B. कमल
C. राजीव D. आम्र

15. A. कोयल B. पिक
C. काग D. वनप्रिय

16. A. गंगा B. देवनदी
C. गोदावरी D. भागीरथी

17. A. गणेश B. एकदन्त
C. देवराज D. गणपति

18. A. घर B. निलय
C. निकेतन D. झोपड़ी

19. A. चाँद B. हिमांशु
C. विनायक D. सुधांशु

20. A. नदी B. तरणी
C. तटिनी D. सरिता

21. A. पक्षी B. चिड़िया
C. सुमन D. विहग

22. A. पवन B. अचला
C. वात D. वायु

23. A. समीर B. पृथ्वी
C. भू D. भूमि

24. A. पानी B. समीर
C. अम्बु D. जल

25. A. पुत्र B. तनया
C. तनय D. सुत

26. A. पुत्र B. तनया
C. सुता D. कन्या

27. A. गृहिणी B. आदमी
C. पुरुष D. नर

28. A. मधु B. फूल
C. पुष्प D. सुमन

29. A. माधव B. तरु
C. पेड़ D. वृक्ष

30. A. माता B. अम्बु
C. अम्मा D. जननी

उत्तरमाला

1. D	2. D	3. D	4. D	5. A
6. A	7. C	8. B	9. B	10. D
11. B	12. D	13. D	14. D	15. C
16. C	17. C	18. D	19. C	20. B
21. C	22. B	23. A	24. B	25. B
26. A	27. A	28. A	29. A	30. B

अभ्यास-4

निर्देशः *गहरे काले शब्द के विलोम शब्द का चयन कीजिए:*

1. उसे हर काम में **सफलता** मिल रही है।
A. असफलता B. सफल
C. कुशलता D. निपुणता

2. कभी किसी की **निन्दा** नहीं करनी चाहिए।
A. गुणगान B. स्तुति
C. प्रशंसा D. यशोगान

3. आलस्य व्यक्ति का सबसे बड़ा **दुश्मन** है।
A. शत्रु B. घातक
C. मित्र D. सहायक

4. वे बुढ़ापे से **दुखी** हैं।
A. अप्रसन्न B. सुखी
C. खुश D. नाराज

5. यहाँ उसकी **चतुराई** नहीं चली।
A. चालाकी B. बहादुरी
C. निपुणता D. मूर्खता

6. शहद की **मिठास** कम नहीं होती।
A. मीठा B. तीखा
C. कडुवा D. खट्टा

7. साहसी के **साहस** को देखकर मैं चकित रह गया।
A. हिम्मत B. बहादुरी
C. निडर D. भय

8. फिल्मोत्सव में सर्वश्रेष्ठ **अभिनेता** को पुरस्कार प्रदान किया गया।
A. हीरोइन B. नेत्री
C. मीनाक्षी D. अभिनेत्री

9. नाटक में नायक और **नायिका** की भूमिका महत्वपूर्ण होती है:
A. हीरो B. नायक
C. नेत्र D. नेता

10. कवि-सम्मेलन में एक कवि और एक **कवयित्री** को आमंत्रित किया गया था।
A. लेखक B. सम्पादक
C. नेता D. कवि

11. विद्यालय के वार्षिकोत्सव के लिए नेता और एक **नेत्री** को आमंत्रित किया गया।
A. अभिनेता B. विद्वान्
C. विदुषी D. नेता

12. **मोहन बहुत चतुर है।**
A. निपुण B. तेज
C. सुस्त D. मूर्ख

13. सोहन अब पूर्ण **स्वस्थ** है।
A. प्रसन्न B. खुश
C. अस्वस्थ D. अप्रसन्न

14. पक्षी **आकाश** में उड़ते हैं :
A. गगन B. नभ
C. धरती D. पाताल

15. वह विद्यालय में देर से आया और **अनुपस्थित** हो गया।
A. पूर्व B. उपस्थित
C. प्रवेश D. समयपूर्व

16. **बालक** चाँद की ओर देख रहा है।
A. बालिका B. लड़का
C. बच्चा D. बच्ची

17. मैं उसके विचार से बिल्कुल **सहमत** नहीं हूँ।
A. समर्थन B. सहमति
C. असहमत D. प्रशंसक

18. उसकी हालत **अधिक** खराब है।
A. बहुत B. कम
C. ठीक D. कुशल

19. **धर्म** की सर्वत्र विजय होती है:
A. अधर्म B. ज्ञान
C. भक्ति D. ईमानदारी

20. अच्छे चरित्र के बिना जीवन **निरर्थक** है:
A. व्यर्थ B. अर्थपूर्ण
C. सार्थक D. कुशल

21. **ईमानदारी** बड़ी दुर्लभ वस्तु है:
A. सच्चाई B. भलाई
C. बेइमानी D. परोपकारी

22. एवरेस्ट संसार का सबसे **ऊँचा** पर्वत है:
A. नीचा B. वितल
C. पाताल D. मध्यम

23. वह विश्वास के **योग्य** नहीं है:
A. काबिल B. विश्वासी
C. अयोग्य D. बेकार

24. क्या वह इतना **मूर्ख** है?
A. चालाक B. विद्वान्
C. बुद्धिमान D. धूर्त

25. कितना सुहावना **दृश्य** है!
A. अदृश्य B. दर्शनीय
C. सुन्दर D. व्यर्थ

उत्तरमाला

1. A	2. C	3. C	4. B	5. D
6. C	7. D	8. D	9. B	10. D
11. D	12. D	13. C	14. D	15. B
16. A	17. C	18. B	19. A	20. C
21. C	22. A	23. C	24. C	25. A

अभ्यास-5

निर्देशः नीचे प्रत्येक **काले गहरे शब्द** के चार विलोम दिए गए हैं। इनमें सही विलोम का चयन कीजिए :

1. अग्नि
A. आग B. अनल
C. दहन D. जल

2. अग्रज
A. अनुज B. भ्राता
C. भाई D. अम्बा

3. अच्छा
A. बुरा B. खराब
C. गंदा D. भ्रष्ट

4. अंत
A. प्रारम्भ B. समाप्त
C. शेष D. अल्प

5. अचल
A. विचल B. वितल
C. सजल D. चल

6. अति
A. अधिक B. बहुत
C. अल्प D. कम

7. अत्यधिक
A. अल्प B. अधिक
C. स्वल्प D. न्यूनतम

8. अंधकार
A. अंधेरा B. प्रकाश
C. रात्रि D. दिन

9. अतिवृष्टि
A. अनावृष्टि B. वृष्टि
C. वर्षा D. वर्षण

10. अनाथ
A. नाथ B. स्वामी
C. मासिक D. सनाथ

11. अनुकूल
A. मनोकूल B. प्रतिकूल
C. अनुकरण D. मनस्वी

12. अनुराग
A. राग B. विराग
C. विग्रह D. स्नेह

13. अन्त
A. श्री गणेश B. आदि
C. शुरुआत D. समाप्त

14. अपना
A. अपनत्व B. पराया
C. मित्र D. शत्रु

15. अपमान
A. मान B. सम्मान
C. वर्तमान D. स्वाभिमान

16. अपेक्षा
A. इच्छा B. स्वेच्छा
C. प्रविच्छा D. उपेक्षा

17. अमर
A. मर्त्य B. मृत्यु
C. सुधा D. गरल

18. अल्पायु
A. चिरायु B. उमरदराज
C. नश्वर D. सनातन

19. अस्त
A. उदय B. विकास
C. निर्माण D. सृष्टि

20. आकर्षण
A. प्रतिकर्षण B. विकर्षण
C. सम्मोहन D. विरत

21. आकाश
A. गगन B. नभ
C. वसुन्धरा D. पाताल

22. आगे
A. पीछे B. पूर्व
C. पृष्ट D. पृष्ठ

23. आजाद
A. स्वतंत्र B. स्वतंत्रतता
C. परतंत्र D. गुलाम

24. आदान
A. आयात B. निर्यात
C. प्रदान D. निदान

25. आधुनिक
A. अर्वाचीन B. नूतन
C. प्राचीन D. वर्तमान

उत्तरमाला

1. D	**2.** A	**3.** A	**4.** A	**5.** D
6. D	**7.** C	**8.** B	**9.** A	**10.** D
11. B	**12.** B	**13.** A	**14.** B	**15.** B
16. D	**17.** A	**18.** A	**19.** A	**20.** B
21. D	**22.** A	**23.** D	**24.** C	**25.** C

अभ्यास-6

निर्देशः *नीचे कुछ शब्द दिए गए हैं प्रत्येक शब्द के चार वैकल्पिक अर्थ दिए गए हैं। सही अर्थ का चयन कीजिए :*

1. सुरक्षित
A. कुशल B. घटना
C. दुर्घटना D. बचाव

2. प्रतिभाशाली
A. सज्जन B. कुशाग्र
C. विद्वान् D. वैभवशाली

3. आत्मसमर्पण
A. अपने आप को सौंपना B. समर्पण
C. अर्पण D. त्यागज

4. सिद्धहस्त
A. निपुण B. कर्मठ
C. मेहनती D. परिश्रमी

5. सुशोभित
A. मजेदार B. सुस्वागतम्
C. अच्छा D. शोभा पाना

6. स्वादिष्ट
A. मजेदार B. बेकार
C. मीठा D. तीखा

7. **स्वावलम्बी**
A. निर्भर B. परालंबी
C. आत्मनिर्भर D. अतिथि

8. **उपकरण**
A. साधन B. युक्ति
C. यंत्र D. मशीन

9. **कीमत**
A. क्रय B. विक्रय
C. मूल्य D. बिक्री

10. **संगठन**
A. एकता B. अनेकता
C. समूह D. संस्था

11. **विपत्ति**
A. दुख B. विपदा
C. मुसीबत D. सुख

12. **तृण**
A. तिनका B. धूल
C. धूप D. लकड़ी

13. **आश्चर्य**
A. निरीक्षण B. दृष्टिगोचर
C. हैरानी D. थकावट

14. **हार्दिक**
A. हृदय से B. शरीर से
C. मन से D. मस्तिष्क से

15. **नियति**
A. भाग्य B. किनारा
C. समय D. पवित्र

16. **सुगन्धित**
A. दुर्गन्ध B. खुशबू वाला
C. फूल D. कमल

17. **उत्साह**
A. होश B. हवास
C. जोश D. हिम्मत

18. **सहयोग**
A. मिलन सार B. मेहनती
C. परोपकारी D. आपसी सहायता

19. **मुसीबत**
A. विपत्ति B. सुशोभित
C. सहायता D. मदद

20. **निरक्षर**
A. साक्षर B. दर्शनीय
C. पठनीय D. अनपढ़

21. **उपवन**
A. वन B. तीर
C. जंगल D. बाग

22. **मेघ**
A. बादल B. पंकज
C. राजीव D. मेघनाद

23. **आधुनिक**
A. प्राचीन B. पुरातन
C. भूतकाल D. आज का

24. **तीर**
A. वाण B. धनुष
C. किनारा D. नदी

25. **परीक्षण**
A. जाँच B. पड़ताल
C. परीक्षा D. इम्तहान

26. **अभिवादन**
A. नमस्ते B. प्रणाम
C. बधाई D. शुभकामना

27. **सर्वत्र**
A. नश्वर B. सजीव
C. ईश्वर D. सभी जगह

28. **हलवाहा**
A. चरवाहा B. किसान
C. मजदूर D. हल चलाने वाला

29. **शिखर**
A. पर्वत B. पहाड़
C. टीला D. चोटी

30. **भयानक**
A. डरावना B. भयभीत
C. डरना D. खूँखार

उत्तरमाला

1. D	2. B	3. A	4. A	5. D
6. A	7. C	8. C	9. C	10. A
11. C	12. A	13. C	14. A	15. A
16. B	17. C	18. D	19. A	20. D
21. D	22. A	23. D	24. A	25. A
26. B	27. D	28. D	29. D	30. A

अभ्यास-7

निर्देशः *नीचे कुछ शब्द दिए जा रहे हैं। प्रत्येक शब्द के* **उपसर्ग** *के सन्दर्भ में चार विकल्प दिए गए हैं। आपको सही विकल्प का चयन करना है :*

1. अलबत्ता
A. अ B. अल
C. लब D. त्ता

2. अलगरज
A. अल B. लग
C. गर D. रज

3. कमसिन
A. क B. कम
C. सि D. सिन
4. अनमोल
A. अ B. अन
C. मो D. मोल
5. अनजान
A. अ B. अन
C. जा D. जान
6. अनपढ़
A. अ B. पढ़
C. प D. अन
7. अधखिला
A. अ B. अध
C. ला D. खिला
8. अधजला
A. अ B. ज
C. अध D. ला
9. अधपका
A. अ B. अध
C. पका D. का
10. अघखिला
A. अ B. अघ
C. खिला D. ला
11. उन्नीस
A. उन B. उन्
C. नीस D. स
12. उनसठ
A. उ B. उन
C. सठ D. ठ
13. दुकाल
A. द B. दुक
C. दु D. काल
14. दुबला
A. दब B. दुब
C. ला D. दु
15. निकम्मा
A. नि B. निक
C. कम्मा D. मा
16. निर्लज्ज
A. निर B. निल
C. नि D. लज्ज
17. बिनब्याहा
A. बि B. बिन
C. ब्याहा D. हा
18. भरपेट
A. भर B. पेट
C. पे D. ट
19. भरपाई
A. भ B. र
C. पा D. भर
20. कुपात्र
A. कु B. कुप
C. पा D. पात्र
21. सुजान
A. सु B. सुज
C. सुजा D. जान
22. गैर कानूनी
A. गै B. गैर
C. कानु D. नुनी
23. गैरसरकारी
A. गैर B. सर
C. का D. कारी
24. अपमान
A. अ B. अप
C. मा D. मान
25. अनुशासन
A. अ B. शासन
C. सन D. अनु
26. अविनीत
A. अवि B. अ
C. नी D. नीत
27. अभिमान
A. अभि B. अ
C. मा D. मान
28. अभियान
A. अ B. मान
C. यान D. अभि
29. अध्ययन
A. अध् B. अधि
C. यन D. न
30. निश्चल
A. नि B. निर
C. निस D. चल

उत्तरमाला

1. B	2. A	3. B	4. B	5. B
6. D	7. B	8. C	9. B	10. B
11. A	12. B	13. C	14. D	15. B
16. A	17. B	18. A	19. D	20. A
21. A	22. B	23. A	24. B	25. D
26. B	27. A	28. D	29. B	30. A

अभ्यास-8

निर्देशः *निम्नलिखित शब्दों में प्रयुक्त प्रत्यय सम्बन्धी चार विकल्प दिए गए हैं, सही विकल्प का चयन कीजिए :*

1. भलाई
A. ई B. लाई
C. आई D. भला

2. चतुराई
A. चतु B. रा
C. ई D. आई

3. भूखा
A. भू B. भूख
C. खा D. आ

4. भिड़न्त
A. भिड् B. भि
C. न्त D. अन्त

5. प्यासा
A. आस B. सा
C. आसा D. सा

6. बिकाऊ
A. बिक B. काऊ
C. आऊ D. ऊ

7. तैराक
A. तै B. तैर
C. राक D. आक

8. सन्नाटा
A. सन् B. सन्ना
C. नाटा D. आटा

9. लोहार
A. लोह B. आरा
C. आरी D. आर

10. मिलान
A. आना B. आने
C. आनी D. आन

11. चढ़ाव
A. चढ़ B. चढ़ा
C. आव D. व

12. लगाव
A. लग B. अव
C. आव D. गाव

13. लिखावट
A. लिख B. लिखा
C. वट D. आवट

14. मिलावट
A. मिल B. वट
C. आवट D. ट

15. मिठास
A. मिठ B. ठास
C. आस D. स

16. चिकनाहट
A. चिक B. नाट्ट
C. हट D. आहट

17. सड़ियल
A. सड़ B. यल
C. ड़ियल D. इयल

18. मरियल
A. मर B. यल
C. मरि D. इयल

19. गड़रिया
A. गड़ B. इया
C. रिया D. या

20. सजीला
A. ईला B. इला
C. ला D. स

21. लुटेरा
A. लुट B. एरा
C. ऐरा D. रा

22. लठैत
A. ए B. ऐ
C. ऐत D. त

23. भगोड़ा
A. ओ B. ओड़ा
C. ड़ा D. भगो

24. खपत
A. ख B. प
C. त D. पत

25. जीवट
A. व B. अट
C. जीव D. जी

उत्तरमाला

1. C	**2.** D	**3.** D	**4.** D	**5.** D
6. C	**7.** D	**8.** D	**9.** D	**10.** D
11. C	**12.** C	**13.** D	**14.** C	**15.** C
16. D	**17.** D	**18.** D	**19.** B	**20.** A
21. B	**22.** C	**23.** B	**24.** C	**25.** B

अभ्यास-9

निर्देशः *नीचे कुछ मुहावरे दिए गए हैं। प्रत्येक के अर्थ के लिए चार विकल्प दिए गए हैं। आपको सही विकल्प का चयन करना है :*

1. अक्ल पर पत्थर पड़ना
A. बुद्धि काम न करना B. दुविधा होना
C. संकट में होना D. परेशान होना

2. अपना उल्लू सीधा करना
A. अवसर देखना B. काम निकालना
C. मतलब साधना D. मूर्ख बनाना

3. अपने मुँह मियाँ-मिट्ठू बनना
A. मिठाई खाना B. प्रशंसा करना
C. निंदा करना D. अपनी प्रशंसा स्वयं करना

4. अपने पाँव पर आप कुल्हाड़ी मारना
A. हानि पहुँचाना B. खेद होना
C. अपना पैर काटना D. अपनी हानि स्वयं करना

5. आँखें चुरा लेना
A. भाग जाना B. छिप जाना
C. अनदेखा करना D. मिल जाना

6. अक्ल का दुश्मन
A. मित्र होना B. शत्रु होना
C. महामूर्ख D. महाविद्वान्

7. अंधे की लाठी
A. एक मात्र सहारा B. मित्र होना
C. शत्रु होना D. दुख पहुँचाना

8. आकाश-पाताल एक करना
A. भाग-दौड़ करना B. परेशान होना
C. थक जाना D. कठिन परिश्रम करना

9. घड़ों पानी पड़ना
A. लज्जित होना B. तुच्छ समझना
C. लाभ होना D. थकावट

10. अगर-मगर करना
A. नुकसान करना B. बहाने बनाना
C. बदनाम करना D. कपट करना

11. मुँह की खाना
A. गिर जाना B. हार जाना
C. भाग जाना D. व्यर्थ होना

12. आस्तीन का साँप होना
A. शत्रु B. मित्र
C. कपटी मित्र D. दयालु

13. एक आँख से देखना
A. बुरा व्यवहार B. समान व्यवहार
C. कपट करना D. लज्जित होना

14. बाल-बाँका न होना
A. घायल होना B. साफ बच जाना
C. क्रोधित होना D. स्वस्थ होना

15. दाँतों तले उँगली दबाना
A. उँगली काटना B. चिंतित हो जाना
C. चकित रह जाना D. प्रसन्न हो जाना

16. जान के लाले पड़ना
A. मरने का खतरा होना B. भाग जाना
C. हार जाना D. मुश्किल में पड़ना

17. बोली मारना
A. ताना देना B. सताना
C. मजाक करना D. याद दिलाना

18. अंधों में काना राजा
A. मूर्खों में अल्पज्ञ को विद्वान् माना जाना
B. सबको मूर्ख समझना
C. अत्यधिक महत्त्वपूर्ण
D. काना राजा

19. अक्ल के घोड़े दौड़ाना
A. बुद्धि लड़ाना
B. कल्पना करना
C. तरह-तरह के उपाय सोचना
D. ज्ञान-प्राप्त करना

20. पानी उतर जाना
A. शर्म करना B. लज्जित न होना
C. भाग जाना D. इज्जत करना

21. तीन-पाँच करना
A. तितर-बितर करना
B. वचन देकर फिर जाना
C. घुमा-फिरा कर बातें करना
D. परेशान करना

22. हथियार डाल देना
A. हार जाना B. जीत जाना
C. धोखा देना D. विजय होना

23. आँख खुलना
A. होश में आना B. अत्यन्त प्यार होना
C. उल्टा काम करना D. क्रोध करना

24. कमर सीधी करना
A. थक जाना B. थकावट दूर करना
C. काम करना D. परिश्रम करना

25. पगड़ी रखना
A. चैन की सांस लेना B. अपमान करना
C. दया की भीख माँगना D. अपमान होना

26. लोहा मानना
A. संघर्ष करना B. विजय होना
C. श्रेष्ठता स्वीकार करना D. खुशामद करना

27. काठ मार जाना
A. दुःखी होना B. चुप होना
C. सफल होना D. मर जाना

28. चाँद पर थूकना

A. अपमान करना

B. बढ़कर बातें करना

C. महान पुरुष पर लांछन लगाना

D. महत्त्वाकांक्षी होना

29. उगल देना

A. अपराध स्वीकार कर लेना

B. सच बोलना

C. उल्टी करना

D. अनपच होना

30. हाथ मलना

A. पश्चाताप करना B. सर्दी मिटाना

C. दुख करना D. तैयार होना

उत्तरमाला

1. A	**2.** C	**3.** D	**4.** D	**5.** C
6. C	**7.** A	**8.** D	**9.** A	**10.** B
11. B	**12.** C	**13.** B	**14.** B	**15.** C
16. D	**17.** A	**18.** A	**19.** A	**20.** B
21. C	**22.** A	**23.** A	**24.** B	**25.** C
26. C	**27.** B	**28.** C	**29.** A	**30.** A

अभ्यास-10

निर्देशः *नीचे कुछ वाक्य खण्ड दिए गए हैं, पूरे वाक्य खण्ड के लिए एक शब्द का चयन कीजिए।*

1. जिसका आदि न हो

A. अनंत B. अमर

C. शाश्वत D. अनादि

2. जो कुछ न जानता हो

A. मूर्ख B. महामूर्ख

C. ज्ञानी D. अज्ञ

3. जो अनुकरण करने योग्य हो

A. अनुकरणीय B. अद्वितीय

C. आदरणीय D. अगम

4. जिसका अंत न हो

A. अनंत B. अनादि

C. आदि D. परलोक

5. जो कभी न मरे

A. मर्त्य B. मुर्त्त

C. अर्मुत्त D. अमर

6. जिसके समान दूसरा न हो

A. अनुकूल B. प्रतिकूल

C. कृतज्ञ D. अद्वितीय

7. जो कम बोलता हो

A. मृदुभाषी B. वाचाल

C. अल्पभाषी D. अल्पज्ञ

8. जिसका इलाज न हो

A. मरणशील B. अमरत्व

C. ब्रिमारी D. लाइलाज

9. जिस का विश्वास न किया जा सके

A. विश्वसनीय B. अविश्वसनीय

C. विश्वासी D. धूर्त्त

10. जिसका कोई नाथ न हो

A. सनाथ B. स्वामी

C. नाथ D. अनाथ

11. कम जानने वाला

A. अल्पज्ञ B. अज्ञ

C. विद् D. विद्वान

12. जहाँ जाना संभव न हो

A. दुर्गम B. अगम

C. तल D. वितल

13. कम खाने वाला

A. बहुभोजी B. पेटु

C. कंजूस D. अल्पाहारी

14. जो बात पहले कभी न हुई हो

A. भूतपूर्व B. अभूतपूर्व

C. प्राचीन D. अर्वाचीन

15. जिस स्त्री के सन्तान न हों

A. बाँझ B. कुलटा

C. पतिता D. विधवा

16. जो कहा न जा सके

A. अकथनीय B. अकथ्य

C. करणीय D. सम्भव

17. एहसान न मानने वाला

A. कृतज्ञ B. कृतघ्न

C. आस्तिक D. विश्वासी

18. जिसने देश के साथ विश्वासघात किया हो

A. विश्वासघाती B. द्रोही

C. आतंकवादी D. देश द्रोही

19. जिसने राष्ट्र के हित में अपना जीवन बलिदान कर दिया हो

A. देशभक्त B. शहीद

C. राष्ट्रभूत D. भारतपुत्र

20. वह जमीन जिसमें कुछ भी पैदा न हो

A. ऊसर B. बंजर

C. उर्वर D. पथरीला

21. वह वस्तु जिसकी चाह हो

A. श्रेष्ठ B. आवश्यक

C. इच्छित D. अभीष्ट

22. दूसरों के पीछे चलने वाला
A. अनुयायी B. अनुज
C. अनुचर D. अनुकरणीय

23. जो पहले न पढ़ा हो
A. पठित B. अपठित
C. पठनीय D. अपठनीय

24. जिसके आर-पार दिखाई देता हो
A. अपारदर्शी B. गम्य
C. अगम्य D. पारदर्शी

25. आज्ञा पालन करने वाला
A. शिष्य B. शिष्या
C. अनुचर D. आज्ञाकारी

26. काम से जी चुराने वाला
A. कामचोर B. आलसी
C. कर्मठ D. परिश्रमी

27. प्रतिदिन होने वाला
A. दैनिक B. शाश्वत
C. सनातन D. अमर

28. जिसका कोई अर्थ न हो
A. सार्थक B. निरर्थक
C. आर्थिक D. अनार्थिक

29. उपकार मानने वाला
A. कृतज्ञ B. कृतघ्न
C. विश्वासी D. अनुयायी

30. हाथ से लिखा हुआ
A. पठनीय B. अपठनीय
C. स्पष्ट D. हस्तलिखित

उत्तरमाला

1. D	**2.** D	**3.** A	**4.** A	**5.** D
6. D	**7.** C	**8.** D	**9.** B	**10.** D
11. A	**12.** A	**13.** D	**14.** B	**15.** A
16. A	**17.** B	**18.** D	**19.** B	**20.** A
21. C	**22.** C	**23.** B	**24.** D	**25.** D
26. A	**27.** A	**28.** B	**29.** A	**30.** D

अभ्यास-11

निर्देशः *नीचे कुछ संज्ञा शब्द दिए जा रहे हैं। प्रत्येक के संज्ञा-भेद के लिए चार विकल्प दिए गये है। सही विकल्प का चयन कीजिए :*

1. तुलसीदास
A. जातिवाचक B. भाववाचक
C. व्यक्तिवाचक D. समूहवाचक

2. यमुना
A. व्यक्तिवाचक B. जातिवाचक
C. समूहवाचक D. भाववाचक

3. बच्चा
A. जातिवाचक B. समूहवाचक
C. भाववाचक D. व्यक्तिवाचक

4. मानवता
A. भाववाचक B. जातिवाचक
C. द्रव्यवाचक D. समूहवाचक

5. हिमालय
A. व्यक्तिवाचक B. जातिवाचक
C. भाववाचक D. समूहवाचक

6. भारत
A. जातिवाचक B. भाववाचक
C. व्यक्तिवाचक D. समूहवाचक

7. एशिया
A. व्यक्तिवाचक B. भाववाचक
C. द्रव्यवाचक D. समूहवाचक

8. महाराष्ट्र
A. जातिवाचक B. व्यक्तिवाचक
C. समूहवाचक D. द्रव्यवाचक

9. सूर सागर
A. व्यक्तिवाचक B. भाववाचक
C. द्रव्यवाचक D. समूहवाचक

10. सोमवार
A. जातिवाचक B. व्यक्तिवाचक
C. द्रव्यवाचक D. समूहवाचक

11. खटमल
A. जातिवाचक B. व्यक्तिवाचक
C. द्रव्यवाचक D. समूहवाचक

12. मैना
A. जातिवाचक B. व्यक्तिवाचक
C. द्रव्यवाचक D. समूहवाचक

13. चाँदी
A. द्रव्यवाचक B. समूहवाचक
C. भाववाचक D. व्यक्तिवाचक

14. अच्छाई
A. भाववाचक B. समूहवाचक
C. जातिवाचक D. व्यक्तिवाचक

15. पीतल
A. द्रव्यवाचक B. भाववाचक
C. व्यक्तिवाचक D. जातिवाचक

16. वीरता
A. भाववाचक B. जातिवाचक
C. द्रव्यवाचक D. समूहवाचक

17. रूस
A. जातिवाचक B. व्यक्तिवाचक
C. भाववाचक D. द्रव्यवाचक

18. लम्बाई

A. भाववाचक B. समूहवाचक

C. द्रव्यवाचक D. व्यक्तिवाचक

19. दल

A. जातिवाचक B. व्यक्तिवाचक

C. समूहवाचक D. द्रव्यवाचक

20. मार्च

A. समूहवाचक B. व्यक्तिवाचक

C. द्रव्यवाचक D. जातिवाचक

21. झुण्ड

A. समूहवाचक B. जातिवाचक

C. व्यक्तिवाचक D. द्रव्यवाचक

22. टोली

A. जातिवाचक B. व्यक्तिवाचक

C. समूहवाचक D. द्रव्यवाचक

23. सुभाष चौक

A. जातिवाचक B. समूहवाचक

C. व्यक्तिवाचक D. भाववाचक

24. संघ

A. जातिवाचक B. द्रव्यवाचक

C. समूहवाचक D. भाववाचक

25. गिरोह

A. समूहवाचक B. द्रव्यवाचक

C. जातिवाचक D. भाववाचक

उत्तरमाला

1. C	**2.** A	**3.** A	**4.** A	**5.** A
6. C	**7.** A	**8.** B	**9.** A	**10.** B
11. A	**12.** A	**13.** A	**14.** A	**15.** A
16. A	**17.** B	**18.** A	**19.** C	**20.** B
21. A	**22.** C	**23.** C	**24.** C	**25.** A

अभ्यास-12

निर्देश: *नीचे दिए गए वाक्य में रिक्त स्थान है। प्रत्येक वाक्य के नीचे कारक चिह्न दिए गए हैं। रिक्त स्थान की पूर्ति के लिए उपयुक्त कारक चिह्न का चयन कीजिए :*

1. निम्नलिखित शब्दों........अर्थ बताइए

A. का B. के

C. से D. पर

2. सरकार मुझे नौकरी........मत निकालिए

A. पर B. में

C. से D. को

3. इस कथन........पुष्टि कीजिए

A. को B. से

C. की D. ने

4. छात्र-छात्राएँ राष्ट्र........सम्पत्ति और उसके भावी कर्णधार होते हैं

A. के B. की

C. को D. में

5. प्रत्येक प्रश्न........चार सम्भावित उत्तर दिए गए हैं

A. के लिए B. में

C. के D. से

6. माता बच्चे........पढ़ाती है

A. को B. के

C. की D. से

7. गुरुजी........सबसे छोटे लड़के को एक नारंगी दी

A. ने B. को

C. से D. के लिए

8. मोहन सोहन से मिलने........गया है

A. से B. के

C. को D. के लिए

9. उसने कलम........लिखा

A. के B. में

C. पर D. से

10. मैं ड्राइवर........गाड़ी चलवाता हूँ

A. के B. पर

C. में D. से

11. शिक्षक छात्रों........पुस्तक पढ़वाते हैं

A. के लिए B. मैं

C. पर D. से

12. मैंने दाढ़ी........उसे मुसलमान समझ लिया

A. से B. के

C. को D. के लिए

13. श्याम अपने भाई हरि........आम लाया है

A. के B. के लिए

C. का D. पर

14. मोहन घर........आता है

A. में B. पर

C. से D. का

15. उसे पाँच दिनों........मूर्च्छा आया करती है

A. पर B. से

C. के D. को

16. मेधावी छात्र परीक्षा........चोरी नहीं करते

A. में B. पर

C. से D. के लिए

उत्तरमाला

1. A	**2.** C	**3.** C	**4.** B	**5.** C
6. A	**7.** A	**8.** D	**9.** D	**10.** D
11. D	**12.** A	**13.** B	**14.** C	**15.** B
16. D				

गद्यांश (अपठित-बोध)

गद्यांश 1

यदि हम निरन्तर प्रयत्न करेंगे तो निश्चय ही अपने सभी लक्ष्यों को प्राप्त कर लेंगे, किन्तु प्रायः देखा जाता है कि अधिक आशावादी लोग थोड़ा सा प्रयत्न करके अधिक फल की कामना करने लगते हैं और मनोवांछित फल प्राप्त न होने पर निराश हो जाते हैं। अतः जीवन में सफलता प्राप्त करने के लिए परिस्थितियों के समक्ष घुटने न टेकें, बल्कि दृढ़ता से उनका मुकाबला करें। याद रखें, जितना कठोर हमारा परिश्रम होगा उसका फल भी उतना ही मीठा होगा।

उपर्युक्त गद्यांश को ध्यानपूर्वक पढ़ें और निम्न प्रश्नों के उत्तर के लिए सही विकल्प को चुनें:

1. फल न मिलने पर कौन निराश हो जाते हैं?
A. आशावादी लोग B. कम आशावादी लोग
C. अधिक आशावादी लोग D. निराशावादी लोग

2. लक्ष्य प्राप्ति के लिए क्या किया जाना चाहिए?
A. फल की कामना B. हिम्मत से मुकाबला
C. निरन्तर प्रयत्न D. परिस्थितियों से मुकाबला

3. आशावादी शब्द का विलोम शब्द है:
A. निराश B. निराशावादी
B. दुखी D. अप्रसन्न

4. मनोवांछित शब्द का क्या अर्थ है?
A. इच्छित B. परीक्षित
C. लाभदायक D. मन को खुश करने वाले

5. परिश्रम शब्द का अर्थ है:
A. साहस B. हिम्मत
C. काम D. कठिन मेहनत

गद्यांश 2

पन्द्रह अगस्त 1947 को हमारा देश स्वतंत्र हुआ। स्वतन्त्रता प्राप्ति के बाद विश्व के दूसरे देशों के साथ भारत के राजनयिक एवं सांस्कृतिक सम्बन्ध जुड़े। पर्यटकों के साथ-साथ राजनीतिज्ञों और साहित्यकारों को भी विदेश यात्रा के पर्याप्त अवसर मिले। विभिन्न प्रकार की छात्रवृत्तियों के माध्यम से बहुत से लोग विदेशों में पढ़ने गए। बहुत से लोगों ने विदेशों में उपलब्ध आजीविका के अवसरों का लाभ उठाया। इन सबके परिणामस्वरूप प्रचुर मात्रा में यात्रावृत्तांत लिखे गए। विदेश-विषयक यात्रावृतांत्तों में रूस और स्वदेश-विषयक यात्रावृतांत्तों में लेखकों की दृष्टि कश्मीर से कन्याकुमारी तक व्याप्त हुई।

उपर्युक्त गद्यांश को ध्यानपूर्वक पढ़ें और निम्नलिखित प्रश्नों के उत्तर के लिए सही विकल्प को चुनें:

1. भारत कब स्वतंत्र हुआ?
A. 15 अगस्त 1947 B. 15 अगस्त 1946
C. 15 अगस्त 1948 D. 15 अगस्त 1949

2. स्वतंत्र भारत के अन्य देशों के साथ किस प्रकार के संबंध जुड़े?
A. राजनीतिक
B. राजनयिक
C. धार्मिक
D. राजनयिक एवं सांस्कृतिक

3. आजीविका का क्या अर्थ है?
A. उपार्जन B. वेतन
C. मेहनत D. रोजगार

4. यात्रा-वृत्तांत का क्या अर्थ है?
A. भ्रमण B. पर्यटन
C. सफरनामा D. विदेशभ्रमण

5. स्वतंत्र का विलोम शब्द है:
A. परतंत्र B. आजाद
C. गुलामी D. मुक्ति

गद्यांश 3

युवा वर्ग का मस्तिष्क नई-नई बातों की ओर ज्यादा तेज दौड़ता है। उसमें अन्य वर्ग के व्यक्तियों से अधिक आवेश और शक्ति होती है। इस अवस्था में यदि सही शिक्षा और उचित मार्ग-दर्शन न मिले तो यही शक्ति प्रेरणा और निर्माण के स्थान पर विनाश की ओर ले जाती है। बिगड़ने और बनने की यही आयु होती है। दुर्भाग्य से हमारे देश में शिक्षा पद्धति केवल उपाधि बाँटने का काम ही करती है। एक सम्पूर्ण व्यक्तित्वपूर्ण मनुष्य बनाना आज की शिक्षा पद्धति के लिए मुश्किल है।

उपर्युक्त गद्यांश को ध्यानपूर्वक पढ़ें और निम्नलिखित प्रश्नों के उत्तर के लिए सही विकल्प को चुनें।

1. निर्माण का विलोम शब्द क्या हैं?
A. रचना B. बनावट
C. विनाश D. सृजन

2. मार्ग-दर्शन का क्या अर्थ है?
A. उपाधि B. रास्ता
C. उद्देश्य D. रास्ता दिखलाना

3. शक्ति विनाश की ओर कब अग्रसर होती है?
A. अधिक आवेश और शक्ति के अभाव में
B. सही शिक्षा और उचित मार्ग दर्शन के अभाव में
C. दुर्भाग्यपूर्ण शिक्षा पद्धति के कारण
D. इनमें से कोई नहीं

4. हमारे देश की शिक्षा पद्धति क्या कार्य करती है?
A. मार्ग-दर्शन B. शक्ति प्रेरणा
C. उपाधि देना D. उपर्युक्त सभी

5. दुर्भाग्य का विपरीत शब्द है:
A. भाग्य B. सौभाग्य
C. भाग्यशाली D. भाग्यवान

गद्यांश 4

भिखारी की भाँति गिड़गिड़ाना प्रेम की भाषा नहीं है। यहाँ तक कि मुक्ति के लिए भगवान् की उपासना करना भी अधम उपासना में गिना जाता है। प्रेम कोई पुरस्कार नहीं चाहता। प्रेम सर्वथा प्रेम के लिए ही होता है। भक्त इसलिए प्रेम करता है कि बिना प्रेम किए वह रह ही नहीं सकता। जब तुम किसी मनोहर प्राकृतिक दृश्य को देखकर उस पर मोहित हो जाते हो तो तुम किसी फल की याचना नहीं करते और न वह दृश्य ही तुमसे कुछ माँगता है। फिर भी उस दृश्य का दर्शन तुम्हारे मन को आनंद से भर देता है।

उपर्युक्त गद्यांश को ध्यानपूर्वक पढ़ें और निम्नलिखित प्रश्नों के उत्तर के लिए सही विकल्प का चयन करें:

1. प्रेम का उद्देश्य क्या होता है?

A. मुक्ति B. उपासना
C. भक्ति D. प्रेम

2. मुक्ति का अर्थ है:

A. आजादी B. स्वतंत्रता
C. परतंत्र D. निर्वाण

3. कैसी उपासना अधम मानी गई है?

A. प्रेम की उपासना B. भगवान की उपासना
C. मुक्ति की उपासना D. भक्ति की उपासना

4. मनोहर शब्द हैं:

A. विशेषण B. संज्ञा
C. सर्वनाम D. अव्यव

5. प्राकृतिक शब्द का अर्थ है:

A. ईश्वरीय B. मानव संबंधी
C. प्रकृति संबंधी D. प्रेम संबंधी

गद्यांश 5

कुछ लोग भाग्यवादी होते हैं और सब-कुछ भाग्य के सहारे छोड़कर कर्म से विरत हो जाते हैं। ऐसे लोग समाज के लिए बोझ हैं। वे कभी कोई बड़ा काम नहीं कर पाते। बड़ी-बड़ी खोज, बड़े-बड़े आविष्कार और बड़े-बड़े निर्माण कार्य कर्मशील लोगों के द्वारा ही संभव हो सके हैं। हम अपनी बुद्धि और प्रतिभा तथा कार्य-क्षमता के बल पर सही मार्ग पर चल सकते हैं, किन्तु बिना कठिन श्रम के अपने लक्ष्य तक नहीं पहुँच सकते। कठिन परिश्रम करने के बाद पाई गई सफलता हमारे मन को अलौकिक आनंद से भर देती है। यदि हम अपने कार्य में अपेक्षित श्रम नहीं करते तो हमारा मन ग्लानि का अनुभव करता है।

उपर्युक्त गद्यांश को ध्यानपूर्वक पढ़ें और निम्नलिखित प्रश्नों के उत्तर के लिए सही विकल्प चुनें:

1. ''आविष्कार'' शब्द का अर्थ है :

A. अनुसंधान B. खोज
C. निर्माण D. विनाश

2. **अलौकिक** शब्द का क्या अर्थ है?

A. संसारिक B. भौतिक
C. अमानुषी D. प्राकृतिक

3. सफलता का विलोम क्या है?

A. सफल B. असफल
C. सफलतापूर्वक D. असफलता

4. परिश्रम करने और न करने से हमारे जीवन पर क्या प्रभाव पड़ता है?

A. लोग भाग्यवादी बन जाते हैं
B. कर्म से विरत हो जाते हैं
C. मन में ग्लानि का अनुभव होता है
D. इनमें से कोई नहीं

5. किस प्रकार के लोग समाज के लिए बोझ हैं?

A. भाग्यवादी B. कर्मठ
C. परिश्रमी D. प्रतिभाशाली

गद्यांश 6

वैदिक काल से हिमालय के पहाड़ बहुत पवित्र माने जाते हैं। इसमें कोई सन्देह नहीं कि हिमालय के पहाड़ों का दृश्य अति सुन्दर है। उसकी विशालता को देखकर मन में आनन्द और कृतज्ञता की लहर उठती है। ऐसा लगता है कि यह विशाल सृष्टि प्रभु की अनुपम देन है। सारी सृष्टि के प्रति समभाव जाग्रत होता है। वस्तुतः यह दृष्टि कोरी कल्पनात्मक या आध्यात्मिक नहीं है। देखा जाए तो सारे भारत की जलवायु का समतोल करने वाले यह हिमालय के पहाड़ हैं, विशेषकर उत्तरी भारत को वर्षा और पानी देने वाले ये ही हैं। गंगोत्री, यमुनोत्री, बद्री, केदार को तीर्थ माना जाता है, जो व्यर्थ कल्पना नहीं है। उन स्थानों से निकलने वाली पवित्र नदियाँ ही वास्तव में हमारी प्राणदात्री रही हैं।

उपर्युक्त गद्यांश को ध्यानपूर्वक पढ़ें और निम्नलिखित प्रश्नों के उत्तर के लिए सही विकल्प चुनें :

1. हिमालय के पर्वत बहुत पवित्र कब से माने जाते हैं?

A. पाषाण काल से B. वैदिक काल से
C. प्राचीन काल से D. आधुनिक काल से

2. विशालता शब्द है :

A. जातिवाचक B. भाववाचक
C. विशेषण D. सर्वनाम

3. भारत की जलवायु को समतोल कौन करता है?

A. गंगोत्री B. यमुनोत्री
C. केदार D. हिमालय

4. सृष्टि का समानार्थक शब्द है :

A. सृजन B. रचना
C. प्रकृति D. संसार

5. प्राणदात्री का क्या अर्थ है?

A. गंगोत्री
B. यमुनोत्री
C. प्राणसंचार करने वाली
D. समभाव जाग्रत करने वाली

गद्यांश 7

सच्चा मित्र एक शिक्षक की भाँति होता है। जिस प्रकार शिक्षक अपने छात्र को सन्मार्ग की ही ओर अग्रसर करता है, उसी प्रकार एक सच्चा मित्र अपने मित्र को पाप के गर्त में गिरने से बचाता है। मानव-जीवन अधिक रहस्यपूर्ण है। कभी-कभी जीवन में ऐसे अवसर उपस्थित हो जाते हैं, जब मनुष्य की धर्मबुद्धि नष्ट हो जाती है और उसका मन द्रुत गति से पाप की ओर दौड़ता है। ऐसे समय में मित्र का ही उपदेश अधिक कल्याणकारी सिद्ध होता है। मित्र के उपदेश का जितना प्रभाव हृदय पर पड़ता है, उतना और किसी का नहीं पड़ता है।

उपर्युक्त गद्यांश को ध्यानपूर्वक पढ़ें और निम्नलिखित प्रश्नों के उत्तर के लिए सही विकल्प चुनें :

1. सच्चा मित्र किस प्रकार का होता है?
   A. विपत्ति में सहायता देने वाला
   B. गलत मार्ग पर चलने से रोकने वाला
   C. शिक्षक के भाँति
   D. धार्मिक गुरु की तरह
2. सन्मार्ग शब्द का विपरीत शब्द है :
   A. अग्रसर B. कुमार्ग
   C. सुमार्ग D. मार्गदर्शक
3. व्यक्ति को पाप के गर्त्त में गिरने से कौन बचाता है?
   A. शिक्षक B. भाई
   C. पिता D. सच्चा मित्र
4. मानव पाप की ओर कब दौड़ता है?
   A. जब स्वार्थी बन जाता है
   B. जब धर्म-बुद्धि नष्ट हो जाती है
   C. जब सच्चामित्र साथ छोड़ देता है
   D. जब धनवान बन जाता है
5. उपदेश में कौन-सा उपसर्ग है?
   A. उ B. उप
   C. दे D. देश

गद्यांश 8

सब तरह के भावों को प्रकट करने की योग्यता रखने वाली और निर्दोष होने पर भी यदि कोई भाषा अपना निज का साहित्य नहीं रखती, तो वह रूपवती भिखारिन की तरह कदापि आदरणीय नहीं हो सकती। उनकी शोभा, उसकी बड़ी सम्पन्नता, उसकी मान-मर्यादा उसके साहित्य पर ही अवलम्बित रहती है। उसके विचारों और राजनैतिक स्थितियों का प्रतिबिम्ब देखने को यदि कहीं मिल सकता है, तो उसके ग्रन्थ साहित्य में मिल सकता है। सामाजिक शक्ति या सजीवता, सामाजिक अशक्ति या निर्जीवता और सामाजिक सभ्यता तथा असभ्यता का निर्णायक एकमात्र साहित्य है।

उपर्युक्त गद्यांश को ध्यानपूर्वक पढ़ें और निम्नलिखित प्रश्नों के उत्तर के लिए सही विकल्प चुनें :

1. साहित्य विहीन भाषा किस प्रकार की होती है?
   A. आदरणीय B. भिखारिन
   C. रूपवती D. रूपवती भिखारिन
2. रूपवती का पुल्लिंग रूप है:
   A. रूपवान B. सुन्दर
   C. सुन्दरी D. रूपवत
3. भाषा की मान मर्यादा किस पर निर्भर करती है?
   A. लिपि पर B. साहित्यकार पर
   C. भक्ति पर D. साहित्य पर
4. ''सम्पन्नता'' शब्द का विपरीत शब्द है:
   A. गरीबी B. विपन्न
   C. अमीर D. विपन्नता
5. राजनैतिक, सामाजिक शक्ति का दर्शन हमें किसमें मिलता है?
   A. समाज B. राज्य
   C. नेता D. साहित्य

गद्यांश 9

स्वतंत्र भारत का सम्पूर्ण दायित्व आज विद्यार्थियों के ही ऊपर है, क्योंकि आज जो विद्यार्थी हैं, वे ही कल स्वतंत्र भारत के नागरिक होंगे। भारत की उन्नति, उसका उत्थान उन्हीं की उन्नति और उत्थान पर निर्भर करता है। अतः विद्यार्थियों को चाहिए कि वे अपने भावी जीवन का निर्माण बड़ी सतर्कता और सावधानी के साथ करें। उन्हें प्रत्येक क्षण अपने राष्ट्र, अपने समाज, अपने धर्म, अपनी संस्कृति को अपनी आँखों के सामने रखना चाहिए, जिससे उनके जीवन से राष्ट्र को कुछ बल प्राप्त हो सके। जो विद्यार्थी राष्ट्रीय दृष्टिकोण से अपने जीवन का निर्माण नहीं करते, वे राष्ट्र और समाज के लिए भार-स्वरूप हैं।

उपर्युक्त गद्यांश को ध्यानपूर्वक पढ़ें और निम्नलिखित प्रश्नों के उत्तर के लिए सही विकल्प चुनें :

1. भारत की उन्नति किस पर निर्भर करती है?
   A. युवाओं पर B. नेताओं पर
   C. साहित्यकारों पर D. विद्यार्थियों पर
2. **उन्नति** का समानार्थक शब्द है :
   A. पतन B. उत्थान
   C. विकास D. उदय
3. **उत्थान** का विपरीत शब्द है :
   A. उदय B. पतन
   C. पराजय D. हार
4. किसे अपने जीवन का निर्माण सतर्कता और सावधानी से करना चाहिए?
   A. युवाओं को B. नेताओं को
   C. बच्चों को D. विद्यार्थियों को
5. धर्म, संस्कृति तथा समाज का रक्षक कौन है?
   A. नागरिक B. ग्रामीण
   C. विद्यार्थी D. युवा

गद्यांश 10

हास्य एक ऐसा माध्यम है, जो नीरस-जीवन को भी सुखद बना देता है। हास्य का जादू इतना प्रभावशाली होता है कि वह छूत के रोग की तरह चारों ओर फैल जाता है। जिसने कभी हँसना नहीं सीखा, सचमुच उसने जीना नहीं सीखा। सामान्यतः मनुष्य को जीवन में इतनी मुसीबतें झेलनी पड़ती हैं कि वह अपने जीवन को पहाड़ समझने लगता है। ऐसे दूभर जीवन को यदि जीने योग्य बनाना हो तो उसके लिए आवश्यक है कि जीवन में हँसने की गुंजाइश हो। हँसी के सहारे मनुष्य अपने कष्टों को भुलाने का प्रयत्न करता है। संघर्ष, तनाव, व्यस्तता, घुटने यदि आज के जीवन की सहज देन हैं, तो इनसे बचने के लिए यह आवश्यक है कि हम हँसना सीखें।

उपर्युक्त गद्यांश को ध्यानपूर्वक पढ़ें और निम्नलिखित प्रश्नों के उत्तर के लिए सही विकल्प चुनें :

1. नीरस जीवन को कौन सुखद बना देता है?
A. संगीत B. गीत
C. आमोद प्रमोद D. हास्य

2. **नीरस** का संधि विच्छेद है :
A. नी + रस B. नि + रस
C. निः + रस D. नीः + रस

3. किसका जीवन व्यर्थ है?
A. जिसने रोना नहीं सीखा
B. जिसने हँसना नहीं सीखा
C. जिसने गाना नहीं सीखा
D. इनमें से कोई नहीं

4. **हँसना** शब्द है :
A. संज्ञा B. विशेषण
C. क्रिया विशेषण D. क्रिया

5. तनाव और घुटन से बचने के लिए क्या करना चाहिए?
A. रोना चाहिए B. गाना चाहिए
C. हँसना चाहिए D. काम करना चाहिए

गद्यांश 11

किसी पुस्तक को पढ़ने में जल्दी नहीं करनी चाहिए, जो कुछ लेखक कहता है, उसे समझने की चेष्टा करनी चाहिए। प्रत्येक शब्द का अर्थ समझने की चेष्टा करनी चाहिए। यदि लेखक योग्य है, तो दूसरी बार वह पुस्तक और अधिक आनन्द देगी और तीसरी बार और अधिक। प्रत्येक बार अध्ययन करने पर आपको नवीन सुन्दर और नए विचार मिलेंगे और उसे आप जितना ही पढ़ेंगे, उतना ही स्नेह करने लगेंगे। सहस्रों व्यक्तियों ने गीता और रामायण तथा कुरान और बाइबिल को बार-बार पढ़ा है। उनका अनुभव है कि प्रत्येक बार उन्हें नई सूझ और नए विचार मिलते गए। कुछ लोग तो इस बात पर गर्व करते हैं कि उन्होंने अमुक पुस्तक को अनेक बार पढ़ा है, उन्हें कंठस्थ हो गई है।

उपर्युक्त गद्यांश को ध्यानपूर्वक पढ़ें और निम्नलिखित प्रश्नों के उत्तर के लिए सही विकल्प चुनें :

1. किसे समझने की चेष्टा करनी चाहिए?
A. पुस्तक B. रामायण
C. महाभारत D. गीता

2. पुस्तक की सजीवता किस पर निर्भर करती है?
A. लेखक B. प्रकाशक
C. पाठक D. चिन्तक

3. **आनन्द** का विपरीत शब्द है :
A. शोक B. दुख
C. संताप D. खुशी

4. नवीन, सुन्दर और नए विचार हमें कहाँ से प्राप्त होता हैं?
A. पुस्तक को बार-बार पढ़कर
B. सुनकर
C. भाषण से
D. अच्छे व्यक्तियों से मिलने पर

5. **कंठस्थ** शब्द का शब्दार्थ है :
A. कंठ में स्थित B. सुंदर कंठ
C. जबानी याद D. पंडित जी

गद्यांश 12

अहिंसा परम धर्म है और हिंसा आपद् धर्म। मनुष्य बराबर अहिंसा की ओर चलना चाहता है, किन्तु परिस्थितियाँ उससे हिंसा कराती है, अर्थात् परमधर्म की रक्षा के लिए आदमी बराबर आपद्धर्म से काम लेता रहा है। भारत अपनी सेनाओं को विघटित कर दे, तब भी उसका अपमान उससे अधिक होने वाला नहीं, जितना नेफा में हुआ। किन्तु परमधर्म पर टिकने की सामर्थ्य अगर भारत में नहीं है, तो आपद्धर्म पर उसे आना चाहिए। व्यवहारतः आपद्धर्म परमधर्म का विरोधी नहीं, उसका रक्षक है।

उपर्युक्त गद्यांश को ध्यानपूर्वक पढ़ें और निम्नलिखित प्रश्नों के उत्तर के लिए सही विकल्प चुनें :

1. **परमधर्म** का विपरीत शब्द है :
A. महान धर्म B. आपद्धर्म
C. सच्चाधर्म D. इनमें से कोई नहीं

2. आपद्धर्म किसे कहा जाता है?
A. अहिंसा B. सत्याग्रह
C. विपत्ति D. हिंसा

3. मानव से हिंसा कौन करवाती है?
A. लोभ B. स्वार्थ
C. द्वेष D. परिस्थितियाँ

4. **सामर्थ्य** का शब्दार्थ है :
A. संघर्ष B. परिश्रम
C. शक्ति D. पराक्रम

5. **परमधर्म** की रक्षा कौन करता है?
A. अहिंसा B. हिंसा
C. आपदधर्म D. युद्ध

गद्यांश 13

वर्तमान काल विज्ञापन का युग माना जाता है। समाचार-पत्रों के अतिरिक्त रेडियो और टेलीविजन भी विज्ञापन के सफल साधन हैं। विज्ञापन का मूल उद्देश्य उत्पादक और भोक्ता में सीधा सम्पर्क स्थापित करना होता है। जितना अधिक विज्ञापन किसी पदार्थ का होगा, उतनी ही उसकी लोकप्रियता बढ़ेगी। इन विज्ञापनों पर धन तो अधिक व्यय होता है, पर इनसे बिक्री बढ़ जाती है। ग्राहक जब इन आकर्षक विज्ञापनों को देखता है तो वह उस वस्तु-विशेष के प्रति आकृष्ट होकर उसे खरीदने को बाध्य हो जाता है।

उपर्युक्त गद्यांश को ध्यानपूर्वक पढ़ें और निम्नलिखित प्रश्नों के उत्तर के लिए सही विकल्प चुनें :

1. वर्तमान को किसका युग माना जाता है?
   A. फैशन B. विज्ञापन
   C. संगीत D. धन
2. उत्पादक तथा भोक्ता के बीच कौन संबंध स्थापित करता है?
   A. टेलीविजन B. समाचार-पत्र
   C. रेडियो D. विज्ञापन
3. **वर्तमान** शब्द का विपरीत शब्द है :
   A. अर्वाचीन B. आधुनिक
   C. आजकल D. प्राचीन
4. **आकर्षक** का शब्दार्थ है :
   A. विकर्षक B. सुन्दर
   C. मनमोहक D. आश्चर्यजनक
5. भोक्ता किस कारण वस्तुओं को खरीदने के लिए बाध्य हो जाता है?
   A. विज्ञापन
   B. आकर्षक विज्ञापन
   C. लोकप्रियता के कारण
   D. आसानी से उपलब्ध होना

गद्यांश 14

लगभग दो सौ वर्ष की गुलामी ने भारत के राष्ट्रीय स्वाभिमान को पैरों से रौंद डाला, हमारी संस्कृति को समाप्त कर दिया, हमारे विश्वासों को हिला दिया और हमारे आत्मविश्वास को चकनाचूर कर दिया, किन्तु अपने इस बूढ़े देश से प्यार करने वाले, इसके एक सामान्य संकेत पर प्राण न्यौछावर करने वाले दीवानों का अभाव न था। एक आवाज उठी और देखते ही देखते राष्ट्र का दबा हुआ आत्माभिमान उन्मत्त हो उठा। इतिहास साक्षी है जाने और अनजाने सहस्त्रों देशभक्त स्वतंत्रता की अनमोल निधि को पाने के लिए शहीद हो गए।

उपर्युक्त गद्यांश को ध्यानपूर्वक पढ़ें और निम्नलिखित प्रश्नों के उत्तर के लिए सही विकल्प चुनें :

1. **स्वाभिमान** का संधि विच्छेद है:
   A. स्वा + भिमान B. स्वः + अभिमान
   C. स्व + अभिमान D. स्वा + अभिमान
2. भारत का राष्ट्रीय स्वाभिमान किस कारण समाप्त हो गया था?
   A. लम्बे गुलामी से B. निरंकुश शासक से
   C. स्वार्थी मानव से D. धर्म के विनाश से
3. **आत्मविश्वास** का शब्दार्थ है
   A. घमण्ड B. गर्व
   C. अपने पर विश्वास D. अभिमान
4. भारत की अनमोल निधि को पाने के लिए कौन शहीद हो गए?
   A. देशभक्त B. नेता
   C. युवा D. युवती
5. **अनमोल निधि** का शब्दार्थ है:
   A. अनन्त खजाना B. अमूल्य खजाना
   C. बहुमूल्य D. स्वतंत्रता

गद्यांश 15

दुनिया के विभिन्न देशों के विकास पर विहंगम दृष्टि डालने से यह स्पष्ट हो जाता है कि आज जिस देश ने वैज्ञानिक उपलब्धियों के सहारे अपना औद्योगीकरण कर लिया, उसी को उन्नत देश कहा जाता है। जिस देश में औद्योगीकरण का स्तर नीचा है, वह पिछड़ा हुआ देश कहा जाता है। वैज्ञानिक आविष्कारों और औद्योगीकरण के आधार पर ही किसी देश की प्रगति को आँका जाता रहा है। विज्ञान ने मानव को पूरी तरह बदल दिया है।

उपर्युक्त गद्यांश को ध्यानपूर्वक पढ़ें और निम्नलिखित प्रश्नों के उत्तर के लिए सही विकल्प चुनें :

1. **विहंगम दृष्टि** का क्या अर्थ है?
   A. एक झलक B. गहन दृष्टि
   C. गहन चिन्तन D. इनमें से कोई नहीं
2. **विकास** का विपरीत शब्द है :
   A. उत्थान B. उदय
   C. पतन D. विनाश
3. **वैज्ञानिक** शब्द में कौन-सा प्रत्यय हैं?
   A. निक B. वै
   C. ईक D. इक
4. मानव जीवन को किसने बदल दिया है :
   A. विकास B. वैज्ञानिक
   C. विज्ञान D. उद्योग
5. किसी भी देश की स्तर को किससे नापा जाता है?
   A. उपलब्धियों पर B. औद्योगीकरण से
   C. वैज्ञानिकों से D. आविष्कारों से

गद्यांश 16

विश्व का वर्तमान उन्नत रूप मानव-श्रम की ही कहानी कह रहा है। गगन चुंबी अट्टालिकाएँ, लंबी-चौड़ी सड़कें, बड़े-बड़े विशाल नगर आकाश में उड़ते वायुयान तथा मानव-जीवन को सुखी और समृद्ध बनाने में योगदान करने वाले ज्ञान-विज्ञान के अनन्त रूप-ये सभी मनुष्य के श्रम का जयघोष करते हैं। स्पष्ट है कि मनुष्य और उसका शरीर विधाता की अनुपम रचना है जो निश्चय ही महान उद्देश्यों की संपूर्ति के

लिए दिया गया है। इस दुर्लभ तन को यदि हम आलस्य, प्रसाद अथवा घटिया कामों में गँवा देते हैं तो उस विधाता के प्रति अन्याय करते हैं।

उपर्युक्त गद्यांश को ध्यानपूर्वक पढ़ें और निम्नलिखित प्रश्नों के उत्तर के लिए सही विकल्प चुनें :

1. विश्व का वर्तमान रूप किसका उद्‌योतक है?
   A. चिन्तक का B. नेता का
   C. वैज्ञानिक का D. मानव श्रम
2. **गगन चुंबी अट्टालिकाएँ** का अर्थ है :
   A. आकाश में उड़ने वाला B. आकाश को छूने वाला
   C. बहुमंजिली इमारत D. इनमें से कोई नहीं
3. आकाश का समानार्थक शब्द है :
   A. वसुन्धरा B. धरा
   C. पयोद D. गगन
4. **सुखी** का विपरीत शब्द है :
   A. प्रसन्न B. अप्रसन्न
   C. दुखी D. उदासी
5. विधाता की अनुपम रचना क्या है?
   A. मानव शरीर B. समुद्र
   C. वन D. पृथ्वी

गद्यांश 17

हमारे देश में एक ऐसा भी युग था जब नैतिक और आध्यात्मिक विकास ही जीवन का वास्तविक लक्ष्य माना जाता था। अहिंसा की भावना सर्वोपरि थी। आज पूरा जीवन दर्शन ही बदल गया है। सर्वत्र पैसे की हाय-हाय तथा धन का उपार्जन ही मुख्य ध्येय हो गया है, भले ही धन-उपार्जन के तरीके गलत ही क्यों न हों? इन सबका असर मनुष्य के प्रतिदिन के जीवन पर पड़ रहा है। समाज का वातावरण दूषित हो गया है—

बाह्य वातावरण तो दूषित है ही, आज सब जानते हैं पर्यावरण की समस्याएँ कितनी चिन्तनीय हो उठी हैं। इन सबके कारण मानसिक और शारीरिक तनाव-खिंचाव और व्याधियाँ पैदा हो रही हैं।

उपर्युक्त गद्यांश को ध्यानपूर्वक पढ़ें और निम्नलिखित प्रश्नों के उत्तर के लिए सही विकल्प चुनें :

1. भारत का प्राचीन आदर्श था :
   A. सत्य और अहिंसा B. नैतिक और आध्यात्मिक विकास
   C. धन उपार्जन D. इनमें से कोई नहीं
2. **अहिंसा** का विपरीत शब्द है :
   A. हिंसा B. सत्याग्रह
   C. विनम्रता D. नैतिकता
3. जीवन दर्शन क्यों बदल गया है?
   A. हिंसा के कारण B. अहिंसा के कारण
   C. धन लिप्सा के कारण D. आध्यात्मिक विकास के कारण
4. समाज का वातावरण दूषित क्यों हो गया है?
   A. शारीरिक तनाव B. मानसिक व्याधियाँ
   C. पर्यावरण की समस्याएँ D. धन उपार्जन के गलत तरीके
5. **पर्यावरण** का शब्दार्थ है:
   A. जलमंडल B. स्थलमंडल
   C. वायुमंडल D. वातावरण

उत्तरमाला

गद्यांश 1

1. C	2. D	3. B	4. A	5. D

गद्यांश 2

1. A	2. D	3. D	4. C	5. A

गद्यांश 3

1. C	2. D	3. B	4. C	5. B

गद्यांश 4

1. D	2. D	3. C	4. A	5. C

गद्यांश 5

1. B	2. D	3. D	4. C	5. A

गद्यांश 6

1. B	2. B	3. D	4. A	5. C

गद्यांश 7

1. C	2. B	3. D	4. B	5. B

गद्यांश 8

1. D	2. A	3. D	4. D	5. D

गद्यांश 9

1. D	2. B	3. B	4. D	5. C

गद्यांश 10

1. D	2. C	3. B	4. D	5. C

गद्यांश 11

1. A	2. A	3. A	4. A	5. C

गद्यांश 12

1. B	2. D	3. D	4. C	5. C

गद्यांश 13

1. B	2. D	3. D	4. C	5. B

गद्यांश 14

1. C	2. A	3. C	4. A	5. B

गद्यांश 15

1. A	2. D	3. C	4. C	5. B

गद्यांश 16

1. D	2. C	3. D	4. C	5. A

गद्यांश 17

1. B	2. A	3. C	4. D	5. D

●●●

GENERAL AWARENESS

NATIONAL SYMBOLS

STATE EMBLEM

State Emblem of India is an adaptation from the Sarnath ion Capital of Ashoka. It was adopted by the Government f India on January 26, 1950. In the adapted form, only hree lions are visible, the fourth being hidden from the iew. The wheel (Dharma Chakra) appears in relief in the entre of the abacus with a bull on the right and a horse on he left.

The bell-shaped lotus has been omitted. The words 'Satyameva Jayate'' meaning ''Truth alone triumphs'' are nscribed below the Emblem in Devanagari script.

IATIONAL FLAG

'he National Flag of India is a horizontal tricolour of deep affron (Kesari), white and dark green in equal proportion. n the centre of the white band there is a wheel in navy blue olour. It has 24 spokes. The ratio of the length and the readth of the flag is 3 : 2. Its design was adopted by the Constituent Assembly of India on July 22, 1947.

IATIONAL ANTHEM

Rabindranath Tagore's song 'Jana-gana-mana' was adopted y the Constituent Assembly as the National Anthem of ndia on January 24, 1950.

Jana-gan-mana-adhinayaka jaya he, Bharata-bhagya-vidhata
Punjab-Sindh-Gujarat-Maratha-Dravida-Utkala-Banga
Vindhya-Himachala-Yamuna-Ganga Uchhala-jaladhi-taranga.
Tava subha name jage, Tava subha asisa mange,
Gahe tava jaya gatha,
Jana-gana-mangala-dayak, jaya he Bharata bhagya vidhata,
Jaya he, jaya he, jaya he, Jaya jaya jaya, jaya he.

IATIONAL SONG

Bankim Chandra Chatterji's 'Vande Mataram' which was a ource of inspiration to the people in their struggle for reedom, has been adopted as National Song. It has an equal tatus with the National Anthem.

Vande Mataram
Sujalam, suphalam, malayaja-shitalam,
Shasya shyamalam, Mataram
Shubhrajyotsna,pulkita yaminim,
Phulla kusumita drumadalashobhinim,
Subhasinim sumadhura—bhashinim,
Sukhadam, Varadam, Mataram.

NATIONAL CALENDAR

It is based on the Saka era with Chaitra as its first month and a normal year of 365 days. It was adopted from March 22, 1957. Dates of the national calendar have a permanent correspondence with dates of Gregorian calendar as Chaitra I falls on March 22 in a normal year and March 21 in a leap year. In official communications, both Saka and Gregorian calendar dates are written. Months of the national calendar are Chaitra, Vaishakha, Jaishtha, Ashada, Shravan, Bhadra, Ashvina, Kartika, Margashirsha, Pausha, Magha and Phalguna.

NATIONAL ANIMAL

The magnificent tiger — Panthera tigris (Linnaeus) is the national animal of India. Tiger is found in several parts of the country and is known for its grace, strength, agility and enormous power. 'Project Tiger' was launched in 1973 to check their dwindling population in India.

NATIONAL BIRD

The Indian Peacock — Pavo Christatus (Linnaeus) is the national bird of India. It is a colourful, swan-sized bird with a fan-shaped crest of feathers on its head and a long-slander neck. The male species is more colourful with blue breast and a spectacular bronze-green train of around 200 elongated feathers.

National Flower—Lotus

National Tree—Banyan

National Fruit—Mango

National Currency—Rupee '₹' (One Rupee = 100 Paise)

National Aquatic Animal—Dolphin

BOOKS AND AUTHORS

Name of Book	Author
in-e-Akbari	Abul Fazal
nand Math	Bankim Chandra Chatterjee
n Unknown Indian	Nirad C. Chaudhuri
Arthshastra	Kautilya
Coolie	Mulk Raj Anand
Das Kapital	Karl Marx

Name of Book	Author
Discovery of India	Jawaharlal Nehru
Eternal India	Mrs. Indira Gandhi
Godan	Prem Chand
Gitanjali	Rabindranath Tagore
Gora	Rabindranath Tagore
ìeet Govinda	Jayadeva
Iarsha Charit	Bana Bhatta
Iindu View of Life	Dr. S. Radhakrishnan
ndia Wins Freedom	Maulana Abul Kalam Azad
obs of Millions	V.V. Giri
ungle Book	Rudyard Kipling
ìamayani	Jai Shankar Prasad
ìadambari	Bana Bhatta
ife Divine	Sri Aurobindo
ast days of Netaji	G.D. Khosla
es Miserables	Victor Hugo
Iahabharat	Veda Vyas
Iacbeth	William Shakespeare
Iein Kempf	Hitler
Ieghduta	Kalidas
Iother (Maa)	Maxim Gorky
Iother India	Katherine Mayo
Iy Experiments with Truth	Mahatma Gandhi
Iy Presidential Years	R. Venkataraman

Name of Book	Author
Neeti Shatak	Bhartrihari
Nehru and His Vision	Dr. K.R. Narayanan
Old Man and the Sea	Ernest Hemingway
One World	Wendell Wilkie
Panchtantra	Vishnu Sharma
Paradise Lost	John Milton
Ramayana	Valmiki (in Sanskrit)
Raghuvansham	Kalidas
Rajtarangini	Kalhan
Ram Charit Manas	Tulsi Das
Abhijnan Shakuntalam	Kalidas
Satanic Verses	Salman Rushdie
Saket	Maithili Sharan Gupta
Speed Post	Shobha De
The God of Small Things	Arundhati Roy
Treasure Island	R.L. Stevenson
Twelfth Night	William Shakespeare
Train to Pakistan	Khuswant Singh
Uttara Ram Charitra	Bhava Bhuti
Vanity Fair	W.M. Thackeray
War and Peace	Leo Tolstoy
Wealth of Nations	Adam Smith
Wake up India	Annie Besant

INVENTIONS AND DISCOVERIES

iscovery	Discoverer
ìeographical Discoveries	
merica	Columbus
razil	Cabral
Iorth Pole	Robert Peary
verest (Conquered)	Tabie Junko
lanetary Motion	Kepler
awaiian Islands	Captain Cook
outh Pole	Amundsen
olar System	Copernicus
hemistry and Physics	
tom Bomb	Otto Hahn
tomic Theory	Dalton
tomic Numbers	Moseley
osmic Rays	R.S. Millikan
ynamite	Alfred Nobel
lectrons Theory	Bohr
lectricity (current)	Volta
lectric Telegraphy (Code)	S. Morse
ravitation	Newton
as Light	Murdock
xygen	J. Priestly
hotography	L. Daguerre

Discovery	Discoverer
Printing for the blind	Louis Braille
Radium	Madame Curie
Telegraph	Samuel Morse
Television	J.L. Baird
Telephone	Graham Bell
Wireless	G. Marconi
X-rays	W.K. Roentgen
Mechanical	
Aeroplane	Wright Brothers
Bicycle	Macmillan
Computer	Charles Babbage
Dynamo	Michal Faraday
Diesel Engine	Rudolf Diesel
Engine (Railway)	Stephenson
Fountain Pen	Waterman
Gramophone	Edison
Locomotive Power of Steam	James Watt
Helicopter	Brequet
Life Boat	Henry Greathead
Microscope	Z. Jansen
Printing Press	Gutenberg
Revolver	Colt

iscovery	Discoverer
ewing Machine	Elias Howe
hermometer	Fahrenheit
ransistor	W. Shockley
ypewriter	Sholes
elescope	Hans Lippershey
ank (Military)	Swinton
ledical	
ntiseptic Surgery	Lord Joseph Lister
acteria	Leeuwenhock
rculation of Blood	William Harvey

Discovery	Discoverer
Homoeopathy (Discovered)	Hahnemann
Insulin	F. Banting
Penicillin	Alexander Flemming
Malaria Parasite	Dr. Ronald Ross
Stethoscope	Laennec
Vitamins	Funk
Anti-Rabies Treatment	Pasteur
General	
Nylon	Carouthers
Science of Geometry	Euclids

WORLD'S GEOGRAPHICAL SURNAMES

City of Sky-scrapers—New York • City of Seven Hills—ome • City of Dreaming Spires—Oxford • City of Golden ate—San Francisco • City of Magnificent Buildings—ashington D.C. • City of Eternal Springs—Quito (S. merica) • China's Sorrow—Hwang Ho • Cockpit of rope—Belgium • Dark Continent—Africa • Emerald Isle—eland • Eternal City—Rome • Empire City—New York 'orbidden City—Lhasa (Tibet) • Garden City—Chicago • ate of Tears—Strait of Bab-el-Mandeb • Gift of the Nile—gypt • Granite City—Aberdeen (Scotland) • Hermit ngdom—Korea • Herring Pond—Atlantic Ocean • Holy nd—Jerusalem • Island Continent—Australia • Islands of oves—Zanzibar • Isle of Pearls—Bahrein (Persian Gulf) Key to the Mediterranean—Gibralter • Land of Cakes—otland • Land of Golden Fleece—Australia • Land of Maple Leaf—Canada • Land of Morning Calm—Korea • Land of Midnight Sun—Norway • Land of the Thousand Lakes—Finland • Land of the Thunderbolt—Bhutan • Land of White Elephant—Thailand • Land of Thousand Elephants—Laos • Land of Rising Sun—Japan • Loneliest Island—Tristan De Gunha (Mid-Atlantic) • Manchester of Japan—Osaka • Pillars of Hercules—Strait of Gibraltar • Pearl of the Antilles—Cuba • Playground of Europe—Switzerland • Quaker City—Philadelphia • Queen of the Adriatic—Venice • Roof of the World—The Pamirs, Central Asia • Sugar bowl of the world—Cuba • Venice of the North—Stockholm • Windy City—Chicago • Whiteman's grave—Guinea Coast of Africa • Yellow River—Huang Ho (China) • Sickman of Europe—Turkiye

CURRENCIES OF DIFFERENT COUNTRIES

untry	Currency
istralia	Australian Dollar
ngladesh	Taka
lgium	Euro
itain	Pound (Sterling)
yanmar	Kyat
nada	Canadian Dollar
rmany	Euro
n	Rial
lia	Rupee
Lanka	Rupee
ina	Yuan
ech Republic	Koruna
nmark	Krone
nce	Euro
kistan	**Rupee**

Country	Currency
Poland	Zloty
Spain	Euro
Indonesia	Rupiah
Iraq	Dinar
Italy	Euro
Japan	Yen
Mexico	Peso
The Netherland	Euro
European Union	Euro
Sweden	Krone
Switzerland	Swiss Franc
Turkiye	Lira
U.A.E.	Dirham
U.S.A.	Dollar
Russia	**Rouble**

CAPITAL OF COUNTRIES

Country	Capital	Country	Capital
Austria	Vienna	Kenya	Nairobi
Afghanisatan	Kabul	Kuwait	Kuwait
Algeria	Algiers	Laos	Vientiane
Angola	Luanda	Lebanon	Beirut
Australia	Canberra	Mexico	Mexico City
Argentina	Buenos Aires	Malaysia	Kualalumpur
Bangladesh	Dhaka	Morocco	Rabat
Belgium	Brussels	Mozambique	Maputo
Bolivia	Lapaz	New Zealand	Welington
Bulgaria	Sofia	Netherlands	Amsterdam
Bhutan	Thimpu	Panama	Panama City
Brazil	Brasilla	Portugal	Lisbon
Canada	Ottawa	Poland	Warsaw
China	Beijing	Sri Lanka	Colombo
Cyprus	Nicosia	Sweden	Stockholm
Columbia	Bagota	Switzerland	Bern
Denmark	Copenhegan	Sudan	Khartoum
Ethiopia	Addis Ababa	Sierra Leone	Freetown
Finland	Helsinki	South Africa	Capetown
France	Paris	Saudi Arabia	Riyadh
Germany	Berlin	Spain	Madrid
Greece	Athens	Thailand	Bangkok
Guatemala	Guatemala City	Turkiye	Ankara
Hungary	Budapest	Russia	Moscow
Iran	Tehran	Azerbaijan	Baku
India	New Delhi	Armenia	Yerevan
Indonesia	Jakarta	Latvia	Riga
Iraq	Baghdad	Ukrain	Kiev
Italy	Rome	U.S.A.	Washington
Ireland	Dublin	U.K.	London
Japan	Tokyo	Egypt	Cairo
Combodia	Phnom Penh	Vietnam	Hanoi
Korea (North)	Pyong Yang	Zambia	Lusaka
Korea (South)	Seoul		

INDIAN CITIES AND THEIR RIVERS

City	State	River	City	State	River
Agra	U.P.	Yamuna	Kanpur	Uttar Pradesh	Ganga
Ahmedabad	Gujarat	Sabarmati	Ludhiana	Punjab	Sutlej
Prayagraj	U.P.	Confluence of the Ganga, Yamuna, and invisible Saraswati	Lucknow	Uttar Pradesh	Gomati
			Nasik	Maharashtra	Godavari
			Patna	Bihar	Ganga
			Srinagar	J & K	Jhelum
Alwaye	Kerala	Periyar	Surat	Gujarat	Tapti
Kolkata	West Bengal	Hooghly	Tiruchirapally	Tamil Nadu	Kaveri
Cuttack	Odisha	Mahanadi	Ujjain	Madhya Pradesh	Shipra
Delhi	Delhi	Yamuna	Vijayawada	Andhra Pradesh	Krishna
Haridwar	Uttarakhand	Ganga	Varanasi	Uttar Pradesh	Ganga

WONDERS OF THE WORLD

Seven Wonders of the Ancient World: (1) the Pyramids of Egypt, built in approximately 2700 BC; (2) the Hanging Gardens at Babylon; (3) the temple of Artemis at Emphesus; (4) the statue of Zeus at Olympia; (5) the tomb of Mausolus at Halicarnassus, built in nearly 350 BC; (6) the Colossus of Rhodes, built in nearly 280 BC; (7) the Pharos Lighthouse at Alexandria.

Seven Wonders of the Medieval World: (1) the Colosseum of Rome; (2) the Great Wall of China; (3) the Porcelain Tower of Nanking; (4) the Mosque at St. Sophia (Constantinople); (5) Stonehenge; (6) the Catacombs of Rome; (7) the Leaning Tower of Pisa.

Seven New Wonders of the World: (1) Taj Mahal of Agra (India); (2) Pyramid at Chichen Itza (Mexico); (3) Machu Picchu (Peru); (4) Statue of Christ The Redeemer (Brazil); (5) Great Wall of China; (6) Roman Colosseum, Italy; (7) Ruins of Petra, Jordan.

STATES AND UNION TERRITORIES OF INDIA (CAPITALS, PRINCIPAL LANGUAGES)

States/Union Territories	*Capitals*	*Principal Languages*
■ Andhra Pradesh	Amravati	Telgu and Urdu
■ Arunachal Pradesh	Itanagar	Monpa, Adi, Nissi etc.
■ Assam	Dispur	Assamese and Bengali
■ Bihar	Patna	Hindi and Maithili
■ Chhattishgarh	Raipur	Hindi
■ Goa	Panaji	Konkani
■ Gujarat	GandhiNagar	Gujarati
■ Haryana	Chandigarh	Hindi
■ Himachal Pradesh	Shimla	Hindi and Pahari
■ Jharkhand	Ranchi	Hindi
■ Kerala	Thiruvananthpuram	Malyalam
■ Karnataka	Bengluru	Kannada
■ Madhya Pradesh	Bhopal	Hindi
■ Maharashtra	Mumbai	Marathi
■ Meghalaya	Shillong	Khashi, Jayantia and Garo
■ Manipur	Imphal	Manipuri
■ Mizoram	Aizawl	Mizo and English
■ Nagaland	Kohima	Naga, Assamese and English
■ Odisha	Bhubaneshwar	Odiya
■ Punjab	Chandigarh	Punjabi
■ Rajasthan	Jaipur	Hindi, Rajasthani
■ Sikkim	Gangtok	Sikkimese and Lepcha
■ Tamil Nadu	Chennai	Tamil
■ Tripura	Agartala	Bengali, Tripuri
■ Uttar Pradesh	Lucknow	Hindi
■ Uttarakhand	Dehradun	Hindi
■ West Bengal	Kolkata	Bengali
■ Telangana	Hyderabad	Telgu and Urdu
■ Jammu & Kashmir	Srinagar/Jammu	Kashmiri, Dongri, Urdu, Dardi and Pahari
■ Andaman and Nicobar Islands	Port Blair	Hindi, Nicobarese, Bengali, Malayalam, Tamil, Telugu
■ Chandigarh	Chandigarh	Hindi, Punjabi, English
■ Dadar and Nagar Haveli and Daman and Diu	Daman	Gujarati, Hindi
■ Delhi	Delhi	Hindi, Punjabi
■ Lakshadweep	Kavaratti	Malayalam
■ Puducherry	Puducherry	Tamil, Telugu, Malayalam, English and French
■ Ladakh	Leh	Ladakhi

HIGH COURTS IN INDIA

Name	Year	Territorial Jurisdiction	Seat
Allahabad	1866	Uttar Pradesh	Prayagraj (Bench at Lucknow)
Andhra Pradesh	2019	Andhra Pradesh	Amaravati
Bombay	1862	Maharashtra, Goa, Dadar & Nagar Haveli and Daman & Diu	Mumbai (Benches at Nagpur, Panaji and Aurangabad)
Calcutta	1862	West Bengal and Andaman & Nicobar Islands	Kolkata (Circuit Benchs at Port Blair and Jalpaiguri)
Chhattisgarh	2000	Chhattisgarh	Bilaspur
Delhi	1966	Delhi	Delhi
Gauhati	1948	Assam, Nagaland, Mizoram and Arunachal Pradesh	Guwahati (Benches at Kohima, Aizawl and Itanagar)
Gujarat	1960	Gujarat	Ahmedabad
Himachal Pradesh	1971	Himachal Pradesh	Shimla
Jammu & Kashmir and ladakh	1928	Jammu & Kashmir, Ladakh	Srinagar and Jammu
Jharkhand	2000	Jharkhand	Ranchi
Karnataka	1884	Karnataka	Bengaluru (Circuit Benches at Dharwar and Gulbarga)
Kerala	1958	Kerala & Lakshadweep	Ernakulam
Madhya Pradesh	1956	Madhya Pradesh	Jabalpur (Benches at Gwalior and Indore)
Madras	1862	Tamil Nadu & Puducherry	Chennai (Bench at Madurai)
Orissa	1948	Odisha	Cuttack
Patna	1916	Bihar	Patna
Punjab and Haryana	1966	Punjab, Haryana and Chandigarh	Chandigarh
Rajasthan	1949	Rajasthan	Jodhpur (Bench at Jaipur)
Sikkim	1975	Sikkim	Gangtok
Uttarakhand	2000	Uttarakhand	Nainital
Tripura	2013	Tripura	Agartala
Telangana	2019	Telangana	Hyderabad
Meghalaya	2013	Meghalaya	Shillong
Manipur	2013	Manipur	Imphal

FAMOUS HILL STATION

Hill Station	State/UT
1. Almora, Mussoorie Nainital	Uttarakhand
2. Cherrapunji (Shillong), Khasi Hills (Shillong)	Meghalaya
3. Ooty, Kodaikanal Yereaud	Tamil Nadu
4. Dalhousie, Kassauli	Himachal Pradesh
5. Darjeeling	West Bengal
6. Gulmarg, Srinagar	Jammu and Kashmir
7. Mahabaleshwar	Maharashtra
8. Mt. Abu	Rajasthan
9. Panchmarhi	Madhya Pradesh
10. Ranchi	Jharkhand

FAMOUS NATIONAL PARKS

1. Corbett National Park : Nainital, Uttarakhand
2. Dudhwa National Park : Lakhimpur Kheri, UP
3. Kaziranga National Park : Jorhat, Assam
4. Kanha National Park : Jabalpur, Bhedaghat
5. Gir National Park : Rajkot, Junagarh, Gujarat
6. Guindy National Park : Guindy, Chennai, Tamil Nadu
7. Nagairhole National Park : Coorg, Karnataka
8. Bandipur National Park : Mysore, Karnataka

FAMOUS NATIONAL WILDLIFE SANCTUARIES

1. Dachigam Wildlife Sanctuary : Srinagar, Jammu and Kashmir
2. Sariska : Alwar, Rajasthan
3. Hazaribagh Wildlife Sanctuary : Hazaribagh, Jharkhand
4. Tiger Project : Sawai Madhopur, Rajasthan
5. Mudhumali Wildlife Sanctuary : Mudhumalia, Nilgiri, Tamil Nadu
6. **Periyar Wildlife Sanctuary** : Idukki, Kottayam, Kerala

HOLY PLACES IN INDIA

1. Amarnath	Jammu and Kashmir
2. Ayodhya	Uttar Pradesh
3. Badrinath	Uttarakhand
4. Dwarka	Gujarat
5. Haridwar	Uttarakhand
6. Kancheepuram	Tamil Nadu
7. Kedarnath	Uttarakhand
8. Mathura	Uttar Pradesh
9. Puri	Odisha
10. Rameswaram	Tamil Nadu
11. Tirupati	Andhra Pradesh
12. Ujjain	Madhya Pradesh
13. Varanasi	Uttar Pradesh
14. Bodh Gaya	Bihar

SPORTS

Terms Associated With Sports :

Cricket : Ashes, Bye, Bodyline, Bowling, Break, Cover-point, Creases, Chinaman, Chucker, Drive, Duck, Follow on, Googly, Hit-Wicket, Hat-trick, Leg-before-wicket, Leg break, Leg-bye, Maiden over, No ball, Night-watchman, Runner, Run-out, Stumped, Silly-point, Slip.

Football : Handball, Corner kick, Dribble, Free Kick, Hat-trick, Off-side, Penalty Kick, Try, Throw in, Wembley.

Hockey : Bully, Carry, Corner kick, Corner, Penalty stroke, Off-side, Penalty, Roll in scoop, Sticks, Sudden death, Striking circle, Short Corner, Scoop, Tie-breaker, Under-cutting, Hat-trick.

Tennis : Backhand drive, Deuce, Fault, Half-volley, Net, Let, Volley, Smash, Service.

Billiards : Break, Cannons, Cue, Pot, Jigger, Scratch, In Bauk, In, Off.

Bridge : Dummy, Finesse, Grand-slam, Little Slam, Revoke, Ruff slam, Trump, Tricks, Vulnerable.

Volley Ball : Booster, Love, Service, Volley, Smasher.

Badminton : Smash, Drop, Let.

Chess : Check, Checkmate, Gambit, State-mate.

Golf : Bogy, Caddie, Hole, Links, Stymie, Tee, Put.

Polo : Chukker, Mallet, Bunder.

Baseball : Bunting, Diamond, Pitcher, Put-out, Strike, Home.

Boxing : Knockout, Punch, Upper-cut, Jab, Hook.

FAMOUS TROPHIES

Agha Khan Cup	Hockey
Beighton Cup	Hockey
Corbillion Cup	World Table Tennis (Women)
Davis Cup	Lawn Tennis
Duleep Trophy	Cricket
Durand Cup	Football
Ezra Cup	Polo
I.F.A. Shield	Football
Irani Cup	Cricket (India)
Jayalaxmi Cup	Table Tennis (Women)
Lady Rattan Tata Trophy	Hockey (Women)
Nehru Cup	Hockey (India)
Obaidullah Cup	Hockey
Ranji Trophy	Cricket (India)
Rangaswamy Cup	Hockey (India)
Rovers Cup	Football (India)
Santosh Trophy	Football (India)
Subroto Cup	Football
Thomas Cup	Badminton
Uber Cup	Badminton (Women)
Wellington Trophy	Rowing (India)

BIGGEST, LARGEST, TALLEST OF THE WORLD

Largest Desert	Sahara (Africa)
Tallest Statue	Statue of Unity (India)
Rainiest Place	Mowsynram near Cherrapunjee (Meghalaya, India)
Biggest Ocean	Pacific Ocean
Deepest Ocean	Pacific Ocean
Largest Mammal	Whale
Fastest Animal	Cheetah
Lightest Substance	Hydrogen gas
Longest River	Nile
Highest Waterfalls	Salto Angel Falls (Venezuela)
Tallest Animal	Giraffe
Largest Bird (Land)	Ostrich
Hardest Mineral	Diamond
Largest Delta	Sunderbans (W.B. India)
Largest Museum	American Museum of Natural History (New York)
Longest Day	June, 21
Shortest Day	December, 22
Biggest Army	People's Liberation Army, China
Largest Salt Water Lake	Caspian Sea
Highest Mountain Peak	Everest (8848 metre high)
Longest Wall	Great Wall of China
Largest Peninsula	Arabia
Largest Planet	Jupiter
Smallest Continent	**Australia**
Largest Lake	**Caspian Sea**

Deepest Lake	Baikal, 3200 ft.
Finest Harbour	Sydney Harbour
Smallest Planet	Mercury
Largest Continent	Asia
Planet nearest to the Sun	Mercury
Longest Highway Tunnel	Laerdal Tunnel (Norway)
Highest Building	Burj Khalifa, Dubai
Country Biggest	Russia (17075000 sq. km.)
Electorate, Largest	India (over 90 crores)
Longest Epic	Mahabharat
Island, Biggest in the World	Greenland
Population, Largest	China
Longest Railway Platform	Shree Siddharoodha Swamiji Railway Station Hubballi, Karnataka (India)
Swimming Course	English Channel

FIRST IN INDIA

Governor General of Independent India — Lord Mountbatten

Cosmonaut — Sq. Ldr. Rakesh Sharma

Field Marshal — S.H.F.J. Manekshaw

Indian Governor General of Indian Union — C. Rajagopalachari

Indian I.C.S. Officer — Satyendra Nath Tagore

Indian to swim across English Channel — Mihir Sen

Indian Women to swim across English Channel — Miss Arti Saha

Man to climb Mount Everest — Tenzing Norgay

Man to climb Mount Everest without Oxygen — Phu Dorjee

Man to climb Mount Everest twice — Nwang Gombu

Nobel Prize Winner — Rabindra Nath Tagore

President of Indian National Congress — W.C. Banerjee

President of Indian Republic — Dr. Rajendra Prasad

Talkie Film — Alam Ara (1931)

Test Tube Baby (Documented) — Indira

Viceroy of India — Lord Canning

Woman Minister of Indian Union — Rajkumari Amrit Kaur

Woman Governor — Mrs. Sarojini Naidu

Woman President of Indian National Congress — Dr. Annie Besant

Woman Prime Minister — Mrs. Indira Gandhi

Chief of Defence Staff (CDS) — General Bipin Rawat

Woman Speaker of a State Assembly — Mrs. Shanno Devi

Prime Minister of India — Pt. Jawaharlal Nehru

Muslim President of Indian Union — Dr. Zakir Hussain

Speaker of Lok Sabha — G.V. Mavlankar

Women to Climb Mount Everest — Bachhendri Pal

Woman Judge in Supreme Court — Mrs. Meera Sahib Fatima Biwi

Women Chief Justice of a High Court — Smt. Leela Seth

The First Indian Weightlifter to Win bronze medal in Olympics — Karnam Malleshwari (Sydney, in 2000)

World Chess Champion — Vishwanathan Anand

India's First Woman Merchant Navy Officer — Sonali Banerjee

The First Woman Air Vice-Marshal — P. Bandopadhyaya

The First Indian to be appointed as United Nations Civilian Police Advisor — Ms. Kiran Bedi

The First Women to be appointed Deputy Governor of Reserve Bank of India — K.J. Udeshi

The First Indian Lady to win a medal in World Athletic Championship — Anju Bobby George

The First Sikh Prime Minister of India — Dr. Manmohan Singh

IMPORTANT DAYS

✶ **January**

5-11	Road Safety Week
12	National Youth Day
15	Army Day
23	National Day of Patriotism
26	Republic Day
30	Martyr's Day

✶ **FEBRUARY**

1-14	Oil Conservation Fortnight
14	Valentine's Day

✶ **MARCH**

4	National Safety Day
8	International Women's Day
15	Consumers' Day
21	World Forest Day
22	World Day for Water
24	World Meteorological Day

✶ **APRIL**

7	World Health Day
7-13	Handloom Week
14-20	Fire Service Week
18	World Heritage Day
22	World Earth Day

✶ **MAY**

1	May Day
5	National Labour Day
8	World Red Cross Day

11 National Technology Day
15 International Day of the Family
17 World Telecommunication Day
24 Commonwealth Day
31 World No-Tobacco Day

✶ **JUNE**
5 World Environment Day
21 International Day of Yoga
26 International Day against Drug Abuse and Illicit Trafficking

✶ **JULY**
11 World Population Day

✶ **AUGUST**
1-7 World Breast feeding Week
10 Sanskrit Divas
15 Independence Day
20 Sadbhavana Divas

✶ **SEPTEMBER**
1-7 National Nutrition Week
5 Teachers' Day
8 International Literary Day
14 Hindi Diwas
23 World Deaf Day
27 World Tourism Day

✶ **OCTOBER**
2 ✶ Gandhi Jayanti
✶ International Day of Non Violence
✶ Anti-Leprosy Day
4 World Animal Day
6 World Habitat Day (Ist Monday)
8 Indian Air Force Day
14 World Standard Day
15 International Day of Rural Women
16 World Food Day
24 United Nations Day
27 Infantry Day
28 World Thrift Day
31 Anti-Terrorism Day

✶ **NOVEMBER**
2 All Saints Day
14 Children's Day
15-21 National Cooperative Week
19-25 Quami Ekta Week
20 Child Rights Day
26 Constitution Day

✶ **DECEMBER**
1 World AIDS Day
3 World Day for the Disabled
4 Naval Day
7 Flag Day
8 SMRC Day
10 Human Rights Day
14 National Energy Conservation Day

PARLIAMENTS OF IMPORTANT COUNTRIES

Afghanistan	—	Shora
Britain	—	Parliament House of Commons, House of Lords
Denmark	—	Folketing
The Netherlands	—	States General
India	—	Sansad
Israel	—	Knesset
Iran	—	Majlis
Ireland	—	Airetann
Iceland	—	Althing
Japan	—	Diet
Norway	—	Storting
Russia	—	Supreme Soviet
Spain	—	Cortes
Sweden	—	Riksdag
U.S.A.	—	Congress Senate
Germany	—	Bundestag

MINERAL RESOURCES OF THE WORLD

Articles	Producers	Articles	Producers
Aluminium	China	Asbestos	Russia
Boxide	Australia	Chromium	South Africa
Copper	Chile	Cobalt	Congo (Kinshasa)
Diamonds	Russia	Gold	China
Iron-ore	China	Lead	China
Platinum	South Africa	Silver	Mexico
Silicon	China	Sulfur	China
Tin	China	Titanium	China
Tungsten	China		

TEN LARGEST COUNTRIES AND THEIR AREAS

Rank by Area	Country	Area (sq. km.)
1.	Russia	17,075,400
2.	Canada	9,976,139
3.	China	9,561,000
4.	U.S.A.	9,363,123
5.	Brazil	8,511,965
6.	Australia	7,686,848
7.	India	3,287,263
8.	Argentina	2,776,889
9.	Kazakhstan	2,724,900
10.	Algeria	2,381,741

PRESIDENT OF INDIA

He is the constitutional head of the Republic but not the real executive.

Qualifications: (1) Indian citizen; (2) age not less than 35 years; (3) should have qualifications for election to Lok Sabha; (4) should not hold any office of profit; (5) should not be a Member of Parliament or State Legislature.

Election: He is elected by the elected Members of Parliament and State Legislative Assemblies in accordance with the system of proportional representation by means of single transferable vote.

Powers: He makes appointment to all the Constitutional posts. He can address either House of Parliament and send message to them. He can summon and prorogue either House of Parliament and dissolve Lok Sabha. All Bills passed by Parliament must receive his assent to become an Act. He issues Ordinance when Parliament is not in session. No money Bill can be introduced in Lok Sabha without his recommendation. He can grant pardon, reprieve or remit punishment and he can commute death sentences. He can declare national emergency, state emergency and financial emergency.

VICE-PRESIDENT OF INDIA

The Vice-President acts as the ex-officio Chairman of Rajya Sabha and acts as the President when the latter is unable to discharge his functions due to illness, absence or any other reason, or till the election of a new President when a vacancy is caused by the death, resignation or removal of the President.

The Vice-President is elected by an electoral college consisting of the members of both Houses of Parliament in accordance with the system of proportional representation by means of the single transferable vote. He must be a citizen of India, not less than 35 years of age, and should be eligible for election as a member of the Council of States.

COUNCIL OF MINISTERS

Council of Ministers is to aid and advise the President in exercise of his functions. Prime Minister and other ministers are appointed by the President.

Cabinet: Every member of the Council of Ministers is not a Cabinet Minister. Cabinet is a small body consisting of only senior members of Council of Ministers. The Cabinet functions like the executive committee of the Council of Ministers.

PRIME MINISTER OF INDIA

Art. 74(1) of our Constitution states that the Prime Minister shall be at the head of council of ministers. He has the power of selecting and advising the President to dismiss them individually. He is the chairman of the cabinet. Art. 78 provides that it shall be the duty of the Prime minister –

- To communicate to the president all the decisions of the council of ministers relating to the administration of the affairs of the union and proposals for legislation.
- To furnish such information relating to the administration of the affairs of the union and proposals for legislation as the president may call for and
- If the President so requires to submit for the consideration of the council of ministers any matter on which a decision has been taken by a minister but which has not been considered by the council.

THE SOLAR SYSTEM: SOME FACTS

Number of Planets: 8—Mercury, Venus, Earth, Mars, Jupiter, Saturn, Uranus and Neptune.

Largest most

Massive planet .... Jupiter
Brightest planet .... Venus
Brightest star .... Sirius
Fastest orbiting planet .... Mercury
Longest (Synodic) day .... Mercury
Planet with largest moon .... Jupiter
Greatest average density .... Jupiter
Tallest mountain .... Earth
Strongest magnetic fields .... Jupiter
Most circular orbit .... Venus
Shortest (synodic) day .... Jupiter
Hottest planet .... Venus
No moons .... Mercury, Venus
Planet with moon with most eccentric orbit ...... Neptune
Lowest average density .... Saturn
Greatest amount of liquid on the surface .... Earth

THE EARTH: FACTS AND DATA

Composition of the Earth: Aluminium (0.4%), Sulphur (2.7%), Silicon (13%), Oxygen (28%), Calcium (1.2%), Nickel (2.7%), Magnesium (17%), Iron (35%)

Surface area	: 510100500 sq km
Land Surface (29.1%)	: 148950800 sq km
Ocean Surface (70.9%)	: 361149700 sq km
Type of water	: 97% salt, 3% fresh
Total area of water	: 382672000 sq km
Equatorial diameter	: 12753 km
Equatorial Circumference	: 40066 km
Polar Circumference	: 39992 km
Polar diameter	: 12710 km
Equatorial radius	: 6376 km
Polar radius	: 6335 km

Mass (estimated weight)	: 594×10^{19} metric tons
Mean distance from the Sun	: 149407000 km
Earth's orbit speed (around sun)	: 107320 kmph
Period of Revolution (round the sun)	: 365 days 5 hrs 48 min. 45.51 seconds
Time of Rotation (on its axis)	: 23 hrs 56 min 4.09 seconds
Inclination of the axis (to the plane of the ecliptic)	: 23º27'

PRINCIPAL MOUNTAIN PEAKS OF THE WORLD

	Mountains	Height in Metres	Range	Date of First Ascent
1.	Mount Everest	8,848	Himalayas	May 29, 1953
2.	K-2 (Godwin Austen)	8,611	Karakoram	July 31, 1954
3.	Kanchenjunga	8,597	Himalayas	May 25, 1955
4.	Lhotse	8,511	Himalayas	May 18, 1956
5.	Makalu I	8,481	Himalayas	May 15, 1955
6.	Dhaulagiri I	8,167	Himalayas	May 13, 1960
7.	Mansalu I	8,156	Himalayas	May 9, 1956
8.	Chollyo	8,153	Himalayas	Oct. 19, 1954
9.	Nanga Parbat	8,124	Himalayas	July 3, 1953
10.	Annapurna I	8,091	Himalayas	June 3, 1950
11.	Gasherbrum I	8,068	Karakoram	July 5, 1958
12.	Broad Peak I	8,047	Karakoram	June 9, 1957
13.	Gasherbrum II	8,034	Karakoram	July 7, 1956
14.	Shisha Pangma (Gosainthan)	8,014	Himalayas	May 2, 1964
15.	Gasherbrum III	7,952	Karakoram	Aug. 11, 1975

POPULAR NICK NAMES OF SOME FAMOUS PERSONALITIES

Andhra Kesari	T. Prakasam
Anna	C.N. Anna Durai
Bang Bandhu	Sheikh Mujibur Rehman
Bapu	Mahatma Gandhi
Bard of Avon	William Shakespeare
Chachaji	Jawaharlal Nehru
Desh Bandhu	C.R. Das
Frontier Gandhi	Khan Abdul Gaffar Khan
Fuhrer	Adolf Hitler
G.B.S.	George Bernard Shaw
Grand Old Man of India	Dadabhai Naoroji
Grand Old Man of Britain	Gladstone
Guru Dev	Rabindra Nath Tagore
Guruji	M.S. Golwalkar
Iron Man of India	Sardar Patel
Lok Nayak	Jayaprakash Narayan
Lady with the Lamp	Florence Nightingale
Lal, Bal, Pal	Lala Lajpat Rai, Bal Gangadhar Tilak, Bipin Chandra Pal
Little Corporal	Napoleon Bonaparte
Lokmanya	Bal Gangadhar Tilak
Mahamana	Pt. Madan Mohan Malaviya
Maid of Orleans	Joan of Arc
Maiden Queen	Queen Elizabeth I
Missile Man	A.P.J. Abdul Kalam

Man of Destiny	Napoleon Bonaparte	Punjab Kesari	Lala Lajpat Rai
Netaji	Subhash Chandra Bose	Shastriji	Lal Bahadur Shastri
Nightingale of India	Sarojini Naidu	Uncle Ho	Ho Chi Minh
Panditji	Jawaharlal Nehru	Wizard of the North	Walter Scott

FAMOUS INTERNATIONAL ORGANISATIONS, HEADQUARTERS AND YEAR OF ESTABLISHMENT

International Organisations	*Headquarters*	*Year of Establishment*
United Nations Organisations (U.N.O.)	New York	1945
International Monetary Fund (I.M.F.)	Washington D.C.	1945
World Health Organisation (W.H.O.)	Geneva	1948
Food & Agricultural Organisation (FAO)	Rome	1945
International Labour Organisation (ILO)	Geneva	1919
UNESCO	Paris	1946
International Court of Justice	The Hague	1946
Universal Postal Union (UPU)	Berne	1874
International Civil Aviation Organisation (ICAO)	Montreal	1945
UNIDO	Vienna	1966
International Atomic Energy Agency (IAEA)	Vienna	1957
International Finance Corporation (IFC)	Washington	1956
United Nations Development Programme (UNDP)	New York	1965
UNICEF	New York	1946
International Maritime Organisation (IMO)	London	1948
World Meteorological Organisation (WMO)	Geneva	1950
International Telecommunication Union (ITU)	Geneva	1865
Arab League	Cairo	1945
Commonwealth of Nations	London	1949
World Trade Organisation (WTO)	Geneva	1995
International Development Association (IDA)	Washington D.C.	1960
International Bank for Reconstruction and Development (IBRD)	Washington D.C.	1945
World Intellectual Property Organisation (WIPO)	Geneva	1967
Organisation of Islamic Conference (OIC)	Jeddah (Saudi Arabia)	1969
European Union (EU)	Brussels	Changed form of EEC Established in 1958
Red Cross	Geneva	1863
Interpol	Lyons	1923
Asian Development Bank (ADB)	Manila	1966
North Atlantic Treaty Organisation (NATO)	Brussels	1949
Association of South East Asian Nations (ASEAN)	Jakarta	1967

BHARAT RATNA AWARD WINNERS

1. Dr. S. Radhakrishnan	1954	**8.** Dr. D.K. Karve	1958
2. C. Rajagopalachari	1954	**9.** Dr. Bidhan Chandra Roy	1961
3. Dr. C.V. Raman	1954	**10.** Purushottam Das Tandon	1961
4. Dr. Bhagwan Das	1955	**11.** Dr. Rajendra Prasad	1962
5. Dr. M. Visvesvaraya	1955	**12.** Dr. Zakir Hussain	1963
6. Jawaharlal Nehru	1955	**13.** Dr. Pandurang Vaman Kane	1963
7. Govind Ballabh Pant	1957	**14.** Lal Bahadur Shastri	1966

15. Indira Gandhi	1971
16. V.V. Giri	1975
17. K. Kamraj	1976
18. Mother Teresa	1980
19. Acharya Vinoba Bhave	1983
20. Khan Abdul Ghaffar Khan	1987
21. M.G. Ramachandran	1988
22. Dr. B.R. Ambedkar	1990
23. Dr. Nelson R. Mandela	1990
24. Rajiv Gandhi	1991
25. Sardar Vallabhbhai Patel	1991
26. Morarji R. Desai	1991
27. Maulana Abul Kalam Azad	1992
28. Jehangir Ratanji Dadabhai Tata	1992
29. Satyajit Roy	1992
30. Gulzari Lal Nanda	1997
31. Mrs. Aruna Asaf Ali	1997
32. Dr. A.P.J. Abdul Kalam	1998
33. M.S. Subbalakshmi	1998
34. C. Subramaniam	1998
35. Jaya Prakash Narayan	1999
36. Prof. Amartya Sen	1999
37. Pt. Ravi Shankar	1999
38. Gopinath Bardoloi	1999
39. Lata Mangeshkar	2001
40. Bismillah Khan	2001
41. Bhimsen Joshi	2008
42. C.N.R. Rao	2014
43. Sachin Tendulkar	2014
44. Madan Mohan Malaviya	2015
45. Atal Bihari Vajpayee	2015
46. Nanaji Deshmukh	2019
47. Bhupen Hazarika	2019
48. Pranab Mukherjee	2019
49. Karpoori Thakur	2024
50. L.K. Advani	2024
51. Charan Singh	2024
52. P.V. Narasimha Rao	2024
53. M.S. Swaminathan	2024

ART AND CULTURE

☞ Classical Dances

Dance	*State*	*Famous Artists*
Bharat Natyam	Tamil Nadu	Yamini Krishnamurthy, Rukmini Devi Arundale, Swapna Sundari, Sonal Mansingh, Vaijanti Mala, Mrinalini Sarabhai, Chandralekha, Indrani, Ram Gopal, Bal Saraswati
Kathakali	Kerala	Gopinath, K.K. Nayar, Kunju-Kurup, T.K. Chandu
Kuchipudi	Andhra Pradesh/ Telangana	Sapna Sundari, Raja Reddy, Shobha Nayar, Radha Reddy, Vedantam Satyanarayan, Vimpanti Chinna Satyam.
Kathak	North India	Birju Maharaj, Gopi Krishna, Shambhu Maharaj, Sitara Devi, Vishnu Sharma, Durga Lal, Shobhana Narayan
Odissi	Odisha	Kelucharan Mahapatra, Indrani Rehman, Madhavi Mudgal, Pratima Bedi, Samyukta Panigrahi, Sonal Mansingh, Debudas
Manipuri	Manipur	Uday Shankar, Bipin Singh, Suryamukhi, Darohra Jhaveri

☞ Famous Folk Dances

State/UT	*Folk Dance*
Andhra Pradesh/ Telangana	Dandari, Banjara
Assam	Bihu, Keli Gopal, Sataria
Bihar	Chhau, Magahi, Durga dance
W. Bengal	Kirtan, Kalatri, Asweabadh, Brita, Kalidance
Chhattisgarh	Saila, Karama, Bhagoria
Gujarat	Garba, Rasalila, Tippani, Dandia,
Haryana	Damyal, Lahoor
Himachal Pradesh	Dussehra dance, Hikat, Notio
J&K	Dumhal, Kud
Ladakh	Spao, Jabro, Brokpa
Jharkhand	Jhau, Ghumakudia, Jadur, Sarhul, Soharai, Karama, Vaima, Loojhari, Jat-Jatin, Vidayat
Karnataka	Yakshagan, Dolu Kunitha
Kerala	Mohini Attam, Padayuni
Madhya Pradesh	Lota Nritya, Jawara
Maharashtra	Tamasha, Dahi Handi, Gof, Deepak Dindi
Manipur	Dhol Cholam
Meghalaya	Nongakarem
Nagaland	Bamboo dance
Odisha	Chhau, Maya Shabari, Dalachai
Punjab	Gidda, Bhangra, Panihari
Rajasthan	Thumar, Kathaputali, Tera Tali
Tamil Nadu	Terukalathu, Kabalatam, Kargam, Pulivesham
Tripura	Hazagiri
Uttar Pradesh	Rasalila, Nautanki, Thali, Dhurang, Jhumela, Huraka, Bol.
Uttarakhand	Kajari, Karan
Goa	Dhode Modini

MUSIC

Main Schools of Classical Music

- There are two main schools of classical music, namely, the Hindustani and the Carnatic. The Hindustani school of classical music is in vogue in north-western India, eastern India and northern parts of the South India.

Musical Instruments

- *They are:* Tabla, Mridangam, Pakhawaj, Chandai, Dholak, Veena, Sitar, Sarod, Gootuvadhyam, Sarangi, Flute, Nadaswaram, Shehnai, Shringi and Turahi.

FAMOUS INTERNATIONAL AIR SERVICES

Air Service	*Name of Country*	*Air Service*	*Name of Country*
Air India	India	K.L.M. Royal Airlines	The Netherlands (Holland)
British Overseas Airways Corporation	Britain	Lufthansa Airlines	Germany
		Iraqi Airways	Iraq
Trans World Airlines	America	National Airlines	Iran
Russian Airlines	Russia	Quantas Airlines	Australia
Japan Airlines	Japan	Hong-Kong Airlines	Hong-Kong
Pakistan International Airlines	Pakistan	Egypt Airlines	Egypt
Malaysia Airlines	Malaysia	Slovak Airlines	Slovakia
Royal Nepal Airlines	Nepal	S.I.A.	Singapore
Swiss Airways	Switzerland	Garuda Airways	Indonesia
Air France	France	Bangladesh Viman Sewa	Bangladesh
Kuwait Airways	Kuwait	Air Lanka	Sri Lanka
Pan American World Airways	America	Elitalia Airlines	Italy
		Air Canada	Canada

FAMOUS RELIGIONS, FOUNDERS, HOLY BOOKS & PLACES OF WORSHIP

Religion	*Founder*	*Holy Books*	*Place of Worship*
Hinduism	Hinduism has no one Founder. (This religion is based upon the religion of original Aryan Settlers)	Ramayan, Vedas, Puranas and Geeta	Temple
Sikh	Guru Nanak Dev	Guru Grantha Sahib	Gurdwara
Christianity	Jesus Christ	Bible	Church
Islam	Prophet Mohammed	Koran (Quran)	Mosque
Parsi	Zoroaster	Zend Avesta	Fire Temple
Jainism	Adinath Rishavdev	Jain Granth	Jain Temple
Buddhism	Gautam Buddha	Tripitaka	Buddha Temple
Jew	Moosa	Torah	Synagogue

INTELLIGENCE AGENCIES OF SOME PROMINENT COUNTRIES

Country	*Intelligence Agency*	*Country*	*Intelligence Agency*
India	Research & Analysis Wing (RAW), Intelligence Bureau (I.B.),Central Bureau of Investigation (C.B.I.)	U.S.A.	Central Intelligence Agency, Federal Bureau of Investigation
Pakistan	Inter Service Intelligence (I.S.I.)	Britain	Military Intelligence (M.I.)-5 and 6, Special Branch, Ultra, Joint Intelligence Organisation

Country	Intelligence Agency	Country	Intelligence Agency
Israel	Mosad	Iran	Sabak
Egypt	Mukhabarat	Iraq	Al-Mukhabarat
Japan	Nicho	Australia	Australian Security and Intelligence Organisation
Russia	K.G.B. (Komitel Gosudars-tvennoy Bezopasnosty) (Committee for State Security)	France	S.D.E.C.E.
Canada	Security Intelligence Service	Spain	C.E.S.I.D.
S. Africa	Bureau of State Security	Cuba	D.G.I.

SOME PROMINENT RACES OF THE WORLD

Races	Country	Races	Country	Races	Country
Veddas	Sri Lanka	Bantu	Central and South Africa	Lapps	European Tundra
Somaid	West Siberia	Tartars	Siberia	Hausa	Nigeria
Masai	East Africa	Baddu	Arab's Desert	Kirghiz	Steppes (Russia)
Muree	New Zealand	Semang	Malaysia	Bushman	Kalahari Desert
Yakoot	Russian Tundra	Eskimo	Canada, Tundra Region	Red Indian	North America
Papuans	New Guyana				
Pygmy	Congo Basin				

FAMOUS STRAITS OF THE WORLD

Strait	Between	Country
Malacca Strait	Andaman Sea and South China Sea	Indonesia
Palk Strait	Mannar and Bay of Bengal	India-Sri Lanka
Magellan Strait	Pacific and South Atlantic Ocean	Chile
Dover Strait	English Channel and North Sea	England-France
Berring Strait	Berring Sea and Chukasi Sea	Alaska-Russia
Sugaroo Strait	Japan Sea and Pacific Ocean	Japan
Sunda Strait	Java and Indian Ocean	Indonesia
Gibralter Strait	Mediterranean Sea and Atlantic Ocean	Spain
Harmuj Strait	Persia and Bay of Oman	Oman-Iran
Hudson Strait	Bay of Hudson and Atlantic Ocean	Canada

FAMOUS NEWSPAPERS OF THE WORLD

Newspaper	Place of Publishing	Language
Daily News	New York (America)	English
Guardian	London (Britain)	English
Pravada	Moscow (Russia)	Russian
Al-Ahram	Cairo (Egypt)	Arabic
Merdeca	Jakarta (Indonesia)	Indonesian
Times	London (Britain)	English
People's Daily	Beijing (China)	Chinese
New Statesman	Britain	English
Daily Mirror	Britain	English
Hindu, Hindustan, Times of India, Tribune, Statesman, Indian Express, Economic Times	India	English
Hindustan, Nav Bharat Times, Dainik Bhaskar, Dainik Jagaran, Punjab Kesari	India	Hindi

IMPORTANT BOUNDARY LINES

Boundary Line	*Countries*	*Boundary Line*	*Countries*
Durand Line	Pakistan and Afghanistan	Seigfrid Line	Germany-France
Hindenberg Line	Germany-Poland	24th Parallel	India-Pakistan
Maginot Line	France and Germany	17th Parallel	The line which defined the boundary between North Viet-nam and South Vietnam before the two were united.
Mannerhein Line	Russia-Finland	38th Parallel	North Korea and South Korea
Mc Mahon Line	India-China	49th Parallel	U.S.A. and Canada
Order Niesse Line	Germany-Poland		
Radcliff Line	India-Pakistan		

SIGNALS/SIGNS AND MEANING

Signal/Sign	*Meaning*	*Signal/Sign*	*Meaning*
Red Triangle	Family Planning	White Flag	Treaty or Surrender
Red Cross	Medical Help	Yellow Flag	Vehicles with patients of contagious diseases
Red Light	Danger, 'Stop' for the movement of vehicles	Two Bones across with a Skull	Danger of electricity
Green Light	Go	Half mast flown Flag	National mourning
Olive Branch	Peace	Lotus and culture	Sign of civilization
White Pigeon or Dove	Peace	Wheel (Chakra)	Sign of Progress
Black Strip on Arm	(i) Opposition (ii) Sorrow	A blind folded woman with scale in hand	Sign of Justice
Black Flag	Opposition	Reversed flown	National calamity flag
Red Flag	(i) Danger (ii) Revolution		

NATIONAL EMBLEMS OF IMPORTANT COUNTRIES

Country	*National Emblem*	*Country*	*National Emblem*
Australia	Kangaroo	New Zealand	Kiwi, Fern Southern Cross
Ireland	Shamrock	Norway	Lion
Italy	White Lily	Nepal	Kukri
Israel	Candelabrum	Pakistan	Crescent
Iran	Rose	Poland	Eagle
Canada	White Lily	France	Lily
Great Britain	Rose	Belgium	Lion
Chile	Candor and Huemul	Bangladesh	Water Lily
Germany	Corn Flower	Mongolia	The Soyombo
Japan	Chrysanthemum	Russia	Double headed eagle
Zimbabwe	Zimbabwe Bird	Lebanon	Cedar Tree
Denmark	Beach	Sudan	Secretary Bird
Turkiye	Crescent and Star	Syria	Eagle
The Netherlands	Lion	India	Lioned Capital

CONTINENTS : SOME FACTS

Continent	Biggest Counrty	Highest Peak	Longest River
Asia	China	Mt. Everest (8848 m)	Yangtze Kiang
Africa	Algeria	Mt. Kilimanjaro (5895 m)	Nile
North America	Canada	Mt. Mckinley (6194 m)	Mississippi Missouri
South America	Brazil	Mt. Acancagua (6960 m)	Amazon
Europe	Russia	Mt. Elbrus (5642 m)	Ob
Australia	Australia	Mt. Coscuisco (2228 m)	Darling
Antarctica	—	Vinson Massif (5140 m)	—

COMPUTER

The computer is the system of that electronic device through which various informations are processed on the basis of a definite set of instructions called program and mathematical (numerical) and non-mathematical both types of informations are processed.

The first mechanical computer was composed or fabricated by Blaise Pascal in 1642 and it is called Pascalene. But in 1833, Charles Babbage first time conceived an automatic calculator or computer. Charles Babbage is called the father of modern computer. Herman made an electronic tabulating machine based on punch cards which operates automatically.

In 1937, first mechanical computer mark-I was fabricated by Howard Akeen. The most outstanding contribution in the development of modern computer goes to John Wan Newmaan who brought the 2nd revolution in the area of computer in 1951. He discovered EDVAC (Electronic Discrete Variable Automatic Computer) and utilised the stored program and the binary number system in the computer.

FUNCTIONS OF COMPUTER

1. Collection and composition (input) of datas;
2. Storage of datas.
3. Processing of datas.
4. Retrieval or output of the proccessed informations and datas.

UNITS OF COMPUTER

1. Input unit.
2. Central processing unit–CPU.
3. External Memory unit.
4. Output unit.

The CPU of the computer is called brain of the computer and sometimes CPU is also called Micro Processor of the computer. The data is entered through the input unit in the computer and through the central processing unit with the help of External Memory Unit datas are arranged and processed. Ultimately by the output unit these datas or informations are issued or released.

PARTS OF COMPUTER

- **Monitor :** The monitor of the computer is like a television in which the picture appears in the form of doted points on the screen and these are called pixcels.
- **Hard Disc and Floppy Disc :** The Hard Disc is the permanent disc in the computers while the Floppy Disc is the disc utilised when datas or informations are to be transferred from one computer to another.
- **Mouse :** The mouse of the computer is like the remote control of TV through which computer is directly regulated or controlled without utilising the key-board.
- **Printer :** The printer is a device which prints any documents or processed informations of the computer.

SOME HIGH LEVEL LANGUAGES

1. **FORTRAN :** This language was developed for solving the mathematical formulae very quickly and conveniently.
2. **COBOL :** This language was developed for the commerical purposes. For the processing of this language a group of sentences is selected called paragraph and all paragraphs composed are called a section, while all sections composed are called a division.
3. **BASIC :** In basic a definite part of the prescribed instruction is only inserted in the computer.
4. **ALGOL :** This was basically fabricated and designed for the complex algebraic calculations.

5. **PASCAL :** It is an amplified and modified form of ALGOL.
6. **COMAL :** This computer language is used for the students of secondary level.
7. **LOGO :** This language is used for children and kids for drawing Graphic line diagrams.
8. **PROLOG :** This language is developed in 1973 in France and this language is used for Artificial Intelligence which is capable and equivalent to the logical program.
9. **FORTH :** This language was invented by Charles Mure which is frequently used in all types of the works in the computer.

COMPUTER VIRUS

The computer virus is an electronic code which is used to abolish or erradicate the inclusive informations or programs of the computer. Some important computer viruses are Micheleanjalo, Dork Avangor, kilo, filip, Macmug, Scores, Casecade, Jeruslem, Date crime, Coloumbs crime, Internet virus, Pachcom, Pach EXE, COM-EXE, Marizuana, C-brain, bloody, Chenge Mungu and Desi etc.

COMPUTER NETWORKING

There are two types of networkings which are usually occur—Local Area Networking (LAN) and Wide Area Networking (WAN). By LAN all the computers of the same buildings are connected like the computers of university premises, computers of offices etc.

By WAN all the comptuers of a large area are connected like the computers of all the offices of a city or town etc. In India a very large computer network namely INDONET has been installing through which all the main towns and cities has to be interlinked.

COMPUTER TERMINOLOGY

- **Bit :** The bit is a unit of measurement of the electronic data. One bit is either 0 or 1 but not both. On composing 8 bits, 1 byte is formed.
- **Bug :** The Bug is the error in the computer program or system and its eradication is called Debug.
- **Byte :** Total eight bits compose a byte. Thus 8 bits = 1 byte.
- **CD-ROM :** A CD like of music CD in which data can be stored substantially called CD-ROM. In a CD with comparison to floppy extremely more datas can be stored but one problem in it is that one time recorded data can not be deleted or modified.
- **Chip :** It is a thin slice on which by a special mechanism a circuit is designed which is normally made from Silicon.
- **Memory System :** The place where computer data and program are temporarily kept is called Memory system. Usually memory is implied from RAM.
- **Modem :** The device which converts digital signals into analogue signals and vice-versa is called Modem.
- **RAM :** It is Random Access Memory (a place) where datas to be processed are kept temporarily and it is unstable memory.
- **ROM :** It is Read Only Memory and it is stable or Non-valatile memory which doesn't ended after power off.
- **Scanner :** It is a device through which graphic image is transformed to digital image and the scanners are of usually two types one desktop and another hand operating.

PROGRAMING

Computers perform phenomenal feats of calculation, but they do not do so in a complicated way. They actually carry out very simple operations, such as addition and subtraction. They achieve their fantastic computing power by carrying out these operations at incredible speed.

The programme, or set of instructions for operating the computer, is therefore written as a sequence of very simple steps. (See box below) Several computer languages have been developed for different applications, including BASIC, COBOL, FORTRAN and PASCAL. Writing programmes is very skilled and time-consuming work. But for most typical computer applications ready-written programmes are available, called "packages".

☞ How A Programme Works

Without a programme to tell it what to do and how to do it, a computer is unable to function. If, for example, you wanted to know how many times the word 'the' appears in this paragraph, or in the whole book, it would not be enough merely to put the text into a computer and then ask it how many times the word appears. For the computer to accomplish the calculations it has to be told what to do in simple steps. The instructions might be:

1. Scan the text until a space followed by 'T' or 't' is found.
2. If the next letter is not 'h', go back to step 1.
3. If the letter is 'h', is the next letter 'e'?
4. If not, go back to step 1. If it is, go to step 5.
5. If 'e' is followed by a space, add 1 to the total.
6. Go back to step 1.

A full computer programme for this operation would need to be broken down into even more simple steps, but a series of such programmes could enable a computer to analyse any amount of text in great detail.

DEFENCE

The Supreme Command of the Armed Forces is vested in the hands of the President of the Country. The responsibility for national defence, however, rests with the Cabinet. All important questions having a bearing on defence are decided by the Cabinet Committee on Political Affairs, which is presided over by the Prime Minister. The Defence Minister is responsible to Parliament for all matters concerning the Defence Services. All the administrative and operational control of Armed Forces are exercised by the Ministry of Defence. The three services – Army, Navy and Air Force function through their respective service headquarters headed by the chief of Staff.

COMMISSIONED RANKS IN DEFENCE SERVICES

Army	*Navy*	*Air Force*
General	Admiral	Air Chief Marshal
Lieutenant-General	Vice-Admiral	Air Marshal
Major-General	Rear-Admiral	Air Vice-Marshal
Brigadier	Commodor	Air Commodor
Colonel	Captain	Group Captain
Lieutenant-Colonel	Commander	Wing Commander
Major	Lt.Commander	Squadron Leader
Captain	Lieutenant	Flight Lieutenant
Lieutenant	Sub-Lieutenant	Flying Officer

INTERNAL SECURITY ORGANISATIONS OF INDIA

S. No.	Name of Organisation	Year of Creation	Headquarters
1.	Assam Rifles (A.R.)	1835	Shillong
2.	Central Reserve Police Force (C.R.P.F.)	1939	New Delhi
3.	National Cadet Corps (N.C.C.)	1948	New Delhi
4.	Territorial Army	1948	In different States
5.	Indo-Tibetan Border Police	1962	New Delhi
6.	Home Guard	1962	In different States
7.	Coast Guard	1978	New Delhi
8.	Border Security Force (B.S.F.)	1965	New Delhi
9.	Central Industrial Security Force (C.I.S.F.)	1969	New Delhi
0.	National Security Guard	1984	New Delhi
1.	Police	—	In different States

COMMANDER-IN-CHIEFS

1. General Sir Rob Lockhart	Aug. 15, 1947 — Dec. 31, 1947
2. General Sir Roy Bucher	Jan. 1, 1948 — Jan. 14, 1949
3. General K. M. Kariappa	Jan. 15, 1949 — Jan. 14, 1953
4. General Maharaj Rajendra Sinhji	Jan. 15, 1953 — March 31, 1955

CHIEF OF DEFENCE STAFF (CDS)

To bring in reform in higher defence management in the country, the post of Chief of Defence Staff (CDS) was created in the rank of a four-star General with salary and prerequisites equivalent to a Service Chief. The Chief of Defence Staff also heads the Department of Military Affairs (DMA), created within the Ministry of Defence and functions as its Secretary. General Bipin Rawat asumed the office as the first CDS of the country from January 1, 2020 for a three-year tenure till his death on December 8, 2021 in a helicopter crash.

ARMY INSTITUTES

1. Sainik Schools upto +2 Level	33 places in India
2. Rashtriya Indian Military College (prepare for entrance to N.D.A)	Dehradun
3. National Defence Academy (three services)	Khadakwasla, Pune
4. Indian Military Academy (Army)	Dehradun
5. Officers Training Academy (3 services) Short Courses	Chennai
6. National Defence College	New Delhi
7. The College of Combat	Mhow
8. The College of Military Engineering	Kirkee
9. Military College of Telecommunication Engineering	Mhow
10. The armoured Corps Centre and School	Ahmed Nagar
11. The School Artillery	Deolali
12. The Infantry School	Mhow and Belgaum
13. College of Material Management	Jabalpur

AIR FORCE INSTITUTIONS

Air Force Academy	Hyderabad
Helicopter Training School	Hakimpet
Flying Instructors School	Tambaram, Chennai
The College of Air Warfare	Secunderabad
Air Force Administrative College	Coimbatore
Air Force Technical College	Jalahalli

DEFENCE PRODUCTION UNITS

1. Bharat Dynamites Ltd.	Hyderabad	8. Mazagaon Dock	Mumbai
2. Praga Tools	Hyderabad	9. Goa Shipyard	Marmugao
3. Mishra Dattu Nigam	Hyderabad	10. Hindustan Shipyard Ltd.	Vishakhapatnam
4. Bharat Electronics Ltd.	Bengaluru	11. Hindustan Aeronautics Ltd.	Bengaluru, Hyderabad, Nasik, Koraput, Kanpur, Lucknow
5. Bharath Earthmovers Ltd.	Bengaluru		
6. Heavy Vehicles Ltd.	Avadi, Chennai		
7. Garden Reach Ship Builders and Engineers Ltd.	Kolkata		

☞ Indian Army Commands

Command	HQ Location	Command	HQ Location
Eastern Command	Kolkata	Western Command	Chandigarh
Northern Command	Udhampur	Southern Command	Pune
Central Command	Lucknow	Training Command	Shimla
South-Western Command	Jaipur		

☞ Indian Air Force Commands

Command	HQ Location	Command	HQ Location
Western Air Command	New Delhi	South-Western Air Command	Gandhinagar
Central Air Command	Prayagraj	Eastern Air Command	Shillong
Southern Air Command	Thiruvananthapuram	Training Command	Bengaluru

☞ Indian Navy Commands

Command	HQ Location	Command	HQ Location
Eastern Naval Command	Vishakhapatnam	Western Naval Command	Mumbai
Southern Naval Command	Kochi		

☞ Missile and Other Weapons

Name	Class	Range	Name	Class	Range
✶ Agni I	SRBM	850 km	✶ Brahmos	Supersonic Cruise Missile	290 km
✶ Agni II	MRBM	2500 km	✶ Brahmos 2	Hypersonic Cruise Missile	290 km
✶ Agni III	IRBM	3500 km-5500 km	✶ Prithvi I	SRBM	150 km
✶ Agni IV *or* Agni II Prime	IRBM	4000 km	✶ Prithvi III	SRBM	350 km
✶ Agni V	ICBM	5000 km-6000 km	✶ Sagarika	SLBM	700 km-2200 km
✶ Agni VI	ICBM	8000 km-10000 km	✶ Shaurya	TBM	700 km-2200 km
✶ Agni 3SL	ICBM	5200 km-11600 km	✶ Astra	Air to Air Missile	80 km-100 km
✶ Dhanush	SRBM	350 km			
✶ Nirbhay	Subsonic Cruise Missile	1000 km			

MULTIPLE CHOICE QUESTIONS

1. Match List-I with List-II and select the correct answer from the codes given below the lists:

List-I

(*a*) Napoleon Bonaparte
(*b*) Jean Jacques Rousseau
(*c*) Croce
(*d*) Madame Roland

List-II

1. 'A history is contemporary history'
2. 'Liberty what crimes are committed in thy name'
3. 'Man is born free but everywhere he is in chains.'
4. 'I am the Child of Revolution'

Codes :

	(*a*)	(*b*)	(*c*)	(*d*)
A.	1	2	3	4
B.	4	3	1	2
C.	3	4	2	1
D.	3	4	1	2

2. Abraham Lincon was elected the President of United States in:
A. 1862 B. 1860
C. 1875 D. 1855

3. Who was known as the 'Prince of Humanists'?
A. Francisco Petrarch B. Dante
C. Boccacio D. Erasmus

4. D-Day is the day when:
A. Germany declared war on Britain
B. US dropped the atom bomb on Hiroshima.
C. Allied Troops landed in Normandy
D. Germany surrendered to the allies

5. Whose teachings inspired the French Revolution?
A. Locke
B. Rousseau
C. Hegel
D. Plato

6. At a time when empires in Europe were crumbling before the might of Napoleon which one of the following Governor-Generals kept the British flag flying high in India?
A. Warren Hastings B. Lord Cornwallis
C. Lord Wellesley D. Lord Hastings

7. Which one of the following statements regarding Fascism in Italy is *not* true?
A. The Fascists came to power as a result of popular uprising
B. In 1926, all political parties except Mussolini's party were banned
C. The Fascists suppressed the Socialist movement
D. The Fascists were hostile to the Communists

8. The fall of Czar Nicholas-II is known as:
A. Bloody Sunday
B. Bolshevik Revolution
C. February Revolution
D. October Revolution

9. Industrial Revolution took place first in:
A. France B. Germany
C. United Kingdom D. Japan

10. The British Prime Minister at the outbreak of World War II was :
A. Churchill B. Baldwin
C. Attlee D. Chemberlain

11. The 'Great Depression' (1929) economic crisis was met by adopting the policy of
A. Stimulus B. Marshall Plan
C. New Deal D. Open Door

12. The slogan "No taxation without representation" was raised during the:
A. American War of Independence
B. Russian Revolution
C. French Revolution
D. Indian Freedom struggle

13. In the nineteenth century the people of Europe started moving from the villages to the cities due to the impact of :
A. Epidemics
B. War
C. Industrialisation
D. Population explosion in villages

14. The important cause of the Civil War in America was:
A. Abolition of slavery
B. Quest for freedom
C. Industrialisation
D. Rebellion by the native Americans

15. Industrial Revolution could not have come about without:
A. Merchant capitalism
B. The Enclosure Movement
C. The services of the proletariat class
D. An agricultural revolution

16. Consider the following statements :
The French Revolution came about mainly due to the :
1. Extreme poverty of the people
2. Impact of the works of great writers
3. Cruelty of the rulers
4. Impact of impulsive reaction

Which of the above statements are correct?
A. 1, 2 and 4 B. 2 and 3
C. 1, 3 and 4 D. 1, 2, 3 and 4

17. Asia's oldest and largest Buddhist monastery is situated in :
A. Tawang (Arunachal Pardesh)
B. Lhasa (Tibet)
C. Trincomallee (Sri Lanka)
D. Ulan Bator (Mongolia)

18. Who was the main architect of the Russian Revolution?
A. Karl Marx B. Lenin
C. Stalin D. Tolstoy

19. V.I. Lenin is associated with :
A. Russian Revolution of 1917
B. Chinese Revolution of 1949
C. German Revolution
D. French Revolution of 1789

20. Which one of the following statements is *not* correct?
A. Voltaire believed in Natural Religion
B. Rousseau wrote *Social Contract*
C. Montesquieu authored *The Spirit of Laws*
D. Necker believed in 'General Will'

21. 6th April, 1930 is well known in the history of India because this date is associated with...........
A. Dandi March by Mahatma Gandhi
B. Quit India Movement
C. Partition of Bengal
D. Partition of India

22. Which ruler enforced the system of 'Price Control' in India?
A. Mohammad Tughlak
B. Razia Begum
C. Alauddin Khilji
D. Sher Shah Suri

23. The concept of 'Din-e-Elahi' was founded by which king?
A. Dara Shikoh B. Akbar
C. Sher Shah Suri D. Shahjahan

24. Who are supposed to be the earliest inhabi-tants of India? Where did they come from?
A. Aryans from Central Asia
B. Dravidians from Mediterranean
C. Negroids from Africa
D. Bhils and the Santhals from West Asia

25. The one chief characteristic of temple architecture of the Gupta Age was :
A. Absence oi dome
B. Huge size
C. Beautiful carvings
D. absence of a covered courtyard for the gathering of worshippers

26. The Rigveda consists of :
A. 1000 hymns B. 2028 hymns
C. 1028 hymns D. 1038 hymns

27. The central point in Ashoka's dharma was :
A. royalty to kings
B. peace and non-violence
C. respect to elders
D. religious tolerance

28. The social evil which was conspicuously absent during ancient India was :
A. *Sati*-System B. *Devadasi*-System
C. Polygamy D. *Purdah*-System

29. Which, among the following, can be accepted as a novelty introduced by Mughal emperors to their buildings?
A. Domes B. Minarets
C. Arches D. Attached gardens

30. The first ruler of India who defeated Muhammud of Ghur was :
A. Mularaja II of Gujarat
B. Prithviraja Chauhan of Delhi
C. Jayachand of Kannauj
D. Parmaldeva of Bundelkhand

31. What important event happened in India in 1911?
A. Bengal was partitioned
B. Non-Cooperation movement was launched
C. India's capital was shifted from Calcutta to Delhi
D. Mahatma Gandhi presided over the Congress session

32. The first phase of the Congress Party (1885-1905) was characterized by its efforts to secure:
A. limited independence
B. complete freedom
C. Indianization of services
D. constitutional reforms

33. The Muslim League demanded a separate homeland for the Indian Muslims openly for the first time at its annual session held in Lahore in the year :
A. 1931 A.D. B. 1936 A.D.
C. 1940 A.D. D. 1941 A.D.

34. Under whose governorship did the East India Company secure the Diwani Rights in Bengal, Bihar and Odisha from Emperor Shah Alam?
A. Lord Cornwallis
B. Lord William Bentinck
C. Lord Clive
D. Lord Wellesley

35. The Simon Commission was generally boycotted by the Indian political parties. What was the reason for this general non-cooperation?
A. the Commission aimed at dividing the people
B. it was an 'all white' Commission
C. it came after the Jallianwala Bagh carnage
D. it was an eye wash

36. Aligarh Muslim University was founded by :
A. Dr. Saifuddin Kitchlu
B. Mohammad Ali Jinnah
C. Sir Syed Ahmed Khan
D. Maulana Mohammad Ali

37. Ibn Batutah was an African traveller visiting India during the time of :
A. Alivardi Khan
B. Ala-ud-din Khalji
C. Iltutmish
D. Mohammad-bin-Tughlaq

38. The battle of Wandiawash was fought in :
A. 1726 B. 1760
C. 1818 D. 1857

39. The abolition of *Sati* by government regulation was at the time of :
A. Warren Hastings B. Lord Wellesley
C. Lord Bentinck D. Lord Ahmerst

40. Pick out the wrong combination :
A. Dilwara Temple : Mt. Abu
B. Pashupati Temple : Kathmandu
C. Padmanabh Temple : Bangalore
D. Minakshi Temple : Madurai

41. Match the following:
(*a*) Chanhudaro (*b*) Kalibangan
(*c*) Lothal (*d*) Surkotada
1. Alleged discovery of the skeleton of horse.
2. Bead making.
3. Traces of a dock and ship on seal.
4. Evidence of ploughing the fields.

The Correct code is :

	(*a*)	(*b*)	(*c*)	(*d*)
A.	2	4	3	1
B.	2	1	3	4
C.	1	2	3	4
D.	2	1	4	3

42. Match the Harappan settlements with the banks of rivers on which they were located :
(*a*) Harappa 1. Ravi
(*b*) Mohenjodaro 2. Indus
(*c*) Ropar 3. Sutlej
(*d*) Kalibangan 4. Ghaggar
(*e*) Lothal 5. Bhogava

Codes :

	(*a*)	(*b*)	(*c*)	(*d*)	(*e*)
A.	1	2	3	4	5
B.	1	2	3	5	4
C.	2	1	3	5	4
D.	2	1	4	3	5

43. The Goddess 'Kannagi' whose many temples were erected during the 'Sangam Age' was the goddess of:
A. Chastity B. Love
C. Prowess D. Wisdom

44. The Jain goal of life is to attain deliverance from the fetters of mudane existence, the way to which lies through three jewels. Which one of the following was not included among the 'three jewels' of Jainism?
A. Right faith B. Right action
C. Right knowledge D. Right conduct

45. The most striking feature of the Ashokan pillar is polish. Name the Ashokan pillar which is considered to be the most graceful of all Ashokan pillars.
A. Sarnath
B. Rampurva
C. Laurya-Nandangarh
D. Rummindei

46. Which are the correct statements?
1. The land grants, started in Satavahana period, paved the way for feudal developments in India.
2. Silk and spices were the Chief Indian export articles of Indo-Roman trade.
3. The Guptas issued the largest number of gold coins in ancient India.
4. The first memorial of a 'SATI' dated 510 A.D. is found at Eran in Madhya Pradesh.

A. 1 and 2 B. 1, 3, and 4
C. 1 and 4 D. 1, 2, 3 and 4

47. Who among the following patronised the 'Gandhara' (Indo-Greek style) School of Art?
A. Ashoka, the Great
B. Harsha Vardhana
C. Kanishka
D. Chandragupta Vikramaditya

48. The Sultanate of Delhi had five ruling dynasties. The dynasty having longest and shortest period were :
A. Ilbari and Khalji
B. Tughlaq and Khalji
C. Tughlaq and Sayyid
D. Ilbari and Lodis

49. Which one of the following events took place at the last during reign of Muhammad-bin-Tughlaq?
A. Introduction of token currency
B. Increase of land-revenue in Doab
C. Transfer of Capital from Delhi to Devagiri.
D. Conquest of Khurasan and Iraq

50. The most learned medieval Muslim ruler who was well versed in various branches of learning including astronomy, mathematics and medicine was :
A. Jalaluddin Khilji
B. Sikander Lodi
C. Ghiyasuddin Tughlaq
D. Muhammad-bin-Tughlaq

51. The 'Sufis' had 12 silsilas. They propounded the idea of Union with God through:
A. Love B. Rituals
C. Fasts D. Prayers

52. Match the following:
(*a*) Peshwa 1. Foreign affairs
(*b*) Panditrao 2. Audit and accounts
(*c*) Amatya 3. Providing grants to scholars
(*d*) Sumant 4. General supervision
5. Military affairs

Select the correct code :

	(*a*)	(*b*)	(*c*)	(*d*)
A.	2	3	4	5
B.	4	1	2	3
C.	4	3	2	1
D.	3	1	4	2

53. The Regulating Act of 1773 can be regarded as the first measure to :
A. assert the right of British Parliament to legislate for India
B. separate the legislature from the executive
C. separate the judiciary from the executive
D. centralise law-making

54. What was the exact constitutional status of the Indian Republic on 26th January, 1950?
A. A Democratic Republic
B. A Sovereign, Democratic Republic
C. A Sovereign, Secular, Democratic Republic
D. A Sovereign, Socialist, Secular, Democratic Republic

55. When the British obtained the grant of Diwani of Bengal, Bihar and Odisha they acquired the right to :
A. maintain law and order in these territories
B. administer civil justice and collect revenue in these territories
C. collect revenue and establish revenue administration in these territories
D. militarily defend these territories

56. Which of the following were responsible for the growth of nationalism in India during the British rule?
1. Economic exploitation of India.
2. Impact of western education.
3. Role of the Press.

Select the correct answer using the codes given below :
Codes:
A. 1, 2 and 3 B. 1 and 2
C. 2 and 3 D. 1 and 3

57. Which one of the following nationalist leaders has been described as being radical in politics but conservative on social issues?
A. G.K. Gokhale
B. B.G. Tilak
C. Lala Lajpat Rai
D. Madan Mohan Malviya

58. Provincial Autonomy in British India was envisaged by the :
A. Act of 1909 B. Act of 1919
C. Act of 1935 D. Act of 1947

59. Dyarchy means :
A. double government
B. a government in which the centre is very powerful
C. a government based on division of power between centre and provinces
D. None of the above

60. The Indian National Congress observed 'Independence Day' for the first time on 26th January in :
A. 1920 B. 1925
C. 1930 D. 1947

61. ....is situated near the banks of Sabarmati River
A. Bhavnagar B. Aurangabad
C. Ahmedabad D. Rajkot

62. Sericulture is:
A. science of the various kinds of serum
B. artificial rearing of fish
C. art of silkworm breeding
D. study of various cultures of a community

63. The most abundant constituents of earth's crust are:
A. Igneous rocks
B. Sedimentary rocks
C. Metamorphic rocks
D. Granite

64. Indian Standard Time is based on:
A. 80°E longitude B. 82½°E longitude
C. 110°E longitude D. 25°E longitude

65. Tides in the oceans are caused by :
A. Gravitational pull of the moon on the earth's surface including sea water
B. Gravitational pull of the sun on the earth's surface only and not on the sea water
C. Gravitational pull of the moon and the sun on the earth's surface including the sea water
D. None of these

66. Nagarjunasagar Project is situated on the river:
A. Tungabhadra
B. Cauvery
C. Krishna
D. Godavari

67. The difference between the Indian Standard Time and the Greenwich Mean Time is:
A. – 3½ hours B. + 3½ hours
C. – 5½ hours D. + 5½ hours

68. Which of the following dams is not on Narmada river?
A. Indira-Sagar Project
B. Maheshwar Hydel Power Project
C. Jobat Project
D. Koyna Power Project

69. Which of the following statements is **not true** about the availability of water on the earth, the crisis for which is going to increase in the years to come?
A. About 97.5 per cent of the total volume of water available on the earth is salty
B. 80 per cent of the water available to us for use comes in bursts as monsoons
C. About 2.5 per cent of the total water available on the earth is polluted water and cannot be used for human activities
D. Possibility is that some big glaciers will melt in the coming ten-fifteen years and sea level will rise by 3-4 metres all over the earth

70. Which of the following is **not** a cash crop?
A. Jute B. Paddy
C. Cashewnut D. Sugarcane

71. Through which States does Cauvery River flow?
A. Gujarat, M.P., Tamil Nadu
B. Karnataka, Kerala, Tamil Nadu
C. Karnataka, Kerala, Andhra Pradesh
D. M.P., Maharashtra, Tamil Nadu

72. Indian Standard Time is the local time of 82½°E which passes through :
A. Guntur B. Delhi
C. Allahabad D. Kolkata

73. The 17th parallel defines the boundary between:
A. North and South Korea
B. USA and Canada
C. North and South Vietnam
D. China and Russia

74. During the period of south-west monsoon, Tamil Nadu remains dry because:
A. the winds do not reach this area
B. there are no mountains in this area
C. it lies in the rain shadow area
D. the temperature is too high to let the winds cool down

75. Which of the following device measures depth of a sea?
A. Fathometer B. Anemometer
C. Altimeter D. Barometer

76. The biggest reserves of thorium are in :
A. India B. China
C. The Soviet Union D. U.S.A.

77. The Girnar Hills are situated in which of the following states?
A. Gujarat B. Karnataka
C. Madhya Pradesh D. Maharashtra

78. During December 22nd the sun is vertically over:
A. Tropic of Cancer
B. Tropic of Capricorn
C. The Equator
D. None of the above

79. Photosphere is described as the :
A. Lower layer of atmosphere
B. Visible surface of the sun from which radiation emanates
C. Wavelength of solar spectrum
D. None of the above

80. Broadly, there are three layers of the earth of the crust, the mantle and the core. The crust forms what percentage of the volume of the earth?
A. 0.5% B. 2.5%
C. 7.5% D. 12.5%

81. The grassland of Argentina is known as :
A. Pampas B. Campos
C. Savanna D. None of the above

82. Different seasons are formed because :
A. Sun is moving around the earth
B. of revolution of the earth around the Sun on its orbit
C. of rotation of the earth around its axis
D. All of the above

83. Eskers and Drumlins are features formed by:
A. underground water
B. running water
C. the action of wind
D. glacial action

84. Match List-I and List-II and select the correct answer using the codes given below the Lists :

List-I *(Rivers)*	**List-II** *(Towns)*
(*a*) Ghaghara	1. Lucknow
(*b*) Brahmaputra	2. Hoshangabad
(*c*) Narmada	3. Ahmedabad
(*d*) Sabarmati	4. Guwahati
	5. Ayodhya

	(a)	(b)	(c)	(d)
A.	4	5	1	2
B.	5	4	2	3
C.	5	4	3	1
D.	3	5	2	1

85. Which of the statements as regards the consequences of the movement of the earth is not correct?
A. Revolution of the earth is the cause of the change of seasons.
B. Rotation of the earth is the cause of days and nights.
C. Rotation of the earth causes variation in the duration of days and nights.
D. Rotation of the earth effects the movement of winds and ocean currents.

86. The world is divided into :
A. 12 time zones
B. 20 time zones
C. 24 time zones
D. 36 time zones

87. The 'Kiel' canal links the :
A. Pacific and Atlantic Oceans
B. Mediterranean Sea and Red Sea
C. Mediterranean Sea and Black Sea
D. North Sea and Baltic Sea

88. Match the following :

List-I	**List-II**
(a) Himadri	1. Outer Himalayas
(b) Shivalik	2. Inner Himalayas
(c) Himanchal	3. Middle Himalayas
(d) Sahyadri	4. Western Ghats

Codes:

	(a)	(b)	(c)	(d)
A.	1	2	3	4
B.	4	2	3	1
C.	2	1	3	4
D.	1	2	3	4

89. The term 'Regur' refers to:
A. Laterite soils
B. Black Cotton soils
C. Red Soils
D. Deltaic Alluvial Soils

90. Location of sugar industry in India is shifting from north to south because of:
A. cheap labour
B. expanding regional market
C. cheap and abundant supply of power
D. high yield and high sugar content in sugarcane

91. Consider the following statements :
1. Ozone is found mostly in the Stratosphere.
2. Ozone layer lies 55-75 km above the surface of the earth.
3. Ozone absorbs ultraviolet radiation from the Sun.
4. Ozone layer has no significance for life on the earth.

Which of the above statements are correct?
A. 1 and 3 B. 2 and 4
C. 2 and 3 D. 1 and 4

92. Which of the following is not a chemical coagulant used in water treatment?
A. Polyaluminium Chloride (PAC)
B. Nitrogen dioxide
C. Aluminium Sulfate (Alum)
D. Aluminium Chloride

93. Darjeeling and Dharamsala would be the right places to visit if one wanted to get a clear view respectively of :
A. Kanchanjunga and Dhauladhar ranges
B. Nandadevi and Dhauladhar ranges
C. Kanchanjunga and Nandadevi ranges
D. Nandadevi and Nanga Parvat

94. Atmosphere exists because:
A. The Gravitational force of the Earth
B. Revolution of the Earth
C. Rotation of the Earth
D. Weight of the gases of atmosphere

95. Victoria lake is located in the continent:
A. Africa
B. Asia
C. North America
D. South America

96. The famous Lagoon Lake of India is :
A. Dal Lake
B. Chilka Lake
C. Pulicat Lake
D. Mansarover

97. Where are most of the earth's active volcanoes concentrated?
A. Indian Ocean
B. Pacific Ocean
C. Aral Sea
D. Atlantic Ocean

98. Through which of the following states does the river Chambal flow?
A. U.P., M.P., Rajasthan
B. M.P., Gujarat, U.P.
C. Rajasthan, M.P., Bihar
D. Gujarat, M.P., U.P.

99. Which country is called the sugar bowl of the world?
A. Cuba B. India
C. Argentina D. USA

100. The area covered by forest in India is about:
A. 46% B. 33%
C. 23% D. 21.71%

101. A closed economy is the one which :
A. does not permit emigration or immigration
B. permits emigration but no immigration
C. engages in no foreign trade
D. engages in no foreign and domestic trade or transit

102. In a developed economy the major share of employment originates in the :
A. primary sector B. tertiary sector
C. secondary sector D. any of the above

103. The Economic and Social Commission for Asia and Pacific (ESCAP) is located at :
A. Bangkok B. Kuala Lumpur
C. Manila D. Singapore

104. Commercial vehicles are not produced by which of the following companies in India?
A. TELCO B. Ashok Leyland
C. DCM Daewoo D. Birla Yamaha

105. What is 'RuPay'?
A. New Currency of RBI
B. New name of Credit Cards of Banks
C. Credit Card for Farmers
D. Card Payment Network

106. The main argument advanced in favour of small scale and cottage industries in India is that:
A. cost of production is low
B. they require small capital investment
C. they advance the goal of equitable distribution of wealth
D. they generate a large volume of employment

107. The most serious economic problems of India are:
A. Poverty and unemployment
B. Stagnation, not poverty
C. Unemployment, not poverty
D. Underdevelopment, not poverty

108. Which of the following is not one of the three central problems of an economy?
A. What to produce
B. How to produce
C. When to produce
D. For whom to produce

109. If saving exceeds investment, the national income will:
A. fall B. rise
C. fluctuate D. remain constant

110. In which of the following industries in India are the maximum number of workers employed?
A. Sugar B. Jute
C. Textiles D. Iron and Steel

111. Terrace Cultivation is practiced mostly:
A. in urban areas
B. on slopes of mountains
C. on tops of hills
D. in undulating tracts

112. Which of the following is a Selective Credit Control method?
A. Bank Rate
B. RBI directives
C. Cash Reserve Ratio
D. Open market operations

113. Which of the following taxes is not shared by the Central Government with the States?
A. Union excise duties
B. Customs duty
C. Income tax
D. Estate duty

114. ICICI is the name of a:
A. Financial Institution
B. Chemical Industry
C. Cotton Industry
D. Chamber of Commerce and Industry

115. Structural Unemployment arises due to
A. Deflationary conditions
B. Heavy industry bias
C. Shortage of raw material
D. Inadequate productive capacity

116. What is the full form of NPA in Context of Banking system?
A. Non-Performing Assests
B. National Productivity Authority
C. National Productivity Association
D. Non-Paying Assets

117. The largest public sector bank in India is:
A. Central Bank of India
B. Punjab National Bank
C. State Bank of India
D. Indian Overseas Bank

118. Which of the following statements best explains the term contraband goods?
A. Goods produced only for exports
B. Goods produced in joint sector only
C. Goods for the trading of which licence is not required
D. Goods that are forbidden, from export, import or even possession, by law

119. Price in the market is fixed by:
A. Stock exchange rates
B. The demand and supply ruling in the market at a particular time
C. The Finance Minister
D. None of the above

120. Devaluation of currency helps to promote:
A. National Income
B. Savings
C. Imports at lower cost
D. Exports

121. Balanced economic growth can be achieved only if:
A. All the sectors of economy grow at the same rate
B. Population growth is arrested
C. All the inter dependent sectors grow in harmony
D. Basic and heavy industries are assigned highest priority

122. P.V. Sindhu is associated with which of the following sport?
A. Badminton
B. Weightlifting
C. Swimming
D. Tennis

123. 'MODVAT' stands for:
A. Ad Valorem tax on output
B. Deduction of cost of inputs from the value of output
C. Reduction in import duties
D. Imposition of tax on professions

124. Who among the following is the first to receive 'Dada Saheb Phalke' award?
A. Shivaji Ganeson
B. Devika Rani
C. Dr. Raj Kumar
D. None of the above

125. The term 'devaluation' means:
A. Reducing the value of a currency in terms of another currency
B. Increasing the value of a currency
C. Revising the value of a currency
D. None of the above

126. Per capita net availability of pulses has shown a tendency of:
A. Increase over time
B. Decrease over time
C. Constant over time
D. First increase then decrease

127. National Income is the same as:
A. Net national product at market price
B. Net domestic product at market price
C. Net national product at factor cost
D. Net domestic product at factor cost

128. Which one of the following is not an example of indirect tax?
A. Goods and Services Tax
B. Excise duty
C. Customs duty
D. Expenditure tax

129. The major aim of devaluation is to:
A. encourage imports
B. encourage exports
C. encourage both exports and imports
D. discourage both exports and imports

130. Structural unemployment arises due to:
A. deflationary conditions
B. heavy industry bias
C. shortage of raw materials
D. inadequate productive capacity

131. When was the Family Planning Programme officially started in India?
A. 1950 B. 1952
C. 1956 D. 1962

132. When was the Reserve Bank of India nationalised?
A. 1947 B. 1949
C. 1950 D. 1951

133. Which of the following is *not* a feature of the Indian economy?
A. High rate of population growth
B. Disguised unemployment
C. Lowest rate of adult literacy
D. High rate of exports

134. The 'Relative Deprivation' approach for measuring poverty has been adopted by:
A. developing countries
B. developed countries
C. under-developed countries
D. None of the above

135. One of the main factors that led to rapid expansion of Indian exports is:
A. Imposition of import duties
B. Liberalisation of the economy
C. Recession in other countries
D. Diversification of exports

136. Sustainable economic development means an increase in the rate of growth of real:
A. total and per capita product
B. total and per capita product and level of literacy rate
C. total and per capita product and life expectancy at birth
D. total and per capita product, taking into account the cost of degradation of the quality of environment in this process

137. Functional unemployment occurs when:
A. unemployed have no qualification for job
B. people frequently change their job
C. people were thrown out from job due to recession
D. None of these

138. Which among the following does **not** have a 'free trade zone'?
A. Kandla B. Mumbai
C. Visakhapatnam D. Thiruvanantpuram

139. Sun Belt of USA is important for which one of the following industries?
A. Cotton textile
B. Petrochemicals
C. Hi-tech electronics
D. Food Processing

140. Commercial banking system in India is
A. unit banking B. branch banking
C. mixed banking D. None of the above

141. Who gives recognition to political parties in India?
A. Parliament
B. President
C. Supreme Court
D. Election Commission

142. The Quorum of the Legislative Council is :
A. one-fourth of its total membership
B. one-third of its membership
C. one-tenth of its membership
D. 25

143. The Indian Constitution is:
A. federal
B. unitary
C. a happy mixture of the federal and unitary
D. federal in normal times and unitary in times of emergency

144. Universal adult franchise implies a right to vote to all:
A. adult residents of the State
B. adult male citizens of the State
C. residents of the State
D. adult citizens of the State

145. When a resolution prefering a charge against the President has been passed by a specified majority in the House, it is sent to the other House for investigation. If, as a result of such an investigation, a resolution is passed through a specified majority by the other House, declaring that the charge has been sustained, the President shall leave his office. The specified special majority must not be less than :
A. two-third of the members present and voting
B. one-third of the members present and voting
C. three-fourth of the members present and voting and two-third of the total membership
D. two-third of the total membership

146. Which one of the following judicial powers of the President of India has been *wrongly* listed?
A. he appoints the Chief Justice and other judges of the Supreme Court
B. he can remove the judges of the Supreme Court on grounds of misconduct
C. he can consult the Supreme Court on any question of law or fact which is of public importance
D. he can grant pardon, reprieves and respites to persons punished under Union Law

147. The Vice-president of India can be removed from his office before the expiry of his term if :
A. the Rajya Sabha passes a resolution by a majority of its members and the Lok Sabha agrees with the resolution
B. if the Supreme Court of India recommends his removal
C. the President so desires
D. None of the above

148. The Chief Justice of a High Court in India is appointed by the :
A. Governor of the State
B. Prime Minister of India
C. Chief Justice of the Supreme Court
D. President of India

149. Which of the following statements is constitutionally not true about the passing of the Union Budgets and Finance Bill in India?
1. Under the law, Finance Bill should be adopted by both the Houses of the Parliament within 45 days of its introduction.
2. If the Finance Bill is not adopted within specified period, the government loses its authority to levy the taxes proposed in the budgets.
3. In the absence of full budget, a vote-on-account gives the power to the government to spend.
4. Government cannot raise revenues without a proper approval of the Finance Bill

A. Only 2 B. Only 3
C. Only 4 D. Only 1, 2 and 3

150. Normally, on whose advice the President's Rule is imposed in a State?
A. Chief Minister
B. Legislative Assembly
C. Governor
D. Chief Justice of High Court

151. Which Article of the Indian Constitution deals with Amendment procedure?
A. Article 368 B. Article 358
C. Article 367 D. All of these

152. Government is the agency through which the will of:
A. the state is expressed
B. the people is expressed
C. the head of the state is expressed
D. the majority is expressed

153. In a unitary system of government :
A. The centre is all powerful
B. The centre is weaker than the states
C. The centre and states stand at par
D. The states and centre are supreme in their respective spheres

154. In Cabinet System of Government the real executive authority rests with :
A. The Council of Ministers
B. The Prime Minister
C. The Constitution
D. The Parliament

155. The Head of the State under a parliamentary government:
A. is an elected representative
B. is a hereditary person
C. is a nominated person
D. may be any one of the above

156. In the event of a ministerial proposal being defeated on the floor of the legislature, under the parliamentary system :
A. the government waits for a general no-confidence motion
B. the minister concerned is taken to task by the Prime Minister
C. the minister is forced to resign
D. the whole Council of Ministers resign

157. The "due process of law" is an essential characteristic of the judicial system of:
A. UK B. France
C. USA D. India

158. Under the Constitution it is :
A. obligatory for the President to accept the advice of the Council of Ministers but is not obliged to follow it
B. obligatory for the President to accept the advice of the Council of Ministers
C. not obligatory for the President to seek or accept the advice of the Council of Ministers
D. obligatory for the President to seek the advice of the Council of Ministers if his own party is in power

159. Which one of the following statements is correct?
A. the Presiding Officer of Rajya Sabha is elected every year
B. the Presiding Officer of Rajya Sabha is elected for a term of two years at a time
C. the Presiding Officer of Rajya Sabha is elected for a term of six years
D. the Vice-President of India is the ex-officio Presiding Officer of Rajya Sabha

160. The introduction of "no confidence" motion in the Lok Sabha requires the support of at least:
A. 50 members B. 70 members
C. 60 members D. 80 members

161. The High Court comes under :
A. State List B. Union List
C. Concurrent List D. None of the above

162. Which one of the following has been wrongly listed as a Fundamental Duty of the Indian citizens?
A. to develop scientific temper, humanism and spirit of inquiry and reform
B. to work for raising the prestige of the country in the international sphere
C. to protect and improve the natural environment
D. to strive towards excellence in all spheres of individual and collective activity

163. Which one of the following is not a Fundamental Duty as outlined in Article 51A of the Constitution?
A. to abide by the Constitution and respect its ideals
B. to defend the country and render national service when called upon to do so
C. to work for the moral upliftment of the weaker sections of society
D. to preserve the rich heritage

164. The main characteristics of the Directive Principles of State Policy given in the Indian Constitution are :
A. not enforceable by any court
B. fundamental in the governance of the country
C. 'Like instruments, instructions, political manifesto and a code of moral precepts which have to guide governors of the country'
D. no law can be passed, which is opposed to these principles

165. Of the following which are true?
A. In a State, the Legislative Council is dominant with regard to non-financial bills and the Legislative Assembly with regard to financial (money) bills
B. Vidhan Parishad can virtually block legisla-tion even if the same is passed by the Vidhan Sabha
C. In case, of a tie between the two Houses, the Governor is duty-bound to call a joint session of the two Houses to have the issue settled on a majority verdict

D. If a Bill is twice approved by the Vidhan Sabha, it becomes law even if rejected by the Vidhan Parishad

166. Which one of the following types of emergency can be declared by the President?
A. Emergency due to threat of war and external aggresion
B. Emergency due to break-down of constitu-tional machinery in a State
C. Financial emergency on account of threat to the financial credit of India
D. all the three emergencies

167. The chairman of which of the following parliamentary committees is invariably from the members of ruling party?
A. Committee on public undertakings
B. Public accounts committee
C. Estimates committee
D. Committee on delegated legislation

168. Which of the following is not a formally prescribed device available to the members of parliament?
A. Question hour
B. Zero hour
C. Half-an-hour discussion
D. Short duration discussion

169. Which of the following is not a tool of executive control over public administration?
A. Power of appointment and removal
B. Line agencies
C. Appeal to public opinion
D. Civil services code

170. If the Speaker of the State Legislative Assembly decides to resign, he should submit his resignation to the:
A. Judges of the High Court
B. Deputy Speaker
C. Chief Minister
D. Finance Minister

171. The President of India can nominate to the Rajya Sabha:
A. 6 members B. 9 members
C. 15 members D. 12 members

172. India is a Federal State because of:
A. dual judiciary
B. dual citizenship prevalent here
C. share of power between the Centre and the States
D. rigid Constitution

173. Residuary Subjects are those subjects which are:
A. contained in the State list
B. contained in the Union list
C. contained in the Concurrent list
D. not covered by any of the three lists

174. Which of the following writs can be issued, by the Supreme Court, to enforce Fundamental Rights?
A. Writ of Habeas Corpus
B. Writ of Mandamus
C. Writ of Quo Warranto
D. All of these

175. When the offices of both the President and the Vice-President of India are vacant, who will discharge their functions?
A. Prime Minister
B. Home Minister
C. Chief Justice of India
D. The Speaker

176. The Supreme Court tenders advice to the President of India on a matter of law or fact:
A. on its own
B. only when such advice is sought
C. only if the matter relates to some basic issue
D. only if the issue poses a threat to the unity and integrity of the country

177. Six months shall **not** intervene between two sessions of the Indian Parliament because :
A. it is the customary practice
B. it is the British convention followed in India
C. it is an obligation under the Constitution of India
D. None of the above

178. The States of the Indian Union can be recognised or their boundaries altered by:
A. the Union Parliament by a simple majority in the ordinary process of legislation
B. two-thirds majority of both the Houses of Parliament
C. two-thirds majority of both the Houses of Parliament and the consent of the legisla-tures of concerned States
D. an executive order of the Union government with the consent of the concerned State governments

179. The Basic Feature theory of the Constitution of India was propounded by the Supreme Court in the case of:
A. Minerva Mills Vs. Union of India
B. Golaknath Vs. State of Punjab
C. Maneka Gandhi Vs. Union of India
D. Keshavananda Vs. State of Kerala

180. Which one of the following writs is issued by a court in case of illegal detention of a person?
A. Habeas corpus
B. Mandamus
C. Certiorari
D. Quo-warranto

181. Name the instrument with the help of which a sailor in a submarine can see the objects on the surface of the sea.
A. Telescope B. Periscope
C. Gycroscope D. Stereoscope

182. 'HEMOPHILLIA' is the disease of ....
A. liver B. blood
C. brain D. bones

183. Vitamin A is abundantly found in ....
A. Brinjal B. Tomato
C. Carrot D. Cabbage

184. .... is not soluble in water.
A. Vitamin A B. Vitamin B
C. Vitamin C D. None of these

185. The blood vessels with the smallest diameter are called ....
A. capillaries B. arterioles
C. venules D. lymphatics

186. Out of the following .... has the greatest elasticity.
A. steel B. rubber
C. aluminium D. annealed copper

187. Cooking gas is a mixture of which of the following two gases?
A. Carbon Dioxide and Oxygen
B. Butane and Propane
C. Carbon Monoxide and Carbon Dioxide
D. Methane and Ethylene

188. The substance most commonly used as a food preservative is:
A. sodium carbonate B. tartaric acid
C. acetic acid D. benzoic acid

189. Normally, the substances that fight against diseases in human systems are known as:
A. dioxyribonucleic acids
B. carbohydrates
C. enzymes
D. antibodies

190. The SI unit of temperature is ....
A. Kelvin B. Celsius
C. Fahrenheit D. None of the above

191. One of the common fungal diseases of man is :
A. plague B. ringworm
C. cholera D. typhoid

192. A clear sky is blue because:
A. red light is scattered more than blue
B. ultraviolet light has been absorbed
C. blue light is scattered more than red
D. blue light has been absorbed

193. Jenner introduced the method of making people immune to :
A. small pox B. rabies
C. cholera D. polio

194. The largest cell in the human body is :
A. Nerve cell B. Live cell
C. Muscle cell D. Kidney cell

195. What is the device that steps up or steps down the voltage?
A. Dynamo B. Conductor
C. Inductor D. Transformer

196. The protein deficiency disease is known as :
A. Kwashiorker B. Cirrhosis
C. Eczema D. Clycoses

197. Iron deficiency causes :
A. rickets B. anaemia
C. cirrhosis D. goitre

198. Blood group of an individual is controlled by :
A. Haemoglobin B. Shape of RBC
C. Shape of WBC D. Genes

199. In a normal man the amount of blood pumped out by the heart per minute is about :
A. 1 litre B. 3 litres
C. 4 litres D. 5 litres

200. Red/green colour blindness in man is known as :
A. Protanopia
B. Deutetanopia
C. Both A and B above
D. Marfan's syndrome

201. The blue colour of the water in the sea is due to :
A. Reflection of the blue light by the impurities in sea water
B. Reflection of the blue sky by sea water and scattering of blue light by water molecules
C. Absorption of other colours by water molecules
D. None of the above

202. The image formed on the retina of the eye is:
A. upright and real
B. larger than the object
C. small and inverted
D. enlarged and real

203. Unit of loudness of sound is:
A. bel B. decibel
C. phon D. none of these

204. Oil rises up the wick in a lamp :
A. because oil is volatile
B. due to the capillary action phenomenon
C. due to the surface tension phenomenon
D. because oil is very light

205. The 'stones' formed in human kidney consist mostly of :
A. calcium oxalate
B. sodium acetate
C. magnesium sulphate
D. calcium

206. We hear the sound later, while the light is seen earlier:
A. because light's speed is more than that of sound
B. because lights travel in a straight direction while sound in a zigzag direction
C. because sound's frequency is lower than light
D. All of the above

207. Which part of an eye is transplanted?
A. Cornea B. Retina
C. Iris D. Sciera

208. The Universal donor group of blood is:
A. O B. A
C. B D. AB

209. The green colour of the leaf is due to :
A. Presence of Chloroplast
B. Presence of Chromium
C. Presence of Nicoplast
D. Presence of excess of oxygen

210. Voice of a child is more shrill than that of an elderly person because:
A. the pitch of the child's voice is higher than that of the person
B. the pitch is lower
C. the child is more energetic
D. None of the above

ANSWERS

1	2	3	4	5	6	7	8	9	10
B	C	D	C	B	C	A	C	C	D
11	12	13	14	15	16	17	18	19	20
C	A	C	A	A	D	A	B	A	D
21	22	23	24	25	26	27	28	29	30
A	C	B	C	D	C	B	D	D	B
31	32	33	34	35	36	37	38	39	40
C	D	C	C	B	C	D	B	C	C
41	42	43	44	45	46	47	48	49	50
A	A	A	B	C	D	C	B	B	D
51	52	53	54	55	56	57	58	59	60
A	C	A	B	B	A	B	C	A	C
61	62	63	64	65	66	67	68	69	70
C	C	B	B	C	C	D	D	D	B
71	72	73	74	75	76	77	78	79	80
B	C	C	C	A	A	A	B	B	A
81	82	83	84	85	86	87	88	89	90
A	B	D	B	C	C	D	C	B	D
91	92	93	94	95	96	97	98	99	100
A	B	A	A	A	B	B	A	A	D
101	102	103	104	105	106	107	108	109	110
C	B	A	D	D	D	A	C	D	C
111	112	113	114	115	116	117	118	119	120
B	B	B	A	D	A	C	D	B	D
121	122	123	124	125	126	127	128	129	130
C	A	A	B	A	D	C	D	B	D
131	132	133	134	135	136	137	138	139	140
B	B	D	A	B	D	B	D	D	C
141	142	143	144	145	146	147	148	149	150
D	C	D	D	D	B	A	D	C	C

151	**152**	**153**	**154**	**155**	**156**	**157**	**158**	**159**	**160**
A	B	A	A	A	D	C	B	D	A
161	**162**	**163**	**164**	**165**	**166**	**167**	**168**	**169**	**170**
B	B	C	B	D	D	C	B	B	B
171	**172**	**173**	**174**	**175**	**176**	**177**	**178**	**179**	**180**
D	C	D	D	C	B	C	A	D	A
181	**182**	**183**	**184**	**185**	**186**	**187**	**188**	**189**	**190**
B	B	C	A	A	A	B	D	D	A
191	**192**	**193**	**194**	**195**	**196**	**197**	**198**	**199**	**200**
B	C	A	A	D	A	B	D	D	A
201	**202**	**203**	**204**	**205**	**206**	**207**	**208**	**209**	**210**
B	B	B	B	A	A	A	A	A	A

2408-SP